Writers of the 21st Century

ROBERT A. HEINLEIN

Edited by
JOSEPH D. OLANDER
and
MARTIN HARRY GREENBERG

robert a.
heinlein

TAPLINGER PUBLISHING COMPANY / NEW YORK

To Katie, with love

First Edition

Published in the United States in 1978 by
TAPLINGER PUBLISHING CO., INC.
New York, New York
Copyright © 1978 by Joseph D. Olander and Martin Harry Greenberg
All rights reserved. Printed in the U.S.A.

Published simultaneously in Canada by
BURNS & MACEACHERN, LIMITED, TORONTO

Library of Congress Cataloging in Publication Data
Main entry under title:
Robert A. Heinlein.

(Writers of the 21st century)
Bibliography: p.
Includes index.
CONTENTS: Williamson, J. Youth against space.—Samuelson, D.N. Frontiers of the future.—Gaar, A.C. The human as machine analog. [etc.]
    1. Heinlein, Robert Anson, 1907-   —Criticism and interpretation—Addresses, essays, lectures. I. Olander, Joseph D. II. Greenberg, Martin Harry. III. Series.
PS3515.E288Z84   813'.5'4   76-11054
ISBN 0-8008-6801-3
ISBN 0-8008-6802-1 pbk.

Designed by MANUEL WEINSTEIN

CONTENTS

Introduction

Joseph D. Olander and Martin Harry Greenberg

ROBERT A. HEINLEIN is an outstanding figure in modern American science fiction. He has published voluminously, his science fiction sells well, and his work continues to be in print. His *Stranger in a Strange Land* and *Starship Troopers* have sold in the millions, especially in college bookstores. He has been described as one of the "fathers" of modern science fiction. He is also one of the few science fiction writers who have helped in making science fiction well known in "mainstream" literary circles.

But Heinlein is also a writer whose fiction and ideas often lead to strong feelings and reactions. Throughout his work, Heinlein appears to adopt positions favored by the American political right. He attacks "permissiveness" in the various societies he depicts, especially in child-rearing practices and in the "coddling" of criminals and lawbreakers in general. He advocates corporal punishment for social deviants and flogging for speeders and other traffic offenders. He is enthusiastic about what he considers the importance of military-style discipline to hold a community together. He exhibits a strong respect for custom in his work, although he makes it clear that custom must not stand in the way of societal change. When his heroes are in control of society, Heinlein resists criticism with "love it or leave it"; when they are out of power, he becomes a strong advocate of the right of revolution.

To dwell on the content of his advocacy, however, is to miss the opportunity to take advantage of the insights of his science fiction. Among them are perspectives and issues which relate to some of the perennial concerns of philosophy, such as the best form of government, whether and to what extent political utopias are possible, and the dimensions of power, liberty, equality, justice, and order. Sexuality, family, love, and immortality are also major themes in his

7

fiction. The quality of his style certainly comes in for severe criticism, but the treatment of his subject is frequently insightful.

Plots usually center around a protagonist—the famous "Heinlein hero"—who is always tough, just, relatively fearless when it counts, and endowed with extraordinary skills and physical prowess. The protagonist's most noteworthy characteristic—whether male or female—is "competence." Heinlein defines competence partially as success, partially as ability (in fields like mathematics or engineering), partially as capability for fighting—but, most important, as the capacity to survive. For Heinlein, individual or collective survival is the criterion which seems to shape the structure and thematic apparatus of his fiction. Through it, major political, ethical, and moral questions can be examined.

Heinlein's preoccupation with survival in his fiction should not be looked at in a vacuum; it is a logical extension of his assumptions about human nature. Heinlein is sometimes classified as "Hobbesian" since he consistently maintains that human nature is predicated upon competition between individuals for power. Heinlein recognizes that scarcity in regard to material goods can produce competition, conflict, and war, but he also recognizes that some "things"— like power—are scarce by definition and will always be in short supply. For Heinlein, moreover, the human being is by nature a working animal who needs creative labor to remain human. He assumes that man has an evil, aggressive nature and this characteristic makes him basically a "wild animal"—the "roughest creature in the universe."

Here it is important to note a major criticism of science fiction writers—the charge that while they extrapolate trends into the future and treat change as the inevitable product of science and technology, they are reluctant to change radically their assumptions about human nature. It may be that Heinlein's science fiction validates this charge. For him, the animal nature of the human being is a constant that—in the future, as in the present and the past—is governed by the drive to survive and to dominate. Changes in social and political relationships, in technology, and in science may leave this basic nature untouched.

While Heinlein is concerned with the survival of the group and of the race, his emphasis is on the survival of those individuals within society with the talent and the courage to ensure racial survival—the competent. The view that the survival of the fittest equals the survival of the best finds contemporary expression in his science fiction.

Survival for the competent is a prerequisite for the survival of the rest, and from this perspective flows his attitude toward morality.

But one should not be misguided by this simplification, for Heinlein often forces us to recognize basic questions: What kind of political order do we ourselves live in? Does it affirm, reaffirm, or deny our own good qualities as human beings? What instruments, purposes, and values does our own political order serve? What will it serve in the future, and what will it mean in terms of our survival as a species and as individuals? We may be surprised to learn that Heinlein's fiction points less to the importance of technological tools to help us confront the future and more to our need to reexamine ourselves.

In Jack Williamson's opening essay, "Youth Against Space: Heinlein's Juveniles Revisited," Williamson advances the argument that the "juveniles" which Heinlein wrote after World War II and up until the late 1950s may constitute the latter's most enduring work as a writer. These books include *Rocket Ship Galileo, Space Cadet, Red Planet, Farmer in the Sky, Between Planets, The Rolling Stones, Starman Jones, Star Beast, Tunnel in the Sky, Time for the Stars, Citizen of the Galaxy, Have Space Suit—Will Travel*, and, finally, *Starship Troopers*. Any survey of Heinlein's career must include these "juvenile" novels, suggests Williamson, who finds them more aesthetically satisfying—more entertaining and dramatic—than Heinlein's later, more didactic fiction. Williamson's analysis is based upon his own preference for science fiction which restores confidence in our future and in ourselves—and which therefore avoids analysis of what he calls "festering 'inner space.'" Regardless of the debate this position implies, Heinlein's juveniles clearly represent a major step in the development of Heinlein as a writer and in the development of science fiction.

David N. Samuelson, in "Major Frontier Worlds of Robert A. Heinlein: The Future and Fantasy," uses the metaphor of the frontier to analyze Heinlein's future history series and fantasies. Basing the analysis on Heinlein's novel-length fiction and short stories, Samuelson offers a very critical assessment of Heinlein's fiction and of his craftsmanship.

Proceeding from a concern about the lack of equal development between humanity's moral capability and technological progress, Alice Carol Gaar assesses Heinlein's preoccupation with the techniques for human survival. "The Human as Machine Analog: The

Big Daddy of Interchangeable Parts in the Fiction of Robert A. Heinlein" is not only an essay about Heinlein's views on "how things work" but also an inquiry into fundamental ethical questions. *Magic, Inc.*, "*Universe,*" *Methuselah's Children*, *Waldo*, *Starship Troopers*, *Stranger in a Strange Land*, *The Moon Is a Harsh Mistress*, *I Will Fear No Evil*, and *Time Enough for Love* are used to illustrate the analysis.

The concept of progress is closely associated with Heinlein's fiction, and Philip E. Smith II, examines Heinlein's fiction from this perspective. "The Evolution of Politics and the Politics of Evolution: Social Darwinism in Heinlein's Fiction" is explicitly based on the assumption that Heinlein's writing is patterned upon social Darwinism. Smith looks at some of Heinlein's utopian ideals, points out the contradictions in Heinlein's political fantasies, and argues that Heinlein's political values underlie the concept of progress which runs throughout his writing.

Ronald Sarti's "Variations on a Theme: Human Sexuality in the Work of Robert A. Heinlein" deals directly with the question of to what extent—and how well—Heinlein treats the theme of sexuality in his fiction. Sarti divides Heinlein's career into two periods. The first consists of the first twenty years of his writing career (1939-1958), during which he developed mariginal sexual themes and topics. The second period began in 1959, when sexuality began to emerge as thematically significant in practically every work.

Ivor A. Rogers, in "Robert Heinlein: Folklorist of Outer Space," points up Heinlein's paradox as a writer: critics tear Heinlein's fiction apart on grounds of literary criteria but they enjoy—as do millions of readers—his fiction. Arguing that *Time Enough for Love* is patterned after *Caleb Catlum's America* by Vincent McHugh, Rogers concludes that the former is a romance, not a science fiction novel, in an attempt to demonstrate science fiction as folktale.

Stranger in a Strange Land took America's youth by storm when it was published, and Robert Plank, in "Omnipotent Cannibals in *Stranger in a Strange Land*," attempts to answer the question of the novel's appeal. Although he finds the novel lacking in the traditional science fiction satisfaction based upon science and technology, Plank submits that the alternative satisfaction is the breakthrough achieved by the novel in treating taboo areas of sex, cannibalism, and the fantasy of omnipotence. The essay proceeds beyond an analysis of *Stranger* and raises major questions about the role of fantasy in the modern, civilized world in which we live.

Time Enough for Love is given an in-depth analysis by Russell Letson in "The Returns of Lazarus Long." Characterizing the novel as Heinlein's most ambitious work, Letson sets out to ask whether Heinlein meets critical standards and to discover the nature of the ideological problems readers may have with much of his fiction. The myth of the eternal return runs throughout *Time Enough for Love* and its analysis by Letson.

Finally, Frank H. Tucker, in "Major Political and Social Elements in Heinlein's Fiction," summarizes his perceptions of the political, social, and economic threads inherent in Heinlein's fiction. Tucker does not criticize the ideological dimensions of Heinlein's fiction; rather, he describes them and attempts to point out major polarities in Heinlein's political thought.

Writers of the 21st Century
ROBERT A. HEINLEIN

1. Youth Against Space: Heinlein's Juveniles Revisited

JACK WILLIAMSON

To OPEN ON a personal note, Bob Heinlein is an old friend of mine. We met in Los Angeles not long after John Campbell published "Lifeline," his first short story. I was a Saturday-evening guest many times in his Laurel Canyon home at never-formal gatherings of the never-organized Mañana Literary Society, where we sipped dry sherry and talked science fiction. Though I have seen him less often since Pearl Harbor broke up that little group, we have kept in touch. I admire him as one of the foremost shapers of modern science fiction, and I suspect that his most enduring work will turn out to be the dozen juvenile novels he wrote for Scribner's after the war.

Juvenile science fiction, as a labeled category, begins with Heinlein—though in fact most of the earlier magazine science fiction had been written for youthful readers and censored of anything likely to give offense. There had been new inventions, too, in Tom Swift and the dime novels, but no real futurology. The Heinlein series was a pioneer effort, quickly imitated.

He was feeling his way with the first two books, finding his stride only with *Red Planet*, but that and the following novels represent his craftsmanship at its best. Based on solidly logical extrapolations of future technology and future human history, they are cleanly constructed and deftly written, without the digressions and the preaching that often weaken the drama in his later work.

What I most admire about them is Heinlein's dogged faith in us and our destiny. No blind optimist, he is very much aware of evil days to come. His future worlds are often oppressively misruled, pinched by hunger, and wasted by war. Yet his heroes are always using science and reason to solve problems, to escape the prison Earth, to seek and build better worlds.

Taken altogether, the dozen books tell a generally consistent

15

story of the future conquest of space. The first, *Rocket Ship Galileo*, begins in a backyard shortly after World War II, with three boys testing a primitive rocket motor. The last, *Have Space Suit—Will Travel*, ends with the triumphant return of its young hero from the Lesser Magellanic Cloud, where he has defended the human race before the judges of the Three Galaxies. Nobody has written a more convincing and inspiring future human epic.

Heinlein never writes down. His main characters are young, the plots move fast, and the style is limpidly clear; but he never insults the reader's intelligence. Rereading the novels for this paper, I found them as absorbing as ever; now and then I was deeply moved.

As exemplars of modern literature, they are, of course, open to criticism. None of them reflects the labor and the pain and the dedicated genius that James Joyce put into *Portrait of the Artist*. None of them offers the explicit sex now in fashion—Heinlein used to quarrel with Campbell's taboo on sex in *Astounding Science Fiction*, and I believe he found his juvenile editors equally irksome. None of them looks at the human condition with the dreary pessimism of the New Wave school.

Another limit needs fuller comment. As Damon Knight and Alexei Panshin have remarked, Heinlein's heroes are pretty much alike—all competent people.* The protagonists of the juvenile novels are born bright, and we see them learning how to do everything. They mature into the all-around experts of his adult fiction and finally mellow into such extraordinary oldsters as Jubal Harshaw and Lazarus Long.

These efficient folk reflect Heinlein himself. Swift wrote *Gulliver's Travels* to satirize man's self-important faith in his own reason. Heinlein clearly belongs to the satirized camp, and his people embody the attitudes of the self-confident, reasonable man, the scientist who yearns to know all about the universe and the technologist who toils to control it.

I suspect that this independent individualism can explain Heinlein's often-puzzling bits of irrational mysticism, for example the interludes in heaven in *Stranger in a Strange Land* and the climactic scene in *Starman Jones* when Max has a sense of the dead astrogator standing behind his chair to help him guide the lost ship back through

---

*See Damon Knight, *In Search of Wonder* (Chicago: Advent, 1967), p. 80; and Alexei Panshin, *Heinlein in Dimension* (Chicago: Advent, 1968), p. 129.

the anomaly. Lacking any rational basis for belief in personal immortality, Heinlein and his heroes must either face the inevitability of death or somehow evade it. The long life of Lazarus Long appears to be an evasion, and the flashes of mysticism must be wishful escapes from the rational universe that neither the writer nor his people can finally master.

Actually, I think the supercompetent characters serve Heinlein well. He is no Tolstoy, recording known life. His major motif has always been future technology, treated with some degree of optimism. The theme itself implies people who invent, build, use, and enjoy machines. Technological man has to be rational and competent.

Yet there's a conflict here that I don't think Heinlein has ever fully resolved. As evolving technologies become more and more complex, so does the teamwork needed to support them. Heinlein seems completely aware of this when he is carrying his young protagonists through their education and their rites of initiation, yet he often seems unhappy with the sacrifice of personal freedom that a technological culture seems to require. In *The Rolling Stones*, for instance, his competent people are in full flight from their mechanized environment.

Rocket Ship Galileo, published by Scribner's in 1947, was Heinlein's first book after he returned to Hollywood from his wartime work as an aeronautical research engineer in the Philadelphia Navy Yard. Earlier, there had been almost no market for science fiction outside the category pulps, but now he had already begun widening its popularity with short stories in such high-circulation slicks as *Argosy* and *The Saturday Evening Post*.

A sometimes fumbling experiment, the book does no more than suggest the bright appeal of the later titles. The plot is often trite, and the characters are generally thin stereotypes, with none of the colorful human beings and charming aliens soon to follow. Too, the book has dated badly. Anticipating the first flights to the Moon, it's a poor prediction. The rocket builders work almost alone, on a tiny budget, with no seeming need for the vast NASA organization. The villains are Nazis, an idea perhaps not so badly worn in 1947 as it seems today. The spacecraft land horizontally, like airplanes, rather than on their tails. The action stops for science lectures not related to the story. Yet the book is still readable, with Heinlein's familiar themes already emerging. The military elite of *Starship*

Troopers is implicit in what Cargrave, the atomic scientist, tells the young protagonists:

"American boys are brought up loose and easy. That's fine. I like it that way. But a time comes when loose and easy isn't enough, when you have to be willing to obey, and do it wholeheartedly and without argument."

Space Cadet, published in 1948, is a long step forward. The characters are stronger, and they use more of the wisecracking dialogue that gradually became a Heinlein hallmark. The background is carefully built, original, and convincing, the story suspenseful enough. Set a century after *Rocket Ship Galileo*, it has few of the discrepancies with history that date the first book. Much of the interest comes from the Space Patrol itself, presented with detail and feeling that must reflect Heinlein's own Annapolis days.

Here he is already perfecting the *Bildungsroman* form that shapes the whole series. His heroes are learning, maturing, discovering their social roles. The rite-of-passage pattern shows mostly clearly when Matt goes home from the Space Academy to find himself alienated from his own past.

He finds the house shrunk, his kid brother amused at his spaceman's walk, his mother terrified by his familiarity with orbital bombs, his father smugly certain that the Patrol would never bomb the North American Union, his girl interested in another man. In a moment of self-discovery, he changes his mind about resigning from the Patrol. "It was an accumulation of things—all of them adding up to just one idea, that little Mattie didn't live there any more."

The space aliens are already becoming a vital feature of the series. In the first novel, there is only the incidental discovery that the Moon had once been inhabited. In this one, we hear of the Martians, their ways of thinking different from our own. We see evidence that the asteroids are fragments of a lost planet, shattered half a billion years ago by an explosion set off by intelligent creatures. We meet the Venerian amphibians, whose biology and culture are convincingly drawn, though they lack the character and charm of the later aliens.

Heinlein's intellectual kinship with H.G. Wells appears in the theme of the novel: the idea that common men must be guided and guarded by a competent elite. Like Wells, he is something of a classicist; rejecting the romantic notion that society corrupts, he assumes instead that we need social training to save us. I suppose this feeling was fostered by his own military training. Though stated with most force in *Starship Troopers*, it appears in such early stories as "The Roads Must Roll," and it becomes a basic premise for the *Bildungsroman* pattern of the juveniles—a premise often in conflict with Heinlein's own deep sense of romantic individualism.

The code of the Patrol is the essence of the book, most moving in the tradition of letting the living answer for the dead at muster roll. The plot is built upon the process by which Matt is chosen, trained, and tested. The contrasting weakling is Burke, who scoffs at the code, resigns to join the selfish enterprises of his wealthy father, and gets himself and the Patrol into trouble through dishonorable behavior. *Space Cadet* inspired a successful TV series in the 1950s, and even now, in the antimilitary aftermath of Vietnam, it still reads well.

With *Red Planet*, published in 1940, Heinlein found his true direction for the series. The Martian setting is logically constructed and rich in convincing detail—done well enough to make us forget the failure of the Mariners and Vikings to find Percival Lowell's canals and the beings that built them. The characters are engaging and the action develops naturally. Here, for the first time, Heinlein is making the most of his aliens. Willis, the young Martian nymph, is completely real and completely delightful. The whole tone of the book is set by the contrasts between the selfish human bureaucrats who exploit the settlers and the courteous and benign Martians who save them.

The aliens and robots of science fiction are commonly interesting only as symbols of human traits and feelings, and Heinlein makes his extraterrestrials an important part of the symbolic structure. Sometimes they are antagonists; those in *Starman Jones* and *Time for the Stars* can stand for the hostility of untamed nature. But more commonly they are neutral or friendly, and they often serve as teachers for the maturing heroes.

The essential action of the *Bildungsroman* is the process of conflict and growth that replaces native animal traits with social behavior. In *Red Planet*, the Company and its minions stand for the primitive self, the Martians for society. Like society itself, they are old but timeless, wise, bound by custom and tradition. Some of them are ghosts, transcending individual death as society does.

The Martians in this story have a special interest, because they are the educators of Valentine Michael Smith in another rite-of-passage novel, *Stranger in a Strange Land*. *Red Planet* is set a little later and we get to know the Martians better, but they display the same appalling powers that Smith brings back to Earth.

The Company, here, is pure greed. The colonists have been migrating from hemisphere to hemisphere to escape the savage Martian winters, but now the absentee officials plan to stop the migrations, enabling them to double the human population and make year-round use of the facilities. The harsh schoolmaster and other profit-minded Company men are plotting to sell Willis to the London zoo.

The settlers themselves are rugged frontier types, who wear guns as badges of social maturity. They are at the mercy of the Company, however, until Jim and his pal, with a spectacular assist from the Martians, are able to warn and rescue them. Since the action takes place in only a few days, Jim has little time for significant growth, but the action does test his maturing courage, tolerance, and altruism.

Farmer in the Sky, published in 1950, is a hymn to the pioneer. The sky frontier is on Ganymede, Jupiter's largest moon, but the plot parallels the familiar history of the colonization of America—the torch ship that carries the settlers from Earth is named the *Mayflower*.

As a novel of education, the book shows the creation of a rugged individualist. Heinlein uses point of view of unified action that covers half a billion miles of space and a good deal of time, letting Bill Lermer tell his own story in a relaxed, conversational style. Bill is a Scout—the novel was serialized in *Boy's Life*—and Scout training helps to build his competent self-reliance. The contrasting characters are the incompetent misfits who expect society to solve their problems.

The story has a harsh realism unusual for a juvenile. The migrants leave the overpopulated Earth to escape hunger and the threat of war. They struggle to survive on a world never meant for men. More than half are killed by a destructive quake. They meet no friendly aliens, though, near the end, Bill and his friend discover a cache of machines left long ago by a mysterious space visitor. Not very important in the story, this incident does give the reader a welcome break from the grimly hostile setting.

The characters are live people. Bill's mother is dead; he finds his father's new wife hard to accept but becomes deeply attached to his new stepsister, a frail girl whose body can't adapt to the cruel new world.

Much of the interest comes from Heinlein's careful technological extrapolations. The novel household gadgets of his future century are unobtrusively presented. The torch ship is expertly engineered, and the problems of terraforming Ganymede are dramatized in fascinating detail. The idea of terraforming—of transforming an alien world to fit our Terran needs—goes back at least to the air plants on Burroughs' Barsoom, but nobody in science fiction has explored the process more thoroughly than Heinlein does here. Ganymede, so far from the Sun, must have a heat trap to warm it; ice enough to make a worldwide layer twenty feet deep must be processed for oxygen; rock must be ground to dust and seeded with Terran bacteria for soil.

Between Planets, published in 1951, moves the series still further from its juvenile origins toward grown-up concerns. Though we meet the space-born hero while he is still a schoolboy in New Mexico, at the end of the novel he is a combat-tested fighting man with marriage in view. The magazine version of the story appeared in the general adventure magazine *Blue Book* instead of in *Boy's Life*, and the plot grows from the struggle for individual freedom that has become one of Heinlein's major themes.

His political philosophy, expressed here and in much of his later work, resembles that outlined eighty years ago by Brooks Adams in the *Law of Civilization and Decay*. In Adams' own words, "As the pressure of economic competition intensifies with social consolidation, the family regularly disintegrates, the children rejecting the parental authority at a steadily decreasing age; until, finally, the population fuses into a compact mass, in which all individuals are equal before the law, and all are forced to compete with each other for the means of subsistence." Adams admires the barbarians, whom he sees as family men, respecting women and children and the arts of war. He finds no good in the "economic man," who has lost his primitive virtues and loves only money. On Heinlein's overcrowded and urbanized Earth, the family has given way to the central authority of the oppressive Federation, which rules and exploits all the planets.

Don Harvey unwittingly becomes a courier for a secret group of freedom plotters; unwillingly, he is involved in a revolt of the human colonists on Venus that seems loosely patterned after the American Revolution. Though some of the action is pretty traditional space opera, the characters are ably drawn and Heinlein closes the novel with a vigorous statement of his unhappiness with "the historical imperative of the last two centuries, the withering away of individual freedom under larger and [ever] more pervasive organizations, both governmental and quasi-governmental."

The Venerian "dragons"—Heinlein seems to scorn the euphemistic term Venusian—are among his most appealing and most convincing space aliens, serving as powerful symbols for his freedom theme. "Sir Isaac Newton" is an enormous, long-tailed saurian whose ancestors evolved in the seas of Venus; he has learned to supplement his whistled native "true speech" with an elaborately formal sort of English spoken through a vocoder and with a Cockney accent. He is a brilliant physicist, a courteous host, a staunch defender of individual liberty, and a loyal friend to Don Harvey, whose mother's family came from Venus. The extended family is the Venerian social unit, and Sir Isaac stands for all the city-threatened values that Heinlein and Brooks Adams admire.

Though the theme is strong, it is never allowed to overwhelm the story, as sometimes happens in Heinlein's later work. No matter how much he dislikes the urbanization and the centralized social discipline that seem to be essential for the flowering of technology, he still loves the technological gadgetry itself. The whole background is well imagined, the story told with zest. It hardly matters that Venus is now no longer the humid jungle planet we all used to picture before the space probes began reporting temperatures too high for organic life.

The Rolling Stones, published in 1952, displays an enviable craftsmanship. The narrative is episodic and nearly plotless, a fact that Heinlein emphasizes with the contrast between the lives of his protagonists and the events of the melodramatic adventure serial they are writing about the Galactic Overlord. Discarding most of the standard devices for suspense, he is still able to compel the reader's interest in his lively people and their almost aimless wanderings from Luna City to Mars and the Asteroids and on toward Saturn... and "the ends of the Universe."

They are the Stone family, ranging in age from the apparently immortal Grandmother Hazel, through the teenaged "unheavenly twins," Castor and Pollux, down to Lowell, the infant genius who can already beat his grandmother at chess. Each one is a variation on the brilliantly competent man. Heinlein reveals them indirectly, through action and dialogue. There is no description of Meade, the older sister, but when we learn that her doctor-sculptress mother is modeling her head, we assume that she is attractive.

The story is a dream of personal freedom. The Stones leave Luna City in a secondhand spaceship, with no motives except an impatience with social restraints and an itch to see the universe. With the father in command, as captain of the ship, the family becomes once more the fully independent social unit.

Here, I believe, Heinlein is dramatizing a personal concern that is also a dilemma of our technological world. Advancing technology not only asks competent people to master special skills, but it also asks for smooth cooperation. The increasingly complex division of labor requires a social discipline strong enough to prevent sabotage and acts of terrorism, to restrain the power grabs of narrow selfish interests, to unite workers and managers, to fuse the elite and the mass. The protection of the world machines requires a painful sacrifice of personal freedom which I think Heinlein is reluctant to accept.

But *The Rolling Stones*, unlike such later works as *Farnham's Freehold*, carries its thematic burden lightly. It is a delightful romp through space, brightened with such items as the Martian flat cats, which multiply like the guinea pigs in Ellis Parker Butler's famous funny story ("Pigs is Pigs"), until the money-minded twins find a market for them in the meteor-mining colony.

Much of the effect comes as usual from the sense of an accurately extrapolated future background, with all the new technologies given an air of commonplace reality. The used spaceship, for example, is bought from "Dealer Dan, the Spaceship Man," who is drawn after today's used-car salesmen. Though the meteor miners use radar and rocket scooters, they live like forty-niners.

The pattern of social initiation is not quite so clear here as in the other novels, since the whole family is in flight from organized society. The self-centered twins change only slightly, but they do gain some sense of obligation to a wider humanity. The whole family takes risks to bring the mother's medical skills to sick spacemen.

Starman Jones, published in 1953, is a classic example of the *Bildungsroman* pattern and perhaps my own favorite of the series. Max Jones is a poor, hill farm boy faced with the hard problem of finding the place he wants in a closed society. With Heinlein's reasonably consistent future history moving on, the old torch ship *Einstein* has become the starship *Asgard*, now equipped with Horst-Conrad impellers that can drive her at the speed of light and beyond, to jump her across the light-years through the congruences of a folded universe. Max wants to be a starman, but his way is barred by a rigid guild system that has no room for him.

Good science fiction mixes the known and the new—in more formal terms, it recognizes that we can perceive and respond to those items that can somehow attach to the mental structures we already possess. Heinlein gives us exciting novelties enough in Max's universe, but not without his usual deft preparation. We see Max slopping the hogs and feeding the chickens before he runs away from an intolerable "step-stepmother" and her insufferable new husband to look for his way to the stars.

For all his social handicaps, he has several things going for him: a genius for math, an eidetic memory, a friend named Sam. He has listened to the tales of an uncle who belonged to the Astrogators' Guild and memorized the tech manuals and space charts the uncle left him. Sam is an older man, a figure who neatly complements Max in the role-finding pattern of the novel. Once an Imperial Marine, he has lost his social place because he lacks Max's moral strength. Now a colorful conniver, whose entertaining speech tag is his habit of mixing familiar proverbs, he gives his life at the end of the book in full atonement for his social faults.

The background is worked out with love and skill; though some of the minor characters are stereotypes, they are expertly drawn; Max's young love affair is convincing and appealing. Even on re-reading, I find his social triumphs and defeats really moving.

Though the space aliens play only minor roles, they seem to echo the theme. When the lost ship lands on a new planet, its highly organized alien ecology is as hostile to all men as the closed human social system has seemed to Max.

Aboard the *Asgard* with forged papers provided by Sam, he is always in a precarious position, his social status always in jeopardy, yet he learns to make the most of social opportunity. At the end, when all the other qualified astrogators are dead and the tech manuals and tables are missing, it is Max alone who can take command and pilot the ship through the new congruity, back to galactic civilization.

With its bold symbolism, the book makes a universal appeal. We are all born lonely individualists; we must all make the same struggle, often hard and painful, for a foothold in society. Though there is unlikely coincidence and occasional melodrama in Max's story, such faults don't matter. The novel is a fine juvenile, but also something more. It reflects hopes and fears we all have known.

Star Beast, published in 1954, is vastly different from *Starman*

Jones but equally outstanding. Though part of the Scribner's juvenile series, it ran in *The Magazine of Fantasy and Science Fiction*, the most literate of the category magazines. The actual protagonists are not young John Thomas Stuart and his girl, Betty Sorensen, but rather Mr. Kiku, who is the competently mature Permanent Under Secretary for Spatial Affairs, and Lummox, the star beast herself.

The beast is Heinlein's most charming space alien, a truck-sized, eight-legged, steel-eating monster, brought back to Earth while still only pup-sized by an earlier John Thomas, great-grandfather of the young hero. Lummox is appalling in appearance but entirely amiable, and four John Thomas generations have kept her as a pet.

The book is a wildly delightful comedy grown from Heinlein's continual concern with the able individual in conflict with incompetent pretenders. Most of the fun comes from our anarchistic joy in the successful defiance of rigid social norms and the stupid people who attempt to enforce them. The victims of this satiric exposure range from the Westville city officials to the bumbling politician who is Mr. Kiku's nominal superior.

The comic action begins when Lummox pushes out of her pen to taste some tempting rosebushes. Alarmed by the attacks of frightened neighbors, she causes innocent harm. The Chief and his minions try to destroy her, but find her happily indestructible. Mr. Kiku is involved when Lummox's people come across nine hundred light-years of space to take her home, threatening to vaporize the Earth unless she is surrendered to them. When she is found, she refuses to leave without John Thomas. The whole mad situation enables Heinlein to satirize the faults and follies of every level of human society from the family to the Terran Federation.

John Thomas's mother is among the frustrated plotters against Lummox, and his girl has divorced her own intolerant parents. Mr. Kiku manipulates his political superiors with a superb finesse, allowing Heinlein to lay bare the absurdities of bureaucracy and diplomacy. Lummox is a fine symbol of the romantic individualist, self-impelled, at odds with a corrupt society but undamaged by it. John Thomas and Betty Sorensen enjoy a sort of social immunity borrowed from her, and Mr. Kiku stands tall on his own black feet.

These devastating shots at society and its leaders imply the same reservations about popular rule that H.G. Wells often expressed. Near the end of the book, Mr. Kiku says that the government "is not now a real democracy and it can't be." Majority rule might be good, "But it's rarely that easy. We find ourselves oftener the pilots of a ship in a life-and-death emergency. Is it the pilot's duty to hold powwows with the passengers? Or is it his job to use his skill and experience to bring them safely home?"

But the book is no sermon. Though this familiar theme is stated with force enough, it isn't allowed to spoil the fun, which ends only with the satisfying discovery that the actual pet is not Lummox, but John Thomas himself.

Tunnel in the Sky, published in 1955, lacks the mad fascination of *Star Beast*, though it is built on a wonderful story idea. Life has now become lean on the crowded future Earth, but the star gates are opening on new planets all across the galaxy. Since some of these are dangerous, the schools teach survival. Rod Walker is a high school senior who is dropped with his classmates on an unfriendly new world for a survival test. When a nova explosion disables their gate, the young people are left on their own.

Though the situation is much like that in Golding's *Lord of the Flies*, the development is vastly different. In Golding's book, we watch civilization dissolve into savagery; Heinlein's heroes, before they are rescued, have begun to plant a vigorous new civilization. Golding is a classicist, I think, distrusting the human animal; Heinlein, though half a classicist in making the social adaptation of the naive individual the subject of the whole series, is still I think somehow a romanticist at heart, rejoicing in competent individualism and conceding no more than he must to society.

Another novel of education, *Tunnel in the Sky* begins with both Rod and his teacher uncertain that he is ready for the survival test. On his upward way to leadership in the accidental colony, he must learn to cope with human rivals as well as with an unkind environment. Yet, though the book sometimes seems to have been planned as a parable of man and society, the theme is blurred. The ending strikes me as arbitrary; with the star gate reopened, the young people simply abandon their social experiment.

The problem, I suspect, is another unresolved conflict between Heinlein's romantic individualism and his awareness of the social discipline required by a technological culture. The best writing is in the first half of the book, in which Rod's competence for survival is being developed in conflicts with savage nature and savage-seeming human beings. The latter chapters, in which he is establishing social relationships within the new culture, seem oddly flat and hollow. He avoids sex relationships in a hardly normal way—though his behavior here may have been only Heinlein's concession to his juvenile editors.

In any case, the book simply fails to live up to its initial promises. We are told in the opening that man, "the two-legged brute," is the most dangerous animal in the universe, "which goes double for the female of the species." The first half of the book supports that assumption, but then the human menace fades, leaving only the wilderness planet with its less-than-human threats.

Yet the book is far from bad. The setting, as always, is solidly done. We feel the pinch of want on the overpopulated Earth and we understand the history and the working of the planetary gates that have made migration an alternative to war. Some of the minor characters are memorable, especially Rod's older sister, who is an expert killer, a captain in the Amazons. Most of the story is suspenseful enough, and the weak ending may be only a sign that Heinlein is growing tired of juveniles.

In *Time for the Stars*, published in 1956, Heinlein drops back in history to an age when the torch ships are first venturing beyond the solar system to find room for teeming humanity on new planets. Traveling at less than light-speed, the explorer ships take many years for each crossing between stars, and few of them return.

The plot builds from the idea that telepathy, existing most often between twins, can cross interstellar distances with no time lag. Often in science fiction psionics becomes a wild card allowed to wreck all story logic, but here Heinlein limits and explores it in a completely believable way.

Tom and Pat Bartlett are twins—ignorant of their telepathic gift until tested for service as interstellar communicators. Pat unconsciously fakes an injury that lets him stay safe at home to marry the girl they both love and get rich with their joint earnings, while Tom undertakes the dangerous voyage that may last a hundred years. Tom stays young, moving at relativistic velocities, while Pat grows old. At the end of the story, Tom's mental link at home is no longer Pat but Pat's great-granddaughter.

The story has action enough, including a final struggle with space aliens as mysterious and implacable as the physical universe itself, but the main conflict is Tom's internal battle against the psychological complexes that have allowed Pat to dominate him. He must learn to see the unconscious hate beneath his dutiful love, to break the old habit of always giving in. Heinlein presents this conflict with insight and feeling, giving the story more character drama than usual and building suspense all the way to the final showdown between the old twin and the young.

All the hidden implications of the premise are worked out with Heinlein's usual thoughtful skill. Since such instant mind contact across vast distances is forbidden by Einstein's equations, the equations have to be revised. The logical outcome of these revisions is the "irrelevant" starship, the *Serendipity*, which overtakes the old *Lewis and Clark* in time to jump Tom home for the climactic confrontation with his aged twin and for a twenty-second telepathic courtship with his beautiful great-grandniece.

Beginning on the people-ridden Earth, where parents are taxed for too many children—Tom and Pat were unplanned—the whole story is bleak in tone, with none of the mad comedy of *Star Beast*. Yet it's another fine *Bildungsroman*, given a very original twist. Tom grows up to kill the enemy within and become his own man. If he gets bossed again, it won't be by Pat.

Citizen of the Galaxy, published in 1957, is a sort of epilogue to the whole Scribner's series. The other books, taken together, tell an epic story of the expansion of mankind across the planets of our own Sun and the stars beyond. All that is now past history. The plot action begins off the Earth, in the tyrannic Empire of the Nine Worlds, and carries us on a grand tour of galactic cultures already long established.

The theme springs once more from Heinlein's concern with individual freedom. We meet Thorby as a frightened, whip-scarred child sold at a slave auction. The crippled beggar who buys him is a secret agent of the Exotic Corps, a space police outfit fighting slavery. When the beggar is killed, Thorby escapes to carry information from him to other agents among the space gypsies who call themselves Free Traders, then to the Guard Cruiser *Hydra*, and finally back to legendary Terra, where he is at last identified as the Rubek of Rubek, heir to his own fabulous industrial empire. After a legal battle, he recovers his legacy from the corrupt men in his own company who have been building ships for the slavers and who murdered his parents to avoid detection.

As the story of a young man's education and self-discovery, this clearly fits the classic juvenile pattern, yet the book is adult enough so that John Campbell bought serial rights for *Astounding Science Fiction*. The opening is gripping; the old beggar and the slave boy compel our sympathy; the several settings are detailed with Heinlein's usual captivating skill; the whole novel still reads well.

Yet, for all its ambitious scope, it has major faults. The jumps from one setting to another break it almost into a series of novelettes, each involving Thorby with a new cluster of characters. Toward the end, the suspense collapses—Thorby is only a spectator at the climactic legal battle, which is won by a Jubal Harshaw type (Harshaw, of course, is the brilliant lawyer and a major character in *Stranger in a Strange Land*). Too, I miss the new technologies that add so much genuine wonder to the other books. With the conquest of space already complete, however, I see no real need for new inventions here, and I suppose Heinlein's interests were already shifting from the physical to the social sciences, from gadgets to cultures —the culture of the Free Traders is certainly an anthropologist's delight. In the next novel, anyhow, he comes back to physical science, with one last completely fascinating gadget.

Have Space Suit—Will Travel, published in 1958, brings the series to a highly satisfying climax. The novel opens on a near-future, very familiar Earth. The hero is Kip, another bright and likable boy, who tells his own story in his own breezy style. He wants to go to the Moon, and things begin when he tries for a free trip offered in an advertising giveaway and wins a badly used space suit.

Again we have the rite-of-passage pattern, but done with unusual love and verve. Kip's world is convincingly familiar: he reads *National Geographic* and attends Centerville High and works after school as a soda jerk. His story moves fast. Though he packs it with simplified scientific fact and with philosophic ideas picked up from his individualistic father, he never stops to preach.

The space suit is the essential gadget. It's worthless junk when Kip receives it from the satirized sellers of soap, but he rebuilds it in time to become involved, along with an eleven-year-old girl genius, in a melodramatic space adventure. The girl, Peewee Reisfeld, has been caught by a gang of evil, worm-faced aliens who have also captured the Mother Thing, a furry and appealing creature who is a sort of galactic cop. There is a good deal of routine space opera in the plot action that carries us stage by stage to the Moon, to Pluto, to the Mother Thing's home on Vega V, out to the capital of the Three Galaxies in the Lesser Magellanic Cloud, and finally back again to Earth. With Heinlein's zest and his fine detail, however, the stereotypes are well disguised. Peewee and the Mother Thing are likable people, and the story still holds me.

At the crisis, Kip and Peewee find themselves the spokesmen for the human race before a high court that has already exterminated the worm-faced villains and now charges humanity with being too savage and too intelligent, therefore too dangerous to be left alive. The trial becomes a test of Heinlein's symbolic competent character, perhaps of his own philosophy. Threatened with the extinction of mankind, Kip is defiant. When the judges ask him if he has more to say:

> I looked around the hall. —*the cloud-capped towers... the great globe itself*— "Just this!" I said savagely. "It's not a defense, you don't *want* a defense. All right, take away our star— You will if you can and I guess you can. Go ahead! We'll *make* a star! Then, someday, we'll come back and hunt you down—*all of you!*"

The happy outcome, after an appeal from the compassionate Mother Thing, is that humanity is placed on probation and Kip and Peewee are returned to Earth. Kip is a soda jerk once more, but now with the nerve to toss a chocolate malt into the face of a boy who has bullied him—an incident that Heinlein kept in the book over editorial objection. The series couldn't have had a finer conclusion.

Starship Troopers is a thirteenth juvenile, also written for Scribner's. Following the same story-of-education pattern, it traces the making of a starship soldier. In contrast to *Have Space Suit—Will Travel*, however, it is a dark, disturbing novel, set in a time of vicious space war and devoted to glorification of the fighting man. Though many of its ideas and attitudes had appeared in earlier books of the series, this one was too strong for the editors at Scribner's. They rejected it.

Published by Putnam in 1959, after serialization in *Fantasy and Science Fiction*, it won a Hugo and it still has hearty admirers. Impressed myself by the anthropology of Raymond Dart and Robert Ardrey, I suspect that Heinlein's unpopular emphasis on human savagery is closer to the truth than the cheerier views of his juvenile editors. However that may be, *Starship Troopers* was a turning point in his career, and it began his alienation from a whole school of science fiction criticism. The inspiring theme of space conquest that unifies the dozen Scribner's titles seems complete without it.

Considering the Scribner's books as a group, we can claim for them a major role in the evolution of modern science fiction. Certainly they gave many thousand young readers, and thousands not so young, a delightful introduction to the genre. Built on sound futurology, they still make a fine primer for the new reader. The best of them are splendid models of literary craftsmanship, with more discipline and finish than most of Heinlein's other work. Revealing significant conflicts and shifts of thought, they are relevant to any survey of his whole career.

If their generally optimistic vision of space conquest is not so popular now as it once was, one reason is that we have almost abandoned our real space programs, giving up our grand designs to probe too often into festering "inner space." Our loss of faith in our future and our science and ourselves will surely become a global tragedy if it is not recovered. These books have a spirit too great to be forgotten. They need to be read again.

2. Major Frontier Worlds of Robert A. Heinlein: The Future and Fantasy*

DAVID N. SAMUELSON

THROUGHOUT HIS CAREER, the frontier metaphor has been basic to Heinlein's writing. Only eight of his twenty-eight novels take place primarily on Earth, and four of them concern relations between humans and intelligent extraterrestrial beings, while a fifth concludes on the Moon. This outward spatial movement, coupled with a forward temporal movement, places Heinlein's characters in situations of extremity, facing the unknown and having to learn to understand it, in order just to survive. Whether they are in spaceships or on alien worlds, exploring or settling or righting wrongs, fighting off other species or learning to live with them, their situations parallel those of the American pioneers, for all that they are equipped with advanced technology, "scientific" thinking, and the benefits of historical hindsight. Even in a utopian situation, even in the present or near future here on Earth, even where mental or psi powers are involved, a kind of frontier ethic is invoked, in order to make possible a free exercise of individual initiative, or to justify pragmatically certain measures that in more structured situations, such as those of the society we actually live in, would have to be considered extreme. On the frontier, Heinlein's heroes can be free *from* anything that technology and goodwill can overcome, such as physical slavery, mental bondage, the "prisons" of a single planet and the human body, the limitations of distance and even of death. They can be free *to* roam, explore, discover, earn fame and success, learn things that are useful for the individual or the race, or to achieve self-actualization.

That these freedoms are primarily available to those who can best profit by them, that is, that they represent what Panshin[1] calls

*Reprinted from *Voices for the Future*, Thomas Clareson, ed. (Bowling Green University Popular Press, ©1976).

a "wolfish" sort of freedom for "the Heinlein individual," should not be too surprising, since this is a logical extension of the adolescent dream, especially its American versions. American literature and history are full of famous "wolfish" individuals who pioneered land, technology, and money matters in a society which encouraged everyone to seek, and enabled a few to achieve, their wildest dreams, believing the losses they brought to some were outweighed by the benefits they brought to all. That Heinlein, born in Missouri in 1907, is from a generation and a region which valued those achievements more than many people do today who take them for granted is surely relevant, but so is the fact that in any situation, certain people are more likely to succeed than others. In changing situations, such as the last five centuries of Western civilization, and the various futures Heinlein extrapolates from them, those who succeed are likely to be adaptable, even opportunistic. And Heinlein does not treat freedom, for the most part, as a simple escape. To be sure, some of his works contain large amounts of good-versus-evil melodrama, and lengthy sermons generalizing from inadequate particulars, and most of his work is pitched to the level of a reader of modest intellectual achievement. More often than not, however, the melodrama is subsidiary, the sermons are in character, and freedom is a complex issue, involving both power and responsibility, and requiring various kinds of trade-offs.

By using analogies with situations familiar from history, legend, and personal experience, by anchoring the unfamiliar in specific detail generated by these analogies, Heinlein manages to make his frontier worlds seem real, however weak he may be in plot construction, however limited his range of characters and emotions, however objectionable some of his tics of style, especially in dialogue. In this chapter, I shall examine two major extensions of the frontier metaphor which can be seen in his Future History series and related works from before World War II and in his long run of outright fantasies, in which I have included all of his "adult" novels since 1950. These works I have grouped, in the following discussion, under the subtitles "Frontiers of the Future" and "Frontiers of the Mind." Most of Heinlein's fiction which has appeared in book form will be discussed, leaving out of consideration a handful of stories as well as the original magazine forms of his earliest novel.*

---

*"Frontiers of Youth," a third section omitted here, discusses Heinlein's juveniles and appears in Clareson, ed., *Voices for the Future.*

Frontiers of the Future: Heinlein's Future History Stories

The background chart for Heinlein's Future History series (*Astounding Science Fiction* [hereafter ASF], May 1941; revised 1948; revised 1967) places up to twenty-seven stories in relationship to an assumed time-line stretching from about 1950 to approximately A.D. 2600, suggesting lines of political, scientific, and technological continuity which are only sketchily apparent in the stories themselves. As is immediately apparent in the 1967 omnibus, *The Past Through Tomorrow*, which arranges twenty-one stories and novels in fictionally chronological order, continuity is explicit only from "The Roads Must Roll" to "Requiem" and from "Logic of Empire" to *Methuselah's Children*. The implicit nature of the background, however, extends beyond this series of stories to take in at least three tales not included in the omnibus, as well as a number of novels which assume at least alternative paths in the same general direction. Progress is assumed in both technology (transportation, power sources) and society (toward "The First Human Civilization") with some crossover (psychometrics, semantics), but not as a straight-line projection. Heinlein takes it for granted that power will be abused by some, and that severe setbacks will occur, with a pendulum-like swing between freedom and enslavement (in psychological, as well as physical terms). Against this large-scale movement, individual human dramas will be played out which may support or contradict the slow cultural rise and fall; the Future History concept does not imply a *roman manqué* (like Simak's *City* or Bradbury's *The Martian Chronicles*), but rather a general set of assumptions about the history behind the individual stories. Thus the omission from the omnibus of three tales that definitely do fit ("Sky Lift" and "Columbus Was a Dope" from *The Menace from Earth*, "Let There Be Light" from *The Man Who Sold the Moon*) does not damage the concept, nor does the nonexistence of some five stories once planned as part of the series (for an explanation concerning three of them see "Concerning Stories Never Written: Postscript," *Revolt in 2100*).[2] The unity of the omnibus volume, however, does suffer by the inclusion of at least two stories that really don't fit, and by the aesthetic distance between the prewar stories (which seem to take the continuity seriously) and the postwar stories (which are more elementary in concept, if more polished in style).

"Life-Line" is an appropriate introduction to the omnibus, despite the lack of impact of its devices and characters on the ensuing fictional history (one short reference appears in the closing work). Heinlein's first published story (ASF, August 1939), its subject is ostensibly a machine, invented by Dr. Hugo Pinero, that predicts a person's instant of death. The story is also about the fear of knowledge and about the effects of perfecting such a device. Characters behave melodramatically, but the satire, pointed at scientists, reporters, insurance companies, gangsters, even lovers, is fairly effective. In this position, it points the reader toward the future, and introduces such continuing themes as the forgotten genius, the insanity of complacency, the value of empirical proof versus orthodox theory, and the powerful motivation of financial gain.

The next three stories explore the dimensions of power: technological, economic, and psychological. "The Roads Must Roll" (ASF, June 1940), is memorable for its projection that private cars would so clutter the world that another transportation system would be needed, and for its assumption that the transportation monopoly would have to be watched over by a faceless paramilitary class. But the description of the workings of the moving roads is vague and confusing, the lectures that halt the action are obtrusive, and the final confrontation between Gaines (the perfectionist "Mister Clean") and Van Kleeck (the "little man" who heads the labor "conspiracy") is so overblown and melodramatic as to be ludicrous. "Blowups Happen" (ASF, September 1940) is not so much about atomic power plants as it is about the custodial psychology adumbrated by Gaines and his Transportation Corps. To avoid atomic accidents, psychologists watch technicians, and are themselves observed, making temperamental blowups all the more likely. The situation is declared impossible by a world-famous physicist-psychologist consulted, and becomes more so when it seems the Moon once suffered atomic Armageddon. Power company directors choose to fire the plant superintendent rather than risk the economic chaos of a shutdown, but they are pressured into relocating the plant in orbit, made possible by the subplotted discovery of an atomic rocket fuel.[3] The solutions are simplistic, events happen with miraculous speed and coincidence, but the problems are built up seriously enough to make some melodrama credible, and most of the characters are convincing, if we allow for adventure magazine oversimplification. "The Man Who Sold the Moon" (*The Man Who Sold the Moon*, 1950), also oversimplified by contrast with the immensity of the real space program, is still readable and enjoyable despite its being dated; the chief reason is D.D. Harriman, the millionaire huckster-administrator who harnesses all his resources to a dream he can only realize vicariously. Beneath the wheeling and dealing, the conversations that are great fun but patently unreal, a sharp satirical blade separates Harriman's grandiose goals (which go far beyond a mere Moon landing) from the mundane realities of selling people something none of them really wants.[4] Harriman's gamesmanship enables him to play off against each other the avarice and self-interest of both rich and poor, even at the expense of an occasional minor swindle. It also leads him into the financial trap which keeps him, like Moses (the comparison is explicit), from getting to the promised land. The sense of a legend in the making haunts every scene, most of them are handled with wit and practical realism, and the pace for a change is almost leisurely.

Of the next eleven stories, fictionally bracketing the year 2000, most are compactly and carefully crafted, but dependent for their impact upon a slick manipulation of sentiment, as is appropriate for publication in a mass-circulation, general-interest magazine. "Delilah and the Space-Rigger" (*Blue Book*, January 1949) describes the building of a space station in orbit, but its plot turns on the device of permitting women to be part of the work crew. "Space Jockey" (*The Saturday Evening Post*, April 26, 1947) concerns Jake Pemberton, whose job as a rocket pilot conflicts with his home life. An earlier story, "Requiem" (ASF, January 1940), is just as sentimental, but more clumsily executed.[5] The inordinate fondness many science fiction fans have for this story may be based partly on their own commitment to science fiction and space travel, and partly on its relationship to "The Man Who Sold the Moon." In "Requiem," an aging D.D. Harriman outwits his heirs and the law, and manages to get to the Moon after all, with the aid of two calloused space bums and rickety rocket ship; his triumph is short-lived, for he dies from the physical strain of the flight, but not until he sets foot on the lunar surface. "The Long Watch" (*American Legion Magazine*, December 1949) is a detailed sketch of how a political and military *naif* surprises himself by sacrificing his life to foil a military takeover of a lunar base for atomic missiles.[6] "Gentlemen, Be Seated" (Argosy, May 1948) uses a background of lunar colonization for a low-keyed rescue story, the point of which is plugging an air leak with the seat of one's pants. "The Black Pits of Luna" (*The Saturday Evening Post*, January 10, 1948), another lunar rescue story, depends on our sympathy for a lost child and his brother, the teenage narrator, who locates him. The best of the lot, " 'It's Great to Be Back' " (*The Saturday Evening Post*, July 26, 1947), works on our understanding of the impossibility of ever "going home again," along with our awareness of inanities and discomforts of urban and suburban living, applying them by analogy to the plight of a young scientist couple, dissatisfied with living on the Moon, who find they are really accustomed to it and cannot readjust to life on Earth.

One of the best stories in the volume, " '—We Also Walk Dogs,' " (ASF, July 1941), does not really fit the Future History scheme: other stories show no awareness of gravity neutralization, intelligent aliens from our sister planets, or the type of operation typified by General Services, Inc., the corporate "hero" of this story. Thematically, of course, it exhibits the faith in technology and self-serving behavior which are common Heinlein features, and by its position amid "space" stories, it illustrates that Earth is not completely stagnant all this time. General Services, built up by the desire of people with money to have things done for them, is called upon to make possible an interspecies conference on Earth. The nullification of gravity required is theoretically impossible, but one man might be able to do it. To get his cooperation, since he is only interested in his own research, GS must replicate a famous bowl in the British Museum, and give him the original. All of this must be, and is, accomplished quickly and without publicity; the real focus, though, is on people and motivations. Like Harriman, the GS people are interested in making money, in seeing a job well done, and in something extra. They cynically manipulate a rich dowager, opportunistically rig contractual rights to the gravity neutralizer, and treat the whole operation as a matter of course. But they are humanized, as is the crotchety inventor, by a reverential possessiveness toward the coveted bowl, "The Flower of Forgetfulness," which tempts them, too, to withdraw into abstract contemplation.

With "Searchlight" (commissioned for an advertisement by Hoffman Electronics, August 1962, *Scientific American* and other magazines), the omnibus returns to sentimentality, asking our unearned sympathy for a girl, a blind musical prodigy, lost on the Moon in yet another rescue story. "Ordeal in Space" (*Town and Country*, May 1948), describes a spaceman's earthbound attempts to adapt to his fear of falling; most scenes are well done, especially those tracing his fears, but the accidental cause of his overcoming them is a kitten (!) lost on a window ledge. Sentiment is milked to the last drop in "The Green Hills of Earth" (*The Saturday Evening Post*, February 8, 1947), "the story of Rhysling, the Blind Singer of the Spaceways," which recounts his adventures as a space bum, his dirty songs (supposedly unexpurgated), his romantic visions, and his dying act of heroism, during which he recorded the final version of the title song.

The second definite sequence begins with "Logic of Empire" (ASF, March 1941), a heavily didactic story about the colonization of Venus and the interdependency of freedom and slavery. With the aid of large chunks of lecture, Heinlein tries to convince his readers of the inevitability of slavery in certain colonial situations, and the equally inevitable fight of some men to be free. The hero is Humphrey Wingate, a lawyer disbelieving in Venerian slavery who is then forced to experience it; on his return to Earth, thanks to some happy coincidences, he finds others as hard to convince as he had been. Although the physical enslavement is also real, psychological enslavement permeates the story. Earth people don't want to know anything discomforting, and Wingate runs from one mental prison to another: from disbelief to numbed acceptance to a "devil theory" to the only form in which his memoirs can gain a reading public, the ghostwritten "I Was a Slave on Venus." Lightly foreshadowed is the seventy-year American theocracy, whose overthrow is chronicled after the next story.

Out of sequence is "The Menace from Earth" (*Fantasy and Science Fiction*, August 1957), the girl narrator of which corresponds in age and interests to heroes of the "juvenile" novels of Heinlein's second period.[7] Although Holly Jones's romantic naiveté is hard to credit, her dreams of becoming a rocket designer do not seem entirely farfetched, given the time and study she and her prospective partner devote to them. Her provincialism is logically developed, establishing her expertise in her own backyard (Luna City), her disdain for the visiting media starlet, and her need to be educated about herself and her emotions. The real protagonist of the story, as Panshin points out (p. 79), is Luna City; as so often in Heinlein, and science fiction, the characters and events seem to exist for the sake of giving the reader a tour of the facilities. Holly's blasé acceptance of tourists' idiosyncrasies, of the multileveled warren she lives in (neatly summed up by its single map, huge and three-dimensional), and of the "Bats' Cave" where everyone *flies* for recreation, provides the proper air of understatement such wonders would deserve in their own context and environment. Given Holly's self-involvement, we learn little about the people, politics, or technology of Luna City, but we know a good deal about how it feels to live there.

"'If This Goes On—'" (ASF, February-March, 1940) is impressive as an early long narrative; improved by rewriting for book form (1953), it is still choppy and disjointed, but that is justified to some extent by the viewpoint of the narrator. To tell this story of events leading up to and including the overthrow of the Prophet Incarnate, whose theocracy has ruled for some seventy years over what was once the United States, Heinlein has chosen a young innocent, John Lyle, a recent graduate of West Point dragged into the revolution by his romantic infatuation with an equally young and innocent priestess, or Virgin, about to loose her eponymous quality. The first ten short chapters recount his fleeting romance, his induction into the local unit of the underground "Cabal" (despite its policy of discouraging "romantics"), his inquisition, the rescue of Sister Judith, and Lyle's disguise, travels, and escape to the refuge of General Headquarters in a cavern near Phoenix, at which point he was ordered to write the preceding events in a journal. Continuing the journal for his own interest, apparently, Lyle devotes two long chapters to describing the organizational setup and his own partial reeducation before plunging into a description of as much of the revolutionary action as he saw himself. If Lyle is at all typical of the believing populace, the reeducation of this society will be slow at best, since his innocence is all but invincible, and the techniques of brainwashing are rejected. The blows he strikes for freedom are simple, personal, emotional, leaving theoretical considerations to his friend and mentor, Zebadiah Jones, and other members of the Cabal. Lyle does, however, describe what they tell and show him about the business of revolution, the manipulation of media, and the power of propaganda, thus illustrating in a general sense the powers of the common man. The action scenes are well done, the illusion of expertise is excellent, and the naiveté about women and romance, which was necessary in 1940 (and may have been still, to Heinlein's commercial sense, in 1953), is at least motivated by Lyle's innocent upbringing.

The reeducation of the people does occur, in order for the last three works to take place against a common background of utopian peace and tranquillity. Called "The First Human Civilization" on the Future History chart, this civilization obeys a libertarian rule called "the Covenant," exceptions to which propel the next three stories. "Coventry" (ASF, July 1940) is another sermon in disguise. It shows David MacKinnon, an incompetent brawler educated only in "romantic" literature, learning to appreciate the net of civil interdependence by being forced to live outside of it, in a reservation for malcontents, with three societies far more repressive than what he left. MacKinnon's failures provide low comedy, until he is rescued in a sense by an undercover agent, and proves his own reconditioning by a heroic act of loyalty to the Covenant society. The reservation societies are not detailed in such a short work, but the point is clearly established that, without responsible cooperation, liberty is impossible. "Misfit" (ASF, November 1939), Heinlein's second published story, shows youths who are outside the Covenant, or disobedient to it, pressed into service in a "cosmic Construction Corps." On one such job, turning an asteroid into a space station, among the boys whose talents are apparently not needed on Earth is Andrew Jackson Libby, an intuitive mathematical genius whose skills and stubbornness prove highly valuable. The story is notable for its matter-of-fact detailed sketch of everyday behavior in a setting which still seems right around the corner, technologically if not socially.

Concluding the omnibus volume, the novel *Methuselah's Children* (ASF, July-September 1941; revised for book publication 1958) picks up a number of threads from earlier tales, such as freedom and slavery, practice over theory, progress through experimentation, and the value of administrative competence. References to the Prophet and the Covenant, to Pinero and Harriman, to the rolling road and the colonies on the Moon and Venus establish fictional continuity; even one character is carried over from another story, "Slipstick" Libby, the *idiot savant* of "Misfit." The general thrust of Future History away from Earth, from arbitrary rules and constraints, is extended beyond the solar system, as one hundred thousand people escape a pogrom by stealing a starship designed to support generations of human life. These people comprise the Howard Families, products of a voluntary program of breeding for longevity under way since 1874 (the novel begins in 2136). The fact of their longevity leads to their persecution by a society covetous enough to suspend the Covenant in order to pry from them their "secret," believed to be some sort of chemical treatment. After the melodrama of the novel's first half, the second half is more leisurely; the families experience aimlessness in life in the *New Frontiers*, and on two alien planets, before going home again to try to regain a sense of meaning. Technological extrapolation gives way to fantasy, in Libby's handmade "light-pressure" drive which converts to faster-than-light travel, as well as in the forms and powers of the beings who inhabit the Howards' adopted planets.

That the narrative does not appear as fragmented as it might is due largely to the unity supplied by its central character and its basic theme. Supposedly about a hundred thousand people, the story focuses on only a handful, especially one man, born Woodrow Wilson Smith in 1912, alias Captain Aaron Sheffield, best known as Lazarus Long. The stuff of legends, he has already lived through many careers, but not to boredom or passivity; action-oriented, where his relatives are security-conscious, he is capable of carrying out that action, as he proves. Far older than any other surviving member of the Families, he is a precursor of what longevity could bring: problems of memory storage, but also zest for life, and the ability to combine and utilize several "lifetimes" worth of experience. As he is an unlikely model for the Families, so are they to the people on Earth who, in their absence, perfect the nonexistent treatments they once sought, making the whole human race potentially "Methuselah's Children." A compendium of ideas for other possible stories, *Methuselah's Children* obviously was meant to strike sparks, not to provide any definitive answers. Placed at the end of *The Past Through Tomorrow*, it not only sums up the past (our immediate future), but also opens up the further future in space as well as time.

With its hundred thousand people, the *New Frontiers* could have served as a microcosm of the human race, but that theme was reserved for two stories about her sister ship the *Vanguard*, the story of which is told in "Universe" (ASF, May 1941) and "Common Sense" (ASF, October 1941), later packaged and sold as a novel (*Orphans of the Sky*, 1963). In this alternative view of starship travel, incorporated into the Future History chart, a mutiny killed off the knowledgeable crew and technicians, and the people developed a self-contained society, with science downgraded to superstition, and mutants or renegades either fed to the nuclear converter or left to roam in packs in the upper (inner) levels of the ship. "Universe," generally regarded as the classic version of the starship as microcosm, develops this background primarily by suggestion, telling the story of how Hugh Hoyland met the two-headed mutant, Joe-Jim Gregory, and learned the true nature of the ship. "Common Sense," a blood-and-thunder adventure story, fills in specific details of the background and editorializes heavy-handedly about the blindness of people who depend on common sense. After its climactic battle Hoyland leads a small band to escape in the last functioning lifeboat, landing by blind luck on a conveniently passing planet where they can set up housekeeping anew.

Since the omnibus volume introduces the main themes and sums up the central concerns of Heinlein's writing, closing with an open-ended consolidation of prior progress, it is fitting that this parable be excluded. Although it has always been included at the end of the Future History chart, it represents only one alternative future for a small segment of mankind. Other stories and novels which are not on the chart could just as easily be accommodated as alternative paths in the same general direction, with clear exceptions being made for a number of early fantasies (to be discussed later). Four works remaining from before 1950 which are clearly science fictional in nature illustrate this point.

"Solution Unsatisfactory" (ASF, May 1941) became outdated rather quickly, probably to the immense relief of John Campbell. Set in the years 1943-51, it concerns the establishment of a pax Americana to end World War II, making permanent the temporary weapons superiority of the U.S.A., which has developed a lethal radioactive dust. Guard duty is turned over eventually to an international Peace Patrol, so that each country is guarded by foreign nationals. Told by a participant-observer, this story is partly a lecture on some hard truths and responsibilities; its Campbellian title and editorial conclusion indicate Heinlein's belief at the time that this would be a road not taken.

"Waldo" (ASF, August 1942), on the borderline of fantasy, is in some ways similar to "'—We Also Walk Dogs'"; it has an eccentric inventor, a profit motive, a sequential series of problems, and the suggestion of an air of contemplation. The inventor is Waldo, a cranky hermit with a fat but undeveloped body, who has created for himself an orbiting, gravity-free home called "Freehold," and a number of tools requiring little strength to operate them with which he designs and builds things. Logically cornered by the one person he trusts, his doctor, who impresses on him his dependence on other people, Waldo agrees to try to find a solution for the problem causing the failures of the De Kalb motors which power most of Earth's sky traffic. Finding the solution requires two "impossibilities": Waldo must be brought down to Earth in a gravity-absorbing tank, and he and others must learn to accept the existence of an unknown source of power which seems to be what we normally call magic. Accepting the evidence of his senses, rather than clinging to scientific theory, Waldo not only solves the engines' power problems, he also solves his own; the beginning and end of the story find him soppy and sentimental, a celebrated gymnastic dancer. Magic, a different kind of frontier, does not belong to the Future History framework, however pragmatically workable it may be stated to be, but Waldo's floating home, the best part of the story, and his pragmatic approach to problems, would be right at home.[8]

A trivial story on a serious theme, "Jerry Was a Man" (*Thrilling Wonder Stories*, October 1947) takes up another alternative not incorporated into Heinlein's Future History, the shaping and altering of animals by genetic manipulation. While shopping for a winged horse, and buying incidentally a twenty-inch elephant, Mrs. Bronson van Vogel, the "world's richest woman," discovers that the intelligent neochimpanzees are treated as slaves, and made into dog food when they can no longer work. Adopting the aging chimp, Jerry, she arranges for him to bring suit which successfully establishes his "humanity" in a court of law. Stereotyped characters and actions, and cliché-ridden language, both formal and would-be-funny colloquial, almost turn this story into a Heinlein self-parody; for all that it has a serious point to it.

Finally, *Beyond This Horizon*, (ASF, April-May 1942; revised for book publication 1948), Heinlein's one clearly utopian novel, explores some of the possibilities implied by the Covenant society and the general ambience of *Methuselah's Children*. The society depicted could pass for the Future History's "First Human Civilization." Not only does it have world government, peace, security, and technological comforts, but it is also blessed with an institutionalized breeding program which has lengthened life spans and eliminated numerous physical disabilities. And it features a libertarian life-style, including sexual freedom, marriage contracts, and the custom of going armed (a practice which sharpens reflexes and ensures a certain degree of politeness). An essentially static society, however, breeds boredom; some seek continual distraction, others plan a revolution, others look for life to have more meaning.

Hamilton Felix, the hero, provides them with amusement attractions, but his own boredom goes deeper. For excitement, he becomes a double agent, helping to bring down the revolutionaries, a Hitlerian bunch demanding absolute discipline and genetically based hierarchical specialization. He, himself, is the end product of several generations of selective breeding, but he does not choose to have children unless he can see some meaning to this life, as would be demonstrated by proof for or against the belief in survival after death. Partly because of Felix, and involving him as a participant, the government undertakes the Great Research, a series of long-range projects aimed at finding scientifically verifiable answers to such problems as the origin and destiny of the universe, the existence of intelligent beings other than on Earth, the possibility of direct communication without symbols, as well as the existence of an afterlife. Felix agrees to marry, and his first child becomes a living proof of the last two hypotheses; Felix remains the novel's focal point, although the last part of the book is quite diffuse.

Maintaining utopia by avoiding stagnation is the unifying theme which pulls together disparate strands in this narrative. It underlies not only Felix's boredom and these various quests for knowledge, but also the love affairs of Felix and his friend Monroe-Alpha Clifford, and the sensation caused by the discovery of a man from the past (1926), accidentally kept in stasis for "several centuries" who reintroduces some of his (that is, our) quaint customs. A response of a sort to *Brave New World*, echoes of which are obvious, *Beyond This Horizon* has neither the depth nor art of its predecessor; as one of the worst examples, the romance scenes are far too coy and gawky to be credible. However, it does put up a good argument, it is an impressive piece of magazine science fiction (especially for 1942), and it serves as a kind of touchstone for the ideals of which societies in other Heinlein novels fall short. Arguably Heinlein's best prewar work, it unarguably demonstrates the value of the Future History scheme as a set of assumptions and metaphors important beyond the confines of the official chart. Deemphasizing technology and all but ignoring the frontiers of outer space, *Beyond This Horizon* complements the Future History stories by its emphases on "inner space" and the frontiers of knowledge.

These stories and novels set the pattern by which Heinlein has been known in science fiction throughout the years. Generally compact in size, even concise in expression, they are for the most part matter-of-fact evocations of specific moments in the future, the larger currents of history eddying in the background behind these incidents involving specific individuals. The tone is generally authoritative, frequently resulting from the story's being told in first person by a participant who has learned something from the events being narrated. Didacticism is usually overt, but seldom overwhelming, and the masses of humanity are not yet as overtly distrusted as they will be in later works, although the protagonists are almost always among the talented elite, and openly aware of that fact. Construction is slick in the 1947-49 stories, but the bones sometimes stick out in others, and style is not a primary consideration where the writer does not call attention to himself. The overall effect, clearly achieved, is that of presenting anecdotes as if they really came from a history not yet realized.

Frontiers of the Mind: The Explicit Fantasies

Since the earliest days of Heinlein's writing career, his published works have included stories that were unabashed fantasies, which some readers even prefer to his more probable pieces. Why that should be is not immediately apparent, since most of his fantasies show much less care about composition and craftsmanship than do his science fictions. But insofar as science fiction is a rationalizing process, its emotional burden rests largely in the fantasies that underlie the rationalizations. Heinlein's prose is rarely emotional, but his themes usually are. Commercial reasons surely are involved, but presumably there are personal reasons why he prefers certain emotional themes to others, and why he has risked alienating his traditional public in recent years by stripping the rationalizations, especially the science fictional rationalizations, down to barest minimums. Before examining these later, apparently more serious fantasies, it should be instructive to review his earlier, often more frivolous ones.

"'And He Built a Crooked House'" (ASF, February 1941) is sheer horseplay, a *tour de force* about an innovative house shifted by an earthquake into the form of a tesseract, resulting in people's finding all their directions wrong in going from room to room. Its analogy to a nightmare of being lost in labyrinthine rooms should be apparent. The fear of superior beings playing with man is dramatized in "Goldfish Bowl" (ASF, March 1942). Two would-be explorers of newly risen stationary waterspouts in the Pacific wind up in an unearthly prison of sorts, under observation analogous to that suggested by the title, and hammered home by the parallel of pet goldfish left behind by one of the men. This well-wrought story, connecting a variety of uncanny phenomena, has an unnerving Kafkaesque conclusion: the body of one of the scientists reappears, his skin self-mutilated with the message, "Creation took eight days." Another threatening puzzle is only sketched in "The Year of the Jackpot" (*Galaxy Science Fiction*, March 1952): a large number of social and natural cycles are peaking all at the same time. The protagonist is a statistician who acquires a new girlfriend, first because she's a statistic, an unconscious participant in a new "fad" of stripping in public. As the figures indicate increasing reasons for concern, they leave Los Angeles in a hurry, just before the bombs start to fall, only to discover, once they are in their rural retreat, that the sunspot cycle spells disaster for all human life.

In at least six early stories, the defeat of absolute evil by means of superior technological or mental powers is central, in what does not always escape comic-strip quality. "Magic, Inc." (*Unknown Worlds*, September 1940) explicitly brings in devils and witches; in a parallel universe where magic works, a minor devil takes over a crime syndicate, and is defeated only by a female white witch who invades Hell and makes Satan call off his underling. In "Elsewhen" (*ASF*, September 1941), five students and a professor of metaphysics "experiment" with traveling to parallel subjective universes. One becomes an angel, two take part in a revolution against enslavement, while the other two, and eventually the professor, take up Sybaritic residence in a Roman-like, hedonist empire. Stereotyped cops and robbers, and the professor's escape from arrest, through mental powers, supply most of the action. "Lost Legacy" (*Super Science Stories*, November 1941) finds a psychologist, a brain surgeon, and a girl student all disgraced for testing, and proving, the efficacy of mental powers, then running off to California's mysterious Mount Shasta, where they come upon a band of mystics who give them advanced training. After an idyllic period, the three of them try to infiltrate the whole nation by means of a Boy Scout Jamboree, then are forced and helped to overcome the evil controllers of the world. A detective couple, like Mr. and Mrs. North, in "The Unpleasant Profession of Jonathan Hoag" (*Unknown Worlds*, October 1942), get involved in another melodramatic tussle for souls, this time with an organization called "sons of the bird" who operate through the looking glasses of the world. Confusing action culminates in a lengthy explanation that these men were an early sketch by the artist of this world, which he failed to erase when he revised his work. Mr. Hoag is an "art critic" who decides to eliminate them and spare us, thanks to his enjoyment of the tastes of this world, especially the tragicomedy of human love.

More science fictional in nature, *Sixth Column* (ASF January-March 1941) is still recognizably a fantasy because of the basic premise of John Campbell, which Heinlein developed for a quick sale, that six American military scientists, hidden in a mountain installation, can overcome a successful "Pan-Asian" occupation by means of supertechnology and a religious front organization that the invaders are too stupid to see through. Written before Pearl Harbor, this has obvious propaganda value, labeling the enemy as indistinguishable Asians, and touting the superiority of American technology, but has little to offer a mature reader. Also ostensibly science fiction, "Gulf" (ASF, November-December 1949) is an ill-constructed botch composed of roughly equal parts of nonsensical melodrama, educational philosophy (including much talk about semantics, speeded-up language, and freedom), and illogical wrap-up. The superman concept has a certain fascination about it, perhaps especially because it does not rest upon "superpowers" but seems reachable by means of education, but the story as a whole is poorly told, as might be expected of a tale commissioned rather than volunteered. Each of these six tales appeals to basic fears, desires, and prejudices of many readers, and may have been turned out simply as a potboiler. They do not seem to have involved the author enough for him to finish the job of writing, but the ideas—superpowers, black-and-white conflicts—come back more insistently in later years, in works of a more serious nature.

Three of Heinlein's fantasies, however, are reprinted with some regularity, presumably because of their theme, but also because their presentation is expert enough to disarm even a critical reader. "They" (*Unknown Worlds*, April 1941) appears to be a classic study of paranoia, until a trick ending shows that the entire world really was constructed to confuse the narrator and force him to believe other people like himself actually exist. More playful, "By His Bootstraps" (ASF, October 1941) recounts how a young man, stymied over his thesis on mathematics and metaphysics and the impossibility of time travel, is drawn into a future time by his own later self, thus triggering the actions which lead inevitably to the act that opens the sequence. Future and past interact physically, not just subjectively, and the hero's personal sense of determinism seems to control the lives of others. The whole adventure, which results in his becoming a presumably benevolent dictator over long-enslaved people far in the future, can be regarded as another solipsistic fantasy, if not of the hero, at least of the author. Combining solipsism and time travel, "'All You Zombies'" (*Fantasy and Science Fiction*, March 1959) also adds an uncomfortable degree of self-awareness and a hint of real personal terror. Fast-paced, the story is told in perhaps too few words, since the Temporal Bureau's context and functions are a bit vague, but the knots in the tangle appear to be tied tightly, and the emotional impact is strong. Although Heinlein sketches in a few supernumerary characters—an assistant bartender, a Sergeant in the Temporal Bureau, and unidentified hospital and orphanage personnel—all the major characters are the same person, who is his/her own father and mother, as well as the Temporal Bureau employee who makes sure that the paradox is enacted successfully. Construction is particularly important in such a story, and Heinlein's handling is deft, given the necessity for the characters to use dialogue to carry out the exposition. Comprising two-thirds of the wordage, the first section (of eight, each carefully headed by a precise time, date, and place notation) introduces the bartender and the true confessions writer who calls himself "the Unmarried Mother," lamenting his sex change. Hints are dropped that this is more than a simple time travel tale: the bar is called "Pop's Place," the bartender wears a ring displaying the "Worm Ouroboros," with its tail in its mouth, and the jukebox is overheard playing a once popular song, "I'm My Own Granpaw." Six fast passages follow, showing how the Temporal agent arranged things, then the narrator lets the mask drop:

> I felt a headache coming on, but a headache powder is one thing I do not take. I did it once—and you all went away.
> So I crawled into bed and whistled out the light.
> *You* aren't really there at all. There isn't anybody but me—Jane—here alone in the dark.
> I miss you dreadfully!

I don't know that these stories offer the indispensable key to interpreting Heinlein, as Panshin maintains, but they do strike at common human fears; they relate to the significance of freedom and slavery for him, to the scarcity of solid characterizations and the strength of fantasy in his writing.[9] Heinlein is far from unique in exhibiting these qualities, of course; single-character novels are endemic in the twentieth century, solid characterization is rare in anyone's science fiction, and science fiction in general is preoccupied with fantasies of power and control, though often technology-centered. In Heinlein's late work, technology is only minimally developed, the fantasies predominant, with at least a tinge of solipsism in almost every work, as if the writer were overly self-conscious about being the creator of all that goes on in his work. "'All You Zombies'" is an extreme example, prototypical perhaps for the identity problems that have occupied Heinlein, as subject matter at least, since his first postwar adult novel.

The Puppet Masters (*Galaxy Science Fiction*, September-November 1951), is a masterpiece of a horror tale. If freedom is the thing dearest to a Heinlein hero, imagine his recoil against alien beings ("slugs") who fasten themselves parasitically to the nervous system and take over absolute control. Heinlein describes this for us twice, in first person, and also shows them taking over the hero's girlfriend once for good measure. The obvious emotional appeal of the vampire motif should not blind us, however, to the superb storytelling. From the landing of the flying saucers to the humans' mopping-up exercises, the pace never slows as the pseudonymous narrator gives us inside looks at both sides of the war. In the highest echelon of a secret governmental security agency, he is aware of the planning and carrying out of nationwide operations, and also involved personally in specific aspects of most of them. The date of 2007 is arbitrary, since the technology, politics, and mass media involved in the story had a near-future credibility at the time of the writing, while the local color, shock value vignettes, and characterizations are quite convincing enough for a thriller.

The hero's closeness to his father, the head of the agency, and his rigid insistence on a binding marriage to his willing girlfriend could have been explored more fully, especially the latter in a society where temporary contracts are the rule and modesty is no serious barrier to the stripping down required to reveal the slugs. In both cases, however, a conventional 1950s' relationship apparently was assumed in order to increase the shock value of the slugs' temporary control over the hero's closest associates. The emotional values of the theme, in fact, are exploited everywhere, from the hero's own psychological changing of sides under slug control, to the girlfriend's repressed memories of a slug invasion of Venus, to the government's need to take extremely autocratic control measures in order to fight the slugs. The important distinction between the different kinds of control, of course, is that such self-defense measures are essentially voluntary, on the part of the human society if not of every individual, and that they are temporary and reversible. Indeed, Heinlein's virulent opposition to totalitarianism throughout his career seems to me to be based less on political ideology than on this quasi-mystical opposition between "free men" and the "hive" mentality, nowhere more clearly and emotionally illustrated than in this novel.

Loss of identity is not a nightmare, but a dream, in Heinlein's next adult novel, *Double Star* (ASF, February-April 1956), possibly his best crafted example of the long narrative. The other side of the military coin, politics, is the subject of examination, as the actor Lorenzo Smythe ("the Great Lorenzo") is hired, after a gangster-like kidnapping, to impersonate, then required to become, John Joseph Bonforte, leader of the Expansionist Coalition in the world parliament, in a success story worthy of the dreams of any juvenile hero. Heinlein does not minimize the problems of getting away with such an impersonation; Smythe must convince participants in a Martian brotherhood ritual (at the risk of his life), Bonforte's old friend the Emperor (who does see through Lorenzo, but accepts him), the press (in another close call), and the relatively easy-to-fool public. To pull off this feat requires a consummate performer, and Lorenzo, in a highly distinctive first-person narrative, shows us his capabilities. Fully aware of his own tools, experience, and inadequacies, as well as the requirements of the job, he studies carefully the man and his public image until, with the aid of Bonforte's personal staff, reaches the point where he knows better than they what Bonforte would say and do. Standing for tolerance, free trade, expansionism, and general goodness, Smythe-Bonforte also stands in as a representative of any creative person, artist, writer, or politician, doing what he can and must.

Identity problems are also central to *The Door into Summer* (*Fantasy and Science Fiction*, October-December 1956), which might be labeled a story of identity crisis. Three conventional gimmicks identify this novel as science fiction: time travel, cryogenic freezing, and the simple, functionally shaped "service" robots Daniel Boone Davis designs for a living. But they help to construct an adult fairy tale, in which the hero, oppressed by the ugliness and rapacity of the contemporary world, manages to beat the system, almost through no fault of his own. Naively concerned for little else than his beloved designs, he finds himself hustled into cold sleep by his scheming ex-partners, to wake up thirty years later, broke and out of touch with the times. Yet he is able to capitalize on his reputation as a designer, which goes far beyond what memory tells him it should.

In a complex plot—typical of time-travel tales—Dan has his suspicions aroused by discovering his own initials on unfamiliar designs. They deepen when, in looking for Ricky, the little girl who was once his only real friend, he finds she has just checked out of a cold sleep "sanctuary," not alone. Knowing he must have succeeded already, he connives to be sent back in time by a secret device which is normally erratic in terms of temporal direction. Once again in his "own" time, he does the necessary designing, and careful financial planning this time, and sees to it that he and Ricky—closer in age this time—will wake from cold sleep at about the same time thirty years in the future again. In other words, not only does Dan get a second chance, but he uses it carefully, keeping his youth and getting the girl, winning both riches and fame in a world more congenial than the one he left.

Every man's dream, this story is underwritten by Heinlein's usual sense of detail and local color (California and Colorado), by an unusual care for plotting, and an excellent feel for design. Any story of time travel seems to me, technically speaking, a fantasy, but the fairy-tale quality of this one is kept before us by the presence of Dan's cat, Petronius Arbiter or Pete. A literary descendant, I suppose, of Puss-n-Boots, he is Dan's closest companion, even "speaking" when spoken to, who is lost in Dan's first sleep, regained in the second to share in the triumph. Even the book's title derives from Pete's habit, when he and Dan once lived in a Connecticut farmhouse, of trying door after door in a search for one which did not lead into the winter snow and cold outside.[10] And this wintry world, symbolic of our present and near future, chills the tone of the whole novel; for all that it has a happy ending, it is clearly linked to later novels of "alienation."

Nineteen sixty-one brought the book for which Heinlein is now most widely known, the one which established his reputation as a guru, and solidified his alienation from many science fiction critics, though not from the fans, who voted Heinlein his third of four Hugo awards for *Stranger in a Strange Land*. One surprising thing is how well this novel has worn, despite publicity over its being used as a guidebook by the Manson family, and despite the obvious heaviness of its content and delivery.[11] Part satire, part horseplay, part religiosexual parable, this novel has been taken up, and put down, for various extrinsic reasons, to some extent because it is hard to be certain which way the satire is supposed to cut. A dark pessimism underlies the often frivolous tone, and the putdown of contemporary mores is done in the name of a religion itself impossible to take with a perfectly straight face, however appealing it may be to some would-be converts. A confusing book, *Stranger* combines a number of elements from earlier Heinlein works with a new attitude toward human sexuality, a heavy-handed, forced gaiety, as irritating in some ways as the earlier prudery was in others.

The technological content is minimal, reduced to a few comforts and conveniences not unforeseeable as early as 1941, and largely restricted to the first half of the book. Indeed, stylistic differences also support the contention of Moskowitz that the first half was written years before the last.[12] The one essential "science fiction" is a long-standing convention of Heinlein's, the superior mental powers of the inhabitants of Mars, powers such as he previously had attributed to humans only in inconsequential fantasies. There they were also allied to infallible judgment, and used to destroy evildoers, but not connected to the sexual purposes involved here. Though nudity was alluded to, frequently, in earlier works, sexuality was restricted to the innocent kisses and all but kissless romances and even marriages, which were all that science fiction publishing conventions would allow. Sex is a major component in all of the later novels, although its treatment is still unreal, if we assume that characters' speech and behavior should be adequately motivated rather than mere conveniences for the author's didactic purposes. In *Stranger*, the problem is alleviated, but not eliminated, by the integration of sex into the total symbolic fable.

This is of course a *Bildungsroman*, or novel of education, this time one in which the education is that of an innocent superman, with a growing awareness of what it means to be human, as well as to be Martian. His mixture of Martian upbringing with human education—the latter gained primarily from an aged eccentric, Jubal Harshaw; a show-biz religious cult, the Fosterites; and a tour with a carnival—leads, not illogically, to Valentine Michael Smith's founding his own cult of mysticism, sex, and total understanding (or "grokking"), and becoming its first martyr. As innocent as Voltaire's Candide, as amoral and indestructible as Mark Twain's "mysterious stranger," Smith attempts to superimpose Martian customs on human biology and society. Gradually, however, he comes to recognize and even revere human ways, and to recognize the need for his own "discorporation" as both a confession of failure and a rallying symbol. That this is parallel to Christ's death is no accident, but it seems not merely a blasphemy, rather a parody.

The interlocking symbols of water, sex, linguistic patterns, psi powers, godhood, and cannibalism, snakes, and tattoos tap depths of feeling, to be sure. But the carnival showmanship, the silliness of some character reactions, and the ludicrous superimposition of wise-cracking angels in variable heavens direct the reader's attention back to a recognizable world so unregenerate that it can be set right only by fantasies, only in the imagination. The mysticism and joy are pre-sented as being very real, for all the wordy philosophizing and silly avoidance ploys. But the cynicism and satire are also intense, and an unequivocal reading is only possible to someone intent on finding them, from a believing Charlie Manson to a scoffing Robert Plank. Heinlein's most moving book, partly because of the tension between realities and wish fulfillment, it is also as seriously flawed as any of his works, and no more a masterpiece than it is a disaster.[13]

His next adult novel, *Glory Road* (*Fantasy and Science Fiction*, July-September 1963) again strikes out on the archetypal trail made familiar in critical contexts by Frazer, Jung, and Joseph Campbell. Dedicated to friends of *AMRA*, a fan magazine dedicated to sword-and-sorcery fantasies, this novel is superficially a satire of that genre. More precisely, I think it satirizes the traditional romantic yearning for escape, heroism, and deference to authority. Adven-turism, in the Horatio Alger mode, underlies most of the juveniles; this time, Heinlein brings it into the open and turns it against itself. That the adventure episodes are done well may have misled some readers into thinking they were primary, that their essential mean-inglessness is accidental, and that the desultory conversations be-tween the hero and his girl are secondary. But this book has another venerable ancestor, the "road" novel, which generally plays off romance against realism. The hero is hired by means of a classified ad, planted especially for him. He is sexually backward, and satiri-cally so, as representing all Earthmen. His quest is for "the Egg of the Phoenix," an object meaningless to him until after he has won it; it contains the wisdom of the ages, and other characteristics con-tained in the memory patterns of previous "Emperors." His "tools" are supplied by a magic box, four-dimensional apparently, which he promptly loses in a swamp, and inexplicably gets replaced. His "Queen" or "Empress," whom he wins by doing her bidding, turns out to be much older and more powerful than he is. His very success results in his becoming a gigolo and a useless "retired hero." All of these factors seem to me parodic commentaries on the traditional hero-myth, which is contrasted to the "rational" framework of the conversations and the "reality" of the Galactic Empire, with its laissez-faire government and its sexual freedom.

Farnham's Freehold (*IF*, July-October 1964) is a Cold War parable, but not in any simplistic sense. Hugh Farnham is a hard-line cold warrior, a fancier of cats and "freedom," an unconscious stereotype of white male superiority, who has had the foresight to build and stock a bomb shelter that saves his life and that of his family. When the bombs drop on nearby defense installations in Colorado, the third blast knocks them some two thousand years into the future. Set against an idyllic landscape, their pioneer-like survival and growing intrafamiliar rancor are perhaps the best part of the book, despite some regrettable lapses in the cause of sensationalism.[14] The idyll comes to an end, however, when the region's rulers show up; being black, they accept the Farnhams' houseboy, Joe, and enslave the whites. Survival-conscious, Hugh suffers indignities rather than risk the castration normal for slaves not being used for stud purposes, becomes chief historian and bridge partner for the reigning Lord Protector. Meanwhile, he passes messages to Barbara, the friend of his daughter whom he just happens to have impregnated on one try, the night of the bombing, so that they and their twin sons can try to escape. The escape fails, the chief domestic is killed, but nevertheless the four of them are sent back to our time, where subtle differences make possible their surviving the bombing this time, to preserve the limited freedom of the pioneer outpost amid disaster's remnants.

The satire, again, is equivocal. Ostensibly directed at first at those Americans who think they can trust the Communists (and their own government?) not to resort to nuclear war, it carries this line of thinking to what most (white) Americans might think the worst possible social result of such a war. But the Farnham household is satirized, too, in what seems to be a scathing attack on Americans' spoiled way of living, getting whatever they want without struggle, unable to cope with different conditions. Hugh's wife is an alcoholic, his son a mama's boy, his daughter an unwed mother who dies in childbirth, and Hugh himself, for all his technical competence at survival, is neither a master tactician nor a model of civilized adult behavior. He does learn the results of atomic war, he gains perspective on his own culture and his own institutionalized racism, and he senses the futility of overt rebellion for pride's sake and of covert rebellion for freedom's sake. The time-travel device, for which Hugh and Barbara are experimental guinea pigs, does not meet the logic of the plot so much as it gives the reader a vicarious second chance, a chance to see that chauvinism and selfishness may be legitimate only in very particular, circumscribed contexts. Yet the shock treatment and sensationalism Heinlein employs— black rule, enslavement, cannibalism, incestuous desires, voluntary castration, bloody deaths on the part of whites—call a tremendous amount of attention to themselves for their shock value alone. And the flawed construction and extreme talkiness of the book, as of most of Heinlein's novels since and including *Stranger*, are also serious drawbacks, blurring whatever other effects he may have had in mind.

To many readers, *The Moon Is a Harsh Mistress* (*IF*, December 1965-April 1966) seemed a return to the old Heinlein. The setting was the familiar underground lunar colony, the central topic was revolution against repressive Earth imperialism, an inevitable step in the Future History sequence. The handling, however, is by no means inevitable or traditional. The narrator, called "Mannie" or "Man," is a buffoon, who speaks in an unlikely pseudo-Russian dialect;[15] supposedly a leader of the revolution, he conveniently misses key battles. The real hero, as Budrys has pointed out, is a sentient computer named "Mike," who oversees the entire operation of the lunar colony, including life-support systems and media channels.[16] Mike regards his/her/its participation in the revolution as a kind of joke on his nominal bosses, who don't pay any personal attention to its quirky personality. Undertaking a study of humor, Mike is not an entirely trustworthy ally; as the revolution proceeds on course, it keeps reporting that the odds against success are increasing, thus giving rise to the only serious doubts reported in anyone's mind. Mike's loss of sentience after Earth's bombardment of nearby territory is convenient, if the revolutionaries are to consolidate their gains without worrying about the computer's playing games against the new government.

Although the revolution supplies most of the action in this book, it seems perfunctory; certainly it is long overdue in terms of Heinlein's Future History scheme. Yet the lunar life-style, the background which should make the revolution meaningful, isn't all that solid either, for all the experience Heinlein has had in describing it piecemeal in the past. Inconsistencies abound, but some of the main points asserted are the following: its citizens have a heritage of political exile and of scarcity of women; they have a high regard for custom but not for laws; they have an exaggerated sense of chivalry and of free enterprise; they are racially and sexually tolerant of others; they are highly conscious of the thin threads by which their individual and communal survival depend; and they are capable of exerting a united effort only under the stress of an extended propaganda program which emphasizes their oppression by a greedy Earth. Ecologically, this oppression may be very real, threatening to exhaust their resources within seven years, although Heinlein never supports this assertion. Economically, however, they manage to support, on the basis of exports to Earth (primarily of grain), a rather high standard of living and a remarkably "free" society, which is pointedly not a democratic one, either before or after the war. The whole picture, inconsistencies and all, is that of a rather insubstantial dream, incorporating both traditional and unconventional wish fulfillments.

Heinlein does try something new, for him, in his next novel, *I Will Fear No Evil* (*Galaxy Science Fiction*, July-December 1970), but the result is aesthetically little short of disastrous, however successful it may be commercially.[17] Sex is the primary topic, led into by the theoretical premise of transplanting the brain of a dying rich old white man into a new body, that of his nubile young black secretary, killed but left perfectly intact. Some satirical points are made about legal shenanigans establishing identity, about city areas being unpoliceable, about bureaucrats and credit sales and the prison of being rich, but most of the book consists of interminable talk about Joan (for Johann) Eunice (for the secretary) Smith's learning the role of a sensuous woman, in hetero-, homo-, and bisexual combinations. The upshot of it all is that Joan, in the best solipsistic fashion, gets herself pregnant by the banked sperm of Johann, and marries his old lawyer, Jake. The dual consciousness, whose internal dialogues comprise the largest portion of the book, becomes triple when Jake dies.[18] Emigrating to the moon, Joan dies in childbirth, and the three depart from consciousness cheerfully, whether to death or the mind of the newborn child is left indeterminate. Heinlein's career-long dream of escape and off-Earth emigration is extended here to the escape from the limits of a single consciousness and of the mortality of the human body. But, for all that the argument may have serious intent, the cliched characterizations, the simplistic sexual fantasies, and the incredibly arch style make the book all but unreadable; caught between fantasies, it is poorly anchored for science fiction, and too serious and talky to be pornography.

Time Enough for Love (1973), his latest book to date, is not an aesthetically successful work of fiction, either, but it is a revealing document, summing up many of the themes and ideas of Heinlein's *oeuvre*, through its cursory examination of some of the later lives of Lazarus Long, hero and mouthpiece of *Methuselah's Children*.[9] Longer by far than any other Heinlein novel, it is offered as archive records collected over two thousand years from now, comprising stories told by Lazarus out of his past and his selected aphorisms, interspersed with a continuing narrative (with varying viewpoints) of the time in which these records were collected.

Life in the novel's "present," beginning on a world he once founded as a "corporate tyranny" headquartering the Howard Foundation, has some utopian features corresponding to those of early and late Heinlein novels. Long life and its perspective presumably make eminently sensible such wish fulfillments as sexual promiscuity, "logical" distinctions between masculine and feminine roles, and a libertarian government which respects the wishes of the individual (including suicide), in addition to the usual technologically based comforts and conveniences. But this society is becoming too stale and "civilized," more orderly, and the chief administrator, unsure of his course of action, overrules Lazarus' wish to let himself die, in order to record some of his "wisdom" and to share life with him. In the process of settling another new world, the group which surrounds Lazarus takes on some interesting scientific and technological puzzles. They successfully transfer a computer's mind into a "blank" human body, make twin girls out of clones derived from Lazarus, himself, and develop a method of time travel, which really interests him as something new; and everyone loves, and eventually makes love to, everyone else.

Recalling his past lives, Lazarus tells rambling stories, some of which are major building blocks of the novel. As meanderings of this old man, of course, they carry an interest not wholly justified by their structure or the manner of their telling. The first tells of a World War II naval officer who avoided physical labor and danger by using his head; drawn in part from Heinlein's own life experiences, it portrays our century's illogic in ludicrous but loving perspective, showing us Lazarus' view (and apparently Heinlein's) that the life most worth living is that which involves the least effort. The second relates Lazarus' buying and reeducating of a slave couple; brother and sister, but genetically compatible, they marry, settle down, and succeed in the restaurant business, owing it all to him as a surrogate father. The third tells of the one real love of Lazarus' life, love for an "ephemeral" (a girl of our normal life span) on a frontier planet, describing with loving detail the daily joys and hardships of pioneer life. A fourth story emerges from his trip in time, whereby Lazarus finds that he can go home again, to meet his own mother in her youth, and even to make love with her (his own childhood self already existing), before being killed in the trenches of World War I. Of course, he is not really killed, or rather the twins, by means of the time-travel ship, rescue him just before it's too late, assuring him in the book's last words that it was "Just a dream, Beloved. You cannot die."

Given the premise of longevity, going on immortality, it does not seem illogical that for Lazarus Long, having experienced everything, the most important thing in the universe would be love (including, but not limited to sex), that his experiences concerning love would be multifarious, and that his opinions about it would be idiosyncratic. And it is moving to see Heinlein, in what may be the twilight of his career, connecting love and family, struggle and immortality in what is often a direct and personal-seeming narrative, the whole of which suggests that simple pleasures are the best, although we may only be able to gain them fully in our imaginations. But the tales of Lazarus are extremely long-winded and the arch dialogue and giddy behavior of the people in Lazarus' "love-circle" of the fictional present are unconvincing, betraying once more Heinlein's apparent nervousness in writing about sexual matters.[20] And though I can see the need for structural innovations in chronicling (even in representative snippets) a life that spans two thousand years, the shifting points of view, the intrusive narrative voices, the elaborate analogy to a musical composition all seem rather forced.[21]

Heinlein has always had some difficulty dramatizing his fantasies, those that he could not tie down to hard facts by close-order approximation and extrapolation. The early ESP or psychic power stories, for instance, deteriorate into simple melodrama, and the later flights of sexual fantasy, encumbered with talk and disconnected from ordinary character motivation, never get off the ground. On the other hand, *Double Star, The Door into Summer,* and the solipsistic "They" and "'All You Zombies'" are far more successful, because they are anchored to analogies with observable human behavior. A sense of psychological reality, though obscured with symbolism, also keeps *Stranger in a Strange Land* and *Glory Road* from drifting off completely into never-never land. But psychological realities, his own at least, are things that Heinlein often seems to have tried to hide behind such stereotyped emotive labels as "freedom," "power," and "cannibalism." It is not, in fact, until *Time Enough for Love*, for all its faults, that he finally seems to confront that vast territory within the mind, of which such stereotypes are only the most distant frontier outposts.

Conclusion

In analyzing the works of any writer, the critic runs into problems in disentangling his subject's personal contributions from the corporate fantasies of his reading public. In the case of someone like Heinlein, who is unabashedly a writer of commercial fiction, with its often rigid rules and arbitrary editorial straitjackets, this problem is still more complicated. Certainly Heinlein shares with his whole society, including the makers of science fiction, a positive attitude toward the frontier, toward adolescent potential, and toward the proper use of gadgetry. The frontier, with its challenge of the unknown, inviting expansion of man's territory and his knowledge, and often threatening his survival, is a staple of Western literature and philosophy. So is youth, with its romantic dreams, and the volition and potential to learn, in order to achieve them. And the ambivalence of man toward science and technology, his fascination with gadgets coupled with his justifiable fear of their progressive disruption of his way of life, is a key theme continuing through at least the last two centuries in Western civilization. The settings against which these themes are sounded, and to a large extent the manner in which they are presented, Heinlein shares with many other writers of science fiction. Space and the future, instant wisdom and quick technological fixes recur functionally in almost all of his writings, providing the typical science fictional perspective on the present which, it is pretended, allows us to see it whole. Given a single human species, planet, and period in time, differences in race, religion, even sex, and life-style become relatively unimportant.[22] And any single-minded assertion of supremacy, of sex or nation, race or religion, and almost any intolerant attitude (except perhaps one's own) becomes fair game for satire. But Heinlein's own adaptation of these views is also individual, as may be visible in a short historical cross section.

When Heinlein began writing science fiction, escapism was assuredly the name of the game. Readers of science fiction wanted to believe in habitable planets, conquests and utopias, miraculous cures and technological fixes, godlike or demoniacal aliens, and were willing to meet the writer more than halfway.[23] Heinlein was a leader in the adaptation of these fantasies to a fictional world which also allowed for the realities of dining room and boardroom, for the phenomenal effects, direct and indirect, positive and negative, of technological fixes, and for the ornery resistance and resilience of human behavior. As the United States came out of the Depression and into World War II, back into its self-appointed role as savior of the Western democracies, Heinlein helped to develop in the pulp magazines "social science fiction," with its more responsible attitude toward the future modern man and his technology were bringing into being, including the unlikely survival of democracy, except as a label. The prediction-consciousness of Campbell's *Astounding* was echoed in the grand design of Heinlein's Future History which, in its relatively detailed projection of progressive expansion, despite setbacks, in the near future, probably summed up the predominant feeling of the science fiction community.[24]

After the war came initial exuberance, then the Korean War and McCarthyism, and a kind of sinking, by most people, into complacent acceptance of the status quo of Cold War jitters accompanied by unprecedented and ostensibly unlimited growth. Science fiction's critique of this mix of secrecy and stagnation has probably been overrated; certainly Heinlein's view was an oblique one, suggesting by examples of change that apparently stable situations were not permanent. Like other science fiction writers, he also continued to be involved in a kind of special pleading (with which I am in almost complete sympathy) for space travel and expansion off Earth, for technological education and a one-world viewpoint, things emphasized in science fiction of the Forties and Fifties. With the abortive East European revolutions, and increased security-consciousness at home, with the failure of even the first Sputnik to arouse the American competitive spirit to serious educational reform, the dreams of science fiction seemed to fade. The bite of satire, turned against the present, went deeper, but science fiction writers also turned inward, paying more attention to psychological states and to the means by which such states must be expressed in words, language, style. Showing the effects of this same pressure, if in no other way than that he was selling to the same markets, Heinlein's writing became more somber, more sharply satirical, more interested in the individual and his fantasies. Amid these tensions, too, his writing improved, reaching its peak in the mid-Fifties, though he was no longer the pacesetter he had been a decade before.

Introduced by a dream of Camelot and the launching of a crash space program, the Sixties soon bogged down in assassinations, another land war in Asia, mass protests in the streets, worries about overpopulation and ecological imbalance, and the relative boredom of the actual landings on the Moon. Science fiction, corporately, showed the strain, with a continued emphasis on war and conquest, with increasing shrillness concerning overpopulation and ecotastrophe, and with a further shift toward style and "speculative fantasy."[25] Heinlein's interest in the Cold War consciousness as subject matter apparently peaked around the turn of the decade, for his later novels turn away from the social contemporaneity of the Farnham's Freehold frame story toward the fantasies of sex and hedonism already adumbrated by *Stranger in a Strange Land*. An older man now, called by many the "Dean" of science fiction writers (though Leinster, Simak, and Williamson all predate him), Heinlein did not have the incisive style or craftsmanship of younger writers, or their seriousness about brooding, negative themes. His dreams of progress postponed, he fantasized about his dreamworlds and, not unwilling to assume the role of elder statesman, seemed preoccupied with immortality.

In all these phases, Heinlein was an important moving force, speaking at times directly, but mainly through the strength of his example. From the first, there was his sense of realism, of ordinary actions in daily life, of the detailed texture of a limited range of experience, of the continuity between future and current behavior. Then there was his caring about the larger canvas, the Future History so many readers, and other writers, took to heart, only to have a younger generation rebel against it. Having fitted these to the adventure-story formulas that sustained the science fiction magazines, Heinlein then adapted them to the formulas of the mass magazine and juvenile novel markets, selling all the time to the science fiction magazines as well. Finally, as other writers, more competent with words, more careful with design, surpassed him, and gradually did away with the need to follow formulas so faithfully, Heinlein's writing also changed. The results were highly individual, but far from unqualified successes, since Heinlein, shifting more and more from pulp adventure toward philosophical dialogue, did not have the necessary resources of style to fall back on.

Although his latest work shows belated influences of the great "modernist" writers of the earlier part of the century, Heinlein's attitude toward style and manner generally has been, if not antagonistic, at least indifferent; in that, too, he reflects the attitude of most science fiction writers of his generation. In lectures, talks, and articles he emphasized the content, more or less dismissed technique as formula, and deprecated those writers for whom words were more important, mirroring psychological states which often did not have the, for him, requisite, positive outlook.[26] His very mastery of formulas was, in a sense, his downfall, for it obviated the need to create distinctive characters, to explore more than a very narrow emotional range, even to complete the plots and constructs he had begun. Having been successful, too, under formulaic limitations, at suggesting a philosophy rather than spelling it out, he was either unwilling or unable to support his positions more fully in his talky later novels, where no taboos or limits on length were operative. And the authoritative insider manner, replete with wisecracks and homey sayings, he affected in the early Forties, has become dated, while the garrulousness of the Sixties and Seventies has not been an adequate replacement.

Generally a competent craftsman, if nothing else, Heinlein stood out among his contemporaries before the war, and again as a writer of "juvenile" novels, and his high level of consistency overall is probably unmatched except for H. G. Wells. But his best works do not rise above that level as much as his worst fall below it. " '—We Also Walk Dogs,' " "Blowups Happen," and "The Roads Must Roll" are more than competent, as are such postwar stories as "The Green Hills of Earth" and "The Menace from Earth," but all five are dated, in substance or style or both. More universal perhaps because set in the more distant future, *Methuselah's Children* and *Beyond This Horizon* show serious cracks and flaws after thirty years, while the attitudes frozen into "The Man Who Sold the Moon" and *The Puppet Masters* have come to seem somewhat quaint. The "juveniles" stand up as an overall achievement, but none of them really stands out, although my personal preference is for *Citizen of the Galaxy* and *Starship Troopers*, despite my reservations about their philosophical-political underpinnings, over such rollicking jaunts as *The Rolling Stones* and *Have Space Suit—Will Travel*. But Heinlein's best, such stories as " 'It's Great to Be Back,' " "They," and " 'All You Zombies,' " such novels as *Double Star* and *The Door into Summer*, do not seem to me to match the best single novels of a dozen or more other writers, even limiting the list to those whose fame lies mainly in the science fiction field.[27] And his worsts, such as "Elsewhen," "Gulf," "Searchlight," *Rocket*

Ship Galileo, and *I Will Fear No Evil*, are as bad as anything ever
used to show science fiction up as inept and infantile.

Today, Heinlein is known to many, thanks to paperback advertising techniques, as the "Dean" of science fiction writers, not so
much because of his length of service as because of his relationship
to the corporate body of science fiction. He is "historically" important as a pioneer in realistic and extrapolative science fiction,
and as a representative writer whose craftsmanship and technical
knowledgeability were generally quite high. But he may also be a
victim, in a sense, of another basic lesson of the frontier: the earliest
settlers, laying the groundwork, making possible further developments and greater accomplishments, may be indispensable, but frequently they are remembered, if at all, only for being there first.[28]

3. The Human as Machine Analog:
The Big Daddy of Interchangeable Parts in the Fiction of Robert A. Heinlein

ALICE CAROL GAAR

THERE IS a discontinuity between the rate of moral development in the human being and the exponential rate of technological progress. One might state it in a simpler way: The tool grows better and better, while its user is the same old hairless ape. The hairless ape can fly, but emotionally and morally he is still crawling. The machine works very well; maybe we don't work at all. Are the machines getting out of control, or were we never under control?

Robert A. Heinlein has been inspired by the apparent perfections of the cosmic machine to equal it by proving that we can outlive it. However, the human creature can only equal the machine by being like it or like its most efficient products. One may ascribe Heinlein's weakness in characterization—a weakness shared by most science fiction writers—to his overwhelming desire to beat the cosmos at its own game by the clever manipulation of parts. As Alexei Panshin puts it, Heinlein is essentially the engineer and is interested in how things work rather than why.[1] We can criticize Heinlein in an analysis of several of his works on the basis of his interest in process and the mechanics of human survival to see how consistently he carries through his main themes and to what extent they fail or succeed in adding a realistic dimension to his works. Why demand that he re-create a basically nineteenth-century version of a clearly defined individual jeopardized by a milieu either totally indifferent or malign? Today one may see the universe as an ocean of life. The UFO craze suggests that we are a mystery-obsessed people fearful that the apocalypse will pass us by. Heinlein greets the cosmos with a proud "Hello" that says first, "I can live just as long as you," then, "I am possibly God."

However, the very fact that he is competing with what he sees as a giant machine calls into question the conservative view of the pri-

64

mary nature of the individual around whom the cosmos moves and has its being. Heinlein may hail the independent, competent ego as the *sine qua non* of the existing universe, but his own primary interest in process forces a reevaluation of the conservative view of the human being. Process refers to an interlocking network of energies and involves more than just one component, which in turn suggests that we are on the verge of yet another revolution analogous in human terms to the Copernican theory. It is not simply that the human being has lost his central place in the cosmos, already described in lurid and sometimes lugubrious words by writers of the past one hundred and fifty years; but he is transformed into a link in a pattern, a point on a grid, a flow of energy throughout a system. Process implies continuous motion and transformation and that we are ourselves part of a gigantic structure. The real implications of the discoveries of science in the last few centuries are just beginning to filter down into the public maw. It is one thing to regard the human being as a futile creature imprisoned in a hostile world, and quite another to see him as part of a system and necessary in kind to a cosmic ecology. Possibly this reduction to a component is what is eating at Heinlein's vitals. He has been driven to try to come to terms with or outdo the implied systematic analogy. For this he has written his short stories, novels, books, and created Lazarus Long—a symbol of the extrahuman context which like Lazarus goes on and on forever. Such a process makes Lazarus Long a valid symbol of the universe and each component of him and his milieu essential only *in kind.*

Just as the universe is held together by energy in several forms—gravity, electromagnetic attraction, and so forth—so Lazarus Long holds his world together through the abiding power of sexual attraction and activity. But sex means two persons, and where is the second person in the story? In a cosmos that might be really just a gigantic computer, how can one talk in terms of one personality much less two personalities? Or is this question totally irrelevant in a science fiction story? An examination of this question can give us a sharper idea of just what the precise strengths and potentialities of science fiction really are and what the sources of its overriding weaknesses are. Accordingly, I will examine the theme of interchangeable parts and the central figure in the following novels as they are listed in chronological order in Panshin's bibliography: *Magic, Inc.* (appeared as "The Devil Makes the Law" in 1940); "Universe" (1941); *Methuselah's Children* (first appeared in 1941); *Waldo* (first appeared in 1942); *Starship Troopers* (1959); *Stranger in a Strange Land* (1961); *The Moon Is a Harsh Mistress* (first appeared in 1965);[2] and the two novels in the Seventies, *I Will Fear No Evil* (1970),[3] and *Time Enough for Love* (1973).[4] These novels cover three generations. The early ones introduce variations on Heinlein's basic concern with how things work, and the later novels carry his theme to a logical conclusion.

Although Heinlein obviously wrote *Magic, Inc.* tongue in cheek, the work reveals the direction of his interests. Here the unseen energy is present both as an applied commercial resource and as a future potential. The term "Half World"—the source of the magic energy—suggests that our world is also in a sense a half world. As in our own, the powers of that other world are reducible to elements—the demons of earth, fire, water, and air. The laws of homeopathy and contiguity (referred to on page 110 of the book in connection with some second-rate magical "goods") state that the patterns of matter are everywhere, eternal, reproducible, and unbroken. The author thereby confesses his belief not only in the structured nature of the universe, but also in the interrelated natures of his fictional personalities.

Underneath the amusing comments on business and politics is the implication that what we call "reality" must have its complement in order to be symmetrical or complete. That he uses the term "laws" indicates that Heinlein believes in a knowable, predictable universe, whose structure can be understood through applicable formulas. Energy and power are drawn from the total structure. A short, lyrical, even mystical passage demonstrates Heinlein's respect for the innate beauty of energy. Although the salamander has been used to destroy Archie's business (the novel's hero refuses to pay for "protection"), he accepts its neutral or amoral nature, loves its beauty, and desires its presence near him. These is even a delicate sensuousness in the momentary communication between the salamander and Archie with a quality both unknown and concrete. In Archie's appreciation for its perfection, he displays the engineer's love of form and contour. He could characterize the elemental spirit as feminine if he chose, yet it takes the initiative and comes to him. Evidently both humans and the elements may be characterized as having mixed masculine and feminine natures. This short episode foreshadows Heinlein's awareness of the versatility of sexual natures, an awareness which he exploits further in later novels.

The movements of Archie and his friends between worlds serves a metabolic purpose within a larger context. But there is an emotional flatness in their presentation. Archie procures knowledge without paying for it by showing a character change, which indicates that the knowledge obtained has only a superficial effect upon him. When Mrs. Jennings sees danger in Archie's future and warns him that he must let his head rule his heart, there could be the basis for a deeper development that never really appears anywhere in the novels discussed here. In the salamander episode Archie verges on the realization of the fullness of total life. He also displays some sensitivity toward the dynamic flow of events. He may even be suggesting that he is aware that there is an exchange of energy and knowledge between the two worlds which justifies the loss of exact identity.

Both "Universe" and *Methuselah's Children* were first published in 1941 in *Astounding Science Fiction*. Even though the style and plot of "Universe" are far simpler than the works of nearly thirty years later, there are certain basic themes in it that are important for the later novels and serve as the touchstone for the fascination that his works hold. They are the themes of the double personality and of the desire to appropriate a larger space. The personality becomes more complex in order to fill that larger space. Enclosing these two themes is the technology that overwhelms them both. However in "Universe," one of Heinlein's best juveniles, technological enlightenment and mental development are contrasting themes which harmonize well at the end.

The word "universe" means to turn as one unit, which infers that perfection involves motion. The society in the huge spaceship in the short novel is incomplete for many reasons but primarily because motion has gone out of its scheme of things. The "universe" is at first small enough to accomodate only the primitive consciousness of the colonists who have long since forgotten their heritage from the Earth left behind centuries ago. To them their ship *is* the universe since they have no knowledge of anything outside it. The ship delimits their sensibilities and their mentalities. But in this well-written tale of colonists who have long since reverted to a closed hierarchical village culture, the young hero, Hugh Hoyland, finally learns that his ship is merely enclosed within an immensely larger universe. The experience is traumatic for him, but a few lines suffice to describe the effect of the great new insight upon him. He proceeds by logical steps from the awareness that the ship is a thing meant to move from one space to another to the thought that he and the scientists-priests should restore motion to the ship and make it move through the heavens. Because it is based on the principle of pure force-weight and magnetic attraction and there are no moving parts which might cause friction, the great ship is practically indestructible. This can be related to Heinlein's near obsession with human mortality or immortality by applying the idea of frictionless energy to the transplanting of a human from one space to another without destroying anything essential. The individual within that space will be a composite, just as the two-headed Joe-Jim mutant—the most intelligent person whom Hugh meets—is a composite personality.

Since Joe-Jim is more intelligent than anyone else on the ship, he portrays early Heinlein's belief in the superiority of the personality that has more than one part. The viewpoint is a structural one since it requires a controlling pattern. Even in this simple story, change due to doubling fills out a new space. The more complex person, Joe-Jim, who knows that the ship is *in* the universe and not the universe itself, teaches Hugh. At the beginning the young hero has the problem of a space too small for his bursting adventurousness. Then appears the greater intelligence of the individual who can carry on a dialogue with himself. Together they carry on a dynamic interchange within the larger structure of the ship, approaching its weightless section, that is finally seen in the largest structure of all—space.

But although Heinlein thinks of his most important characters as individuals, they are really creatures of the tribe in the sense that they are uncomfortable or unhappy alone with their knowledge. Hugh's first desire is to push his new insights onto his fellows. To this end he plans to forcibly bring them to the Captain's Veranda to reveal outer space to them for the first time.

Methuselah's Children is the most important of the early novels discussed here, since it introduces the Howard Families, who *in toto* represent later the universe delineated in time and space by the person of Lazarus Long. The Howards are Heinlein's answer to the challenge of the machine, and because they appear later in the novel *Time Enough for Love*, one can note the development in his basic ideas over a period of time. The positive behavior of genetic selection seems to be the basic theme of the story, if one assumes that positive behavior produces the near immortality of the Howard conglomerate. The future is based on the physical patterns already present in the genetic makeup, as opposed to accidental choice. In effect, the Howard Foundation *is* choice. As the chooser the Foundation creates an environment rather than just accepting one. The Foundation thereby states that the natural environment—or natural selection—is no longer adequate, although Heinlein sings the praises of the pioneer life as a natural selector of superior characteristics. He has analyzed the larger structure and concluded that a large-scale conscious manipulation is the next step. Certainly there have never been circumstances that suggested that positive thinking enabled beetles, horses, or fish to increase their life span. As far as we know the universe of such creatures is limited almost entirely to instinctual patterns of behavior. The author is trying to analyze the human being's potentiality by comparing him to something that is neither animal nor insect.

Implied by the idea of a long life span granted by favorable genetic conditions is the interlocking, multiple-adult family group that is itself in a real sense time and space. It is the grid of perceptible reality—a continuing pattern as its members multiply and create their own surrounding world increasing in size and depth. But because of persecution and exile there is neither time nor energy within the Howard Families for the suppression of individual characteristics. Indeed, they express the sense of solidarity that comes from shared peril, and their leaders are the oldest ones because they are by definition the strongest and the smartest.

By injecting the reverse values of the Half World into the everyday world, magic in the earlier novel had provided an escape from a culturally static situation. In *Methuselah's Children* the spaceship supplies a challenge by bringing its inhabitants into other dimensions. This in turn presupposes a larger structure whose own dimensions encompass and require constant readjustment. The various discussions between the brilliant mathematician Libby (who pilots them out of the solar system) and the others in the ship refer to the distorted time and space perceptions for a ship moving near the speed of light (pt. 1, chap. 8). Such an experience "smashes" their former dimensions. Yet the individual worlds are not expendable. Among the Howards, longevity is their basic staple and as such the source of their primary "good." Possessing this characteristic they see themselves as members of a family whose identity perseveres in spite of the deaths of individual members. And none of them calls the others expendable. The family is the larger structure, but the healthiness of the Howards is inherent in what they are themselves. Collectively they are in a certain sense healthier than the "ephemerals." They are more adventurous, adaptable, and wiser because they are part of an interlocking of loose family systems which combine both independence and respect for the others.

Since Lazarus Long and Mary Sperling are progenitors of hordes of Howards, who are later quite independent of them, their personalities are singled out early. The Howards live too long to maintain emotional bonds beyond a certain point, even though they care tenderly for the relatively high percentage of subnormal and defective children born into the Families. However, their relationships, founded on the need for mutual benefit, are not emotionally shallow. Over a period of time the sense of identity will become biologically defined, since they will all be more or less related. It follows that the long-lived Howards are very much aware of the fact that they are replaced by huge numbers. And even as individuals they are in a sense analogous to the Families, since the individuals become composites by virtue of organ transplants in the rejuvenation process. Because corporate identity is a physical version of the space continuum, one might conclude that Heinlein is as much interested in corporate identity as in immortality. How does an individual who can speculate on his approaching end really survive in contrast to an insect which is automatically a specialized component of a larger community? Presumably the insect does not consciously create a mental construct of such a community. Are we by instinct less creatures of community, or is the communal mentality far more deeply embedded in the human individual than hitherto realized? The highly specialized insect cannot exist apart from a community because it is inadequate alone. Mary Sperling finally finds immortality by joining the Little People in a mutual relationship. In her, Heinlein is analyzing a human approach to the theme of corporate identity as a form of survival. The individual creates the larger structure in his own mind and thus shares a collective perception. The more persons sharing and shaping this collective perception, the more complex it becomes, a process which enlarges an organizational unit that is itself indissoluble.

In contrast to Mary Sperling's attempt to cope with the idea of death is Lazarus Long, an extreme example of the peculiar genetic gift of the Howards. Yet the author portrays an interesting psychological quirk or strength in Lazarus, who, except for his rather negative state of mind at the beginning of *Time Enough for Love*, does not think about death at all. He inevitably includes all of the women around him within his group by the power of his sexual presence alone, and they in turn bring other men into the group and keep them there. In the later novel sex is the New Evangelism, although it is actually subordinated to the family pattern. It is the universal energy that attracts and holds "bodies" and also the energy that makes communication possible. Although Lazarus expresses his belief in the survival of the fittest, he, like the Howards in general, is neither ruthless nor inhumane, as one can see in the protection of the defective children, who sometimes have special gifts of their own. This means that the family as a real structure is stronger and bigger than the individual weaknesses of a few who accordingly are not regarded as threats. Sex is here an aspect of interfamily identity and dependence and as such is inseparable from the family grouping. And the crucial point is that Heinlein does not delve into the possibilities of unknown, unexplainable power sources in his conception of sex. His use of sex is basically not even really erotic.

As Panshin points out (p. 52) Heinlein does not revert to nonrational explanations of events, and he avoids the mysticism which would contradict his fondness for clear explanations. This is the source ultimately of his shallowness in character portrayal and the flat, opaque quality in the personalities of his characters. Sex reflects energy and love/hate when the individual is almost shattered by the awareness of another will facing him. Mysticism in its most basic sense begins at this point and from there rises into the transcendent regions of religion and speculation. But those devoted to "applied technology" alone avoid the mystery in the beginning. Heinlein's central concern seems to be a unifying pattern or a perpetual energy in human terms. His passion for organization and arrangement is an attempt to analyze the dominating force in the nature of a universe perceived by a living organism. When Lazarus analyzes the alternating despair and hopefulness of the preeminent statesman Slayton Ford (whose protection of the Howards has ruined him), it becomes obvious that the author's main concern is for survival and psychological viability, the *how* rather than the *why* (pt. 1, chap. 8 of *Methuselah's Children*).

The smashed dimensions of the Howards as they move through space and time are merely suggested physical dimensions. Completely missing in Heinlein is the awareness of the tragic levels of life or of tragedy in any form due to guilt or accident. How can there be guilt where there is nothing to sin against, no gods and no sacred mysteries? There is nothing to shake or demolish the psychological, spiritual, or philosophical dimensions within which Heinlein characters move. There is no accident which can utterly destroy *the* machine, because all machines have their duplicates and missing screws can be replaced. Whereas in the classical world tragedy is part of the fortuitous circumstances that humble the mighty and the proud, to many science fiction writers of every level all events are so much a part of an inclusive system (stated or unstated) that the fortuitous event is merely stimulating to the problem-solving intelligence. Even the alien, grotesque as he may be, is in a sense a distant relative, since otherwise he could not be portrayed, he could not be *seen*. Just as our minds have created our universe—a shared, tribal construct— the alien is also a shared, tribal construct. And it is significant that the aliens in *Methuselah's Children* are either hierarchically ordered individuals or corporate components, because that is how we really see ourselves.

The two superior alien peoples are themselves part of a larger hierarchy—the Jockaira, far inferior to the "gods" who have won mastery over temporal and spatial orientations as the Earthmen know them, and the Little People, superior to both the Earthmen and the Jockaira. The individuality of Earthmen evidently makes them (except for some of the subnormal children) unsuitable for mental telepathy. The corporate mentality is baldly set forth in the existence of the Little People, who are not individuals at all. Here for the first time the analogy between human-like creatures and the machine becomes obvious. The universe seems to be a mechanism that includes everything. To conceive of it at all is to conceive of it as a unit, which implies a dimension to our conceptual processes that goes beyond the four that locate a point in time. One might imagine Heinlein's posing of the question to himself: "Why are people not as efficient as machines?" and answering it thus: "Machines have hitherto been seen in a confused manner. People are more efficient than the machine, which is itself inadequate. Of course a person will break down if all of his parts are not functioning correctly. The problem is, how to improve that functioning so that the human being will go on forever, as he was meant to."

One can approach *Methuselah's Children* from the standpoint of a negative argument—the isolated individual is not sufficiently complex. Heinlein *is* on the verge of a metaphysical stance when he includes the individual in a structure which is a source of energy to the individual component but far more than a collective body. He approaches that stance from several aspects; namely, (1) the permanent nature of the larger structure, (2) the interchangeability of its components, (3) the dynamic interaction between those components for growth, and (4) the warping of the physical dimensions that "placed" the smaller structure. The next step is to note carefully how Heinlein "reorganizes" the individual to fit him into that context.

First published in 1942 in *Astounding Science Fiction*, *Waldo* develops Heinlein's cosmic personality by focusing on an individual who is transformed from a physically inferior person (although mechanically brilliant) into someone who is superior in the sense that the new Waldo begins successfully to create the world of men in his own image. The story moves from the self-isolation of the physically inferior, compensating individual to a totally new spatial and temporal orientation on the part of that genius who, as a result of his newly positive attitude toward the rest of humanity, shares his discovery with others. As in "Universe" weightlessness symbolizes the freedom of outer space where one is closer to one's own true nature as a dweller in space. Waldo's genius has lifted him above the physical confines of gravity. Out there he becomes aware of another world which is a source as well as a depository of energy. The Other World is the place where Waldo searches for speed, where he compares electricity to nerve impulses. Waldo proceeds on the assumption that the energy from the Other World is also subject to laws which can be discovered and used if the formulas are known.

Heinlein's shallowness in character portrayal reveals itself here in these machinations. His characters avoid traumatic shock by refusing to confront something unpredictable within a system. Waldo calls Gramps Schneider a hex doctor and then proceeds to work out basic rules for tapping the power source of the unpredictable. Like Heinlein, Waldo is the mechanical genius who avoids the confrontation with the all-encompassing theoretical implications of this new energy. Rambeau really seems more consistent when he loses his sanity because of the traumatic shock to his rigid scientific outlook. Waldo remains, however, a very clever child intrigued by the possibilities and blind to the real import.

But there are some interesting insights in Waldo's attempts to develop a terminal for the power source. When he mentally reduces the Other World to the size of an ostrich egg, he shows his own mastery of a comprehensive structure—a process which in itself becomes the new source of his strength. In this way Waldo has gone beyond the mere sense of another world, as in *Magic, Inc.*, and as an individual, beyond the helpless exposure to other dimensions, as in *Methuselah's Children*. Energy from the Other World makes him into a complete human being who wants nothing more than to be surrounded by other people who like him.

Here again Heinlein's conceptual weakness becomes obvious. The Other World is actually other people, and learning how to manipulate energy corresponds to learning how to interact with the other people, and at the same time, learning how to be a man. But the real interaction with the Other World has to admit its basic mystery, as the theoretician would even while he speculated about it. The author allows the energy exchange between Waldo and his counterpart in the Other World to degenerate into "nerve surgery"—a mechanical and most inadequate description of the process that Waldo thinks he has discovered. The emotional complexity of the exchange is missing, therefore the intimation of the Other World is flat.

Waldo's transformation from an embittered, weak genius into a physical superman is an obvious spin-off from Faust and Nietzschean motifs. The greatness of Goethe's masterpiece is due, among other things, to a consistent following through in the bargain that Faust makes with Mephistopheles. Faust's reign of glory is always in the shadow of the final payment. Every ounce of energy that he receives demands its physical and emotional price. His return to youth at the beginning is balanced by the mistakes of youth and the blindness of old age. The wisdom, wealth, and power that he gains bring with them an emotional winnowing. In the science fiction novel it is the lack of an accompanying developmental trauma that suggests Waldo's powers are spurious. Only in Rambeau's madness and a short description of Waldo's bitter hatred of the "smooth apes" are there the rudiments of an emotional interaction to intense experiences, but these lines are never developed. Though Waldo decides that mental concentration can prevent the myasthenia gravis which is weakening the people below and is the source of his own crippled state, he does not analyze the nature of mental control over the body. His mechanics lead nowhere, and nothing important is really demonstrated. But the positive point made is that Waldo becomes a "real" man, even wants to impress girls (echoing Faust's pathetic wish to fall in love), when he can draw off the energy of the Other World not only to heal himself, but to give himself physical capabilities that others do not possess.

Starship Troopers was first written as a juvenile book, but to my mind it is interesting to adults and one of Heinlein's most successful novels. Its importance for this discussion lies in the way in which the author integrates his hero Rico into a psychologically well-oiled military machine which attracts and animates the hero and gives his life meaning. This novel comes before Heinlein's plunge into the pseudosexual maelstrom, but unlike the other novels discussed here it has a rather carefully analyzed villain who is himself very much like a machine. The major figure of the survivor appears in the person of Rico, who survives his induction into the larger group. Rico's reasons for becoming a soldier reflect the desire to be *part* of a close-knit group. In the beginning hero worship drove him into the military. And his own ego drives him to prove that he is something more than the boss's son, that he is part of something bigger than civilian life has to offer—a Federation citizen who can vote.

This is a further development in the solution to the problem posed in *Magic, Inc.*, where sorcery is accepted tongue in cheek as the key to the Half World, and in *Methuselah's Children*, where longevity is the key to the technology that unlocks ultimate power. Or in *Waldo* where a society is characterized as shaping itself according to the needs of its technology, which can upon occasion be detrimental to the physical makeup of the human being. In *Starship Troopers* a human unit is pitted against the Bugs which are themselves as efficient as machines. They provide the hostile edge to life in this novel, and the human *unit* survives or equals the creatures that symbolize the inscrutable and endless universe around it. The Bugs are streamlined versions of the tentacled monsters of space opera, who are in turn updated versions of the Hydras and Medusas of classical folklore. Huge insects and monsters are all basic symbols of an opponent related to us but also related to the creeping horror of the universe in that they are all imperturbable, unsympathetic, and as pervasive as we. Unindividualized, the Bugs represent an efficient organization which replaces and multiplies immediately what is lost. But they are not mindless, and altogether they compose an intelligence as great as man's and in some respects less vulnerable (chap. 10). The essence of the problem is that the Bugs are the thing that Rico is not, and Rico is not replaceable to himself.

The Bugs seem to be another variation on the theme of the corporate mentality. Actually, groups of the Little People represent or make up one personality, while the Bugs are specialized organisms under the control of a superbrain. But the Little People are just as destructive to the individuality of the Earthmen as the Bugs. The hostility personified in the Bugs stimulates Rico to risk his individuality in a military death. Evidently it is not the single-minded destructiveness of the opponent that terrifies us but its apparent oneness with the surrounding context. Since the author is analyzing the techniques of survival—indifference to death, unity of mind, defense—he has at some point to consider the uses of someone else's hostility. In the alien Bug, Heinlein has drawn a picture of a quintessential soldier's picture of everything unsympathetic in the universe. Rico's decision to go into the military is in contrast to the ininstinctual role of an insect, just as Rico is different from the insect.

How does Rico integrate himself into the unit, and can one really speak of a unit mentality? Common danger and pride in their identity welded the Howards together without destroying their respect for each other's uniqueness, and common pride and an even greater sense of danger weld Rico's combat unit, the Roughnecks, together. In later novels sex takes the place of fear. But all of these forms of emotional reaction and commitment subordinate the survival of the individual to the survival of the larger unit. But it is significant that the Bugs are machine-like in their appearance and in their organization, since they are almost computer controlled. As Dennis E. Showalter states, Rico fights for a network of buddy relationships.[5] We might call that network an extended family, almost an entity in itself held together by a common peril and a common identity rather than blood relationships. This is comparable to the early days of the Howards when they were united by their unique genetic makeup alone. One might argue that Rico has the characteristics of the quintessential human being who wants to belong to a larger unit, since none of Heinlein's heroes in the books discussed here are really loners. Through Rico's desire to integrate himself into the larger unit by fighting the Bugs, Heinlein is analyzing the dynamics of the larger structure.

In spite of the much publicized shift in theme in *Stranger in a Strange Land*, it represents the development of ideas which appear in the earlier novels. The Half World and the Other World are related to the dimension of the Old Ones. The traumatic change in perception in "Universe" appears here. The physical and psychological changes that occur in Waldo, his ability to create his own spatial dimensions occur within the group around Mike, who has learned the techniques of superexistence from the Martians. The "family" that exists in *Methuselah's Children* in the Howards, the Jockaira, and the Little People, and in *Starship Troopers* in the Roughnecks and the Bugs appears in the Martians and Mike's Family. The de facto immortality of the Little People through interchangeable parts leads to the potential immortality of Mike's Family through interchangeable members blessed by association with Mike, by their ritual cannibalism, and by the group sexuality of the love feasts.

Why does Lazarus Long feel such revulsion toward the Little People? It is the total lack of individuation in them that revolts him, the blank character and unstimulating nature of their lives. But the description of the Martians in *Stranger in a Strange Land* is much more detailed because they are captured in the mirror of Mike's personality. The sexual nature which remains such a mystery in the earlier novel and is somewhat more developed in the later is to my mind an aspect of the technological analogy which Heinlein uses and makes increasingly complex. Sex in Heinlein's novels is adolescently shallow because it does not reflect the rich variety of human passions, strengths, weaknesses, virtues, and vices. Instead it mirrors his analysis of the process of group formation and is analogous as such to a kind of magnetic attraction. Here sex is necessary (just as fear and peril) to the formation of a structure larger than the individual and more lasting than the individual. This is in contrast to the real essence of the erotic, namely, the confrontation with another personality which is apart from ourselves—a confrontation which appears rarely in any American fiction.

Heinlein and other science fiction authors who are writing about the possibilities of the vast sociological and psychological changes ahead of us are pioneers on a more superficial level in human relationships out of necessity rather than out of choice. When the group relationships that authors are as yet only playing with, the potentialities of a long life, the implications of the far broader human perspectives are developed in more detail and have a chance to ferment, then the time for a deeper level of experience in conjunction with the inevitable destructive and constructive dimensions of those experiences will have come. At this stage Heinlein can only treat sex like an attraction and differentiate that attraction from other forms of energy. Actually, it is the different sexual orientation of the Martians that prepares Mike for the traumatic shock of Earth sex and thus gives some direction to the rest of the novel. Only by emphasizing sex (and the raw term is most fitting for his approach) can Heinlein create a polar attraction that differentiates the human being from the surrounding universal context. He fully recognizes the natural unity of the physical world and sets up in analogy and as a contrasting figure the dominant masculine characters in lieu of an anthropomorphic god. In this way Mike and his Family and their powers become the source of a new universe with its own laws.

Through the power of his personality Mike is a planet or sun that holds satellites in orbit, just as later Lazarus Long is the creator of his own universe through the manipulation of time and space. The dominant male is God, children (basically through cloning) are the Son, and sex is the Holy Spirit. Or one may compare this trinity to universal energy, the space-time continuum, and electromagnetic attraction. Heinlein wants to compete with and improve upon the universe. However, there is no dynamically dialectical relationship between Mike's satellites. The female figures mirror in no way the mysteries of another presence and there is no overwhelming transcendent reality to smash the preconceived notions of the characters. Mike is a god going nowhere, and it's all just a joke.

The powers that the Martians display and that Mike has learned from them are present in the earlier novels. Heinlein simply reduces the area in which these powers are displayed to the enclosure of the family circle around Mike. "Grok" represents a creative energy control which allows him to recreate the world on his own terms. However, Heinlein remains the engineer who is not concerned with whatever cannot be measured, manipulated, or replaced. This is in contrast to the scientist who has the unknowable gnawing at his vitals. Accordingly, the manipulation of personalities rather than an intense analysis of their basic natures dominates Heinlein's works and that of many science fiction writers. Such manipulations preclude both religion and eroticism since both revolve around objects that cannot be absolutely known on the first person's terms. The author is following through the basic idea that people are interchangeable parts. Rarely does he show interest in the mystery of an unknown reality, and the result is a tautology—a closed circle. Although sex is not the main subject of this chapter, it is relevant to the extent that it reflects in Heinlein the limitations of a mentality trained in applied technology. Which leads us to the next novel, in which line marriages and a dominant computer personality are perfect complements for a successful revolution.

In a discussion of technology in Heinlein one should not ignore the generally engrossing *The Moon Is a Harsh Mistress*, serialized in *IF* in 1965 and published in novel form in 1966. The line marriage, described to some extent in chapter 10, clearly fits into the canon of efficient arrangements which do not interfere with the goal, in this case a successful revolution. It is also capable of lasting *in perpetuum* because of the replacement of component human beings. And obviously the computer Mike is the most compelling and memorable personality in the story though he does come to an end. At the top of a five-level, open, tetrahedral pyramid his purpose is laudable and comprehensible—amusement for himself and the prevention of social disintegration for the sake of his friend Mannie. All of the human characters in the novel are tools for Mike, who plays the game of revolution. The novel illustrates Heinlein's analysis of the human being as a superior tool or mechanism if one accepts Mike as a living character who proves finally that the purpose of life is fun and games. What Mike wants at the beginning of the novel is what Lazarus Long wants in the later novel—amusement and new experiences.

The novels written in the Seventies, *I Will Fear No Evil* and *Time Enough for Love*, push the theme of interchangeable parts within the complete machine to the final conclusion. The first of the two also gives us the ultimate act of nonerotic sex when Joan Eunice, possessing the brain of the physically senile Johann Sebastian Bach Smith, has herself impregnated with his preserved sperm to produce a child at the end. That is the final triumph of the closed system and the omnipotent ego, or one might even call it the act of masturbation taken to its most absurd conclusion. However, this act is merely a baroque continuation of a premise in one of the early novels; for example, the nontheoretical cast of mind shown by Waldo, whose first reaction to the potentialities of the Other World was to make use of its energy and manipulate its powers—all without trying to understand its secrets or touch its mystery. Even in the books of the Seventies sex is nothing but the energy binding space and time and not the communication between profoundly different entities. We have moved from Waldo's ego through the figure of Lazarus, Mike the Martian, then Mike the Computer to the transcendent ego of Johann Sebastian Bach Smith, who by an act of will and with the aid of the latest modern conveniences successfully stamps the "other" sex with his own image and in this way annihilates for the space of the novel the primal mystery of man and woman. Here is a new archetypal family pattern proceeding logically from a figure who like everyone else fears mortality most of all but who simply outlives all those around him. The computer makes possible the transplant of a part from damaged machinery to better machinery. How fitting that the ego should become a member of a somewhat different "sex," since all parts are neutral, nameless, and differentiated only by function.

The title is splendidly ironic. "I will fear no evil" demands the completion of the sentence from the Twenty-third Psalm, "for thou art with me." But the "thou" is not the glorious Eunice (who is not convincing anyway), but rather Smith himself, who is most assuredly an amateur in that role. In spite of the so-called dialogues between two minds in one, the "conversation" is really a dialectical monologue somewhat reminiscent of Joe-Jim's bipartite monologues in "Universe." The computer that had made it all possible provides the glue that holds this self-destructive society together. The ubiquitous nature of the violence in the society as portrayed in the novel indicates that there are no unifying concepts or traditions that can include the mysteries of the world around them and make those mysteries an integral part of the social context. The word "loving" as it is used is meaningless because Joan Eunice really carries on a "dialogue" with him/herself.

Escape from the pressures of another personality's demands is part and parcel of our social heritage, and a genuine female is rarely found in the novels considered here. In chapter 25 the wedding ceremony between Joan Eunice and Jake mirrors the problem that is basic to the works of many writers. The ceremony emphasizes tolerance for one's partner, a tolerance which is equivalent to the body's ability to accept transplants without rejection rather than the soul's devotion to a mystery even larger than itself. In the next chapter technology is identified as the only escape for a dying (if tolerant) race, as well as the true purpose for its existence, and technology is equated in value and importance to the baby that Joan Eunice is carrying. Just as technology had permitted Johann to escape his unbearable physical debility, it is now permitting pioneers to escape an overcrowded Earth and, at the same time, is becoming the excuse for their existence. Or as Jake puts it: "'In the universe, space travel may be the normal birth pangs of an otherwise dying race. A test. Some races pass, some fail'" (26). And the final point of it all has been to produce Joan's baby, who is born in outer space on the Moon—in essence a new Johann S. B. Smith. Thus Heinlein's sole claim to an encounter with the unknown is the space where the baby is born, but the author does not speculate upon that void and its nature.

For Heinlein the only purpose of sex and life is to provide a shelter for children because they are the future. He makes that point very clear in *Time Enough for Love* in the chapter entitled "Agape," where he states that the only excuse for the existence of a family is the protection of the children growing up within its circle. Yet one might ask who the children within that circle are. The twins are Lazarus's clones, "conceived" without his knowledge and in no real sense independent personalities. Heinlein expands upon the premise that eternal migration is the basis for genetic selection, which however is aided by the vast genealogies of the Howard Families, who remain primarily concerned with longevity. And the bulk of the novel is about Lazarus, his recollections, and the attempt to keep him from suiciding by providing him with new experiences. Of course the supreme experience left for him is seduction by his mother, thus returning him to the mirror image of his father—which one might regard as solipsistic or tautological, depending upon his own tastes. Computers and their accompanying technology have brought about this continuation and possibly the conclusion of the Howard Families with Earth's colonization of the galaxies. One might even say that the technology and the colonization are the same mode, far more than merely harmonious. Lazarus himself uses the terms "interchangeable parts" in the chapter "Boondock" in speaking to his two little cloned sisters.

But there is a contrapuntal theme here as befits the musical arrangement of the novel. By far one of the best written and most realistic episodes in his works is "The Tale of the Adopted Daughter," comprising chapters XI and XII in "Variations on a Theme." The episode is in counterpoint to the primary message stating that man is as good as the universal machine because he is a better machine. The tale is an idyllic interlude which extols the hardships and joys of hardy pioneers who find a transcendent meaning for life in their own short existence. Dora gives Lazarus the happiest years of his life because she accepts utterly the fact of her own mortality and of growing old. She refuses rejuvenation, and Lazarus ages willingly to be with her, and from her he learns "that supreme happiness lies in wanting to keep another person safe and warm and happy, and being privileged to try (12). He has learned that the parts which are not interchangeable are the best ones. The most memorable woman out of the multitudes that Lazarus has known is the one who holds a mystery of her own and is as different from him in essence (since she is an "ephemeral") as day is from night. All of the other women in the book seem in effect to be clones of his mother if not of him and reflect nothing more than his self-love, as the twins explain to him in the chapter "Narcissus." Because Dora willingly limits herself to one man, a lifetime of pioneering toil, the bearing of that man's children, and an old age by his side, she is different from the other women in the stories discussed here. It is a traditional tale of a superpioneer's wife with none of the baroque grotesquerie of the New Wave. It is also a lusty story of the Old West, convincing because it is realistic, and realistic because she *is* supremely human, gloriously ephemeral, and determined to live life to the fullest serving husband and children. What comes before and after is interesting, entertaining, even fascinating to some readers, but unreal. The seduction of Lazarus by his mother essentially only completes the circle of the Lazarus theme. What is left for him after the role of an Oedipus without gods but to suffer the punishment of eternal life blind to an escape opening from the endless circle, embracing nothing more than a semidetached, replaceable rib? Along with all of the unreal, replaceable nuts and bolts in the great Cosmic Computer, which are like us because we are unreal and replaceable, there is at least Dora, who wanted to live once rather than just exist many times over.

4. Omnipotent Cannibals in
Stranger in a Strange Land

ROBERT PLANK

I

SCIENCE FICTION is innovative literature. Let us now see what innovations are found in *Stranger in a Strange Land.*[1] They fall clearly into two groups: On the one hand we have the rational innovations, science fiction in the true sense of the word: manned travel to Mars, of course (f.i.p. 9); improvements in comforts and communications, such as "bounce tubes" (f.i.p. 23); automatic air taxis under remote control (f.i.p. 23); "stereovision tanks" (an improved type of TV, apparently; f.i.p. 25); robot kitchens (f.i.p. 25); the Lyle Drive (identified as indispensable for space travel, but not described at all; f.i.p. 29).

None of this is startling. These gadgets, as far as Heinlein says what they are, have already been invented, though not all of them have been developed for general use. More importantly, none of these is essential to the story. Though they give it a certain flavor, the events could clearly unfold, with little inconvenience, if these inventions were never made.

The same is true of the parallel social and political innovations. Two of these are worth noting. For one thing, the emergence of the profession of Fair Witness (f.i.p. 27). Secondly, and of much greater importance, the Federation (f.i.p. 11). The Federation is a superstate established after World War III, comprising roughly the nations that now form the so-called Free World. While it has been said to combine the defects of the United Nations and NATO, it is a real government and has superseded the nation-states.

The supremacy of the Federation is shown, casually and comically, but with telling effect, when the President of the United States appears in the novel, no doubt to the surprise of the readers who

83

have forgotten that there would be such a dignitary. And what does the President of the United States want in the world of *Stranger?* A ticket to a resplendent international conference, that's what he wants. But he no longer rates as a VIP, and the assistant chief of protocol will not admit him. There is nothing for him to do but to stand there, "angry and baffled" (19), until he is sneaked in by Jubal Harshaw (the pugnacious lawyer, hack writer, and universal sage who as Mike's mentor dominates much of the novel).

If there were no Fair Witness, no Lyle Drive, no Federation, the story would have to be told a little differently, but it would be told. The really important innovations are of quite another sort. The book simply could not have been written without them or if it had been, it would have become an entirely different book. These innovations are not extrapolations, they do not represent the future fruition of an ongoing research effort. Nothing in the history of science or technology over the past several thousand years has prepared us to expect them.

Mike, the stranger of the title, was born on Mars. His parents die at his birth, and no human beings are left on Mars. He is raised by Martians—a breed of intelligent beings totally different from man—and trained in the exercise of certain faculties commonplace there but unknown on Earth, though it seems to turn out that more or less any human, with proper instruction, can acquire them. After twenty-five years he is discovered by the next Terran expedition and brought to Earth, the "strange land" of the book's title. The unfolding and use of Mike's powers provide the structure of the novel.

Mike can arbitrarily slow his heartbeat and respiration to practically zero (3). Though psychologists judge him to be a moron (30), he reads three volumes of an encyclopedia in one day (12)(many science fiction writers love to take occasional potshots at psychologists; they credit them with a degree of incompetence that truly is only imaginable in an imaginary society). His mind can leave his body (15). He moves objects by willing them to move (telekinesis; 12) and is of course schooled in using the analogous method of teleportation to move himself by mere wishing, as is customary on Mars (denoted in chapter 8 as "apportation"). He practices levitation (26) and telepathy (26), and so on, and so on.

In short, Mike has those powers that in the border area between science fiction and fantasy—as well as in the literature of the cults that have sprung up in this twilight zone—are called psi powers; and he possesses them more completely than elsewhere ascribed to anybody. They can be defined quite simply: They are the power of achieving any desired change in the real external world by merely wishing it to be so.

It is amazing how often these clear and simple facts are misunderstood. Peter Marin, for example, in an essay review, "Tripping the Heavy Fantastic,"[2] names the books that to him seem to be the favorites of "the young." The list includes five novels (or seven, if we count Tolkien's trilogy as three): *Cat's Cradle, Stranger in a Strange Land, Steppenwolf, Dune,* and *The Lord of the Rings.* He sums up this very mixed lot thus:

> ...those are all "heady" books: not exactly escapist but something close to it—verbal and fantastic trips through other worlds, other realities. Their heroes all possess marvelous or occult talents, the magical tantric and yogic powers of self-control and perception. All of them involve exaggerated but possible states of expanded human "being"—body and soul harmonized and given dominion over time and space. There is a dream-like quality to them all, a quality of wish-fulfillment; each is what Hesse called a "magic theater," and each, like the images in the Tarot deck, must somehow correspond in a rough way to what the young feel is actually happening in themselves.

Faith will move mountains, but it requires a peculiar faith to think of Mike's capabilities as of "exaggerated but possible states."

It is nice to know, though, that this is what "the young" feel is happening in them, especially when we think of the one among Mike's powers that by far exceeds all others: with a "tiny twist" (15), or even without such, just by wishing, he makes things disappear. The word "things" here includes men. At crucial times (for example, 35) it amounts to mass murder—for to speak of "disappearing" is rather an understatement: What Mike wants to disappear ceases to exist. This seems so natural to him that he is quite puzzled when he is asked whether he can bring a certain box back. Of course he can't, because "the box is *not*" (12; the italics are Heinlein's). During much of the novel Mike and his friends are chased by the police and government thugs, and here this power comes in most handy. When an enemy draws his gun at Mike's cornered friend, Mike simply reaches out—and presto, the gunman "is not."

It obviously would often be a great convenience to be able to overcome an obstacle by simply making it disappear; but Mike, strangely, uses his power very sparingly on inanimate objects—with one great exception: clothes. This is his delight; one might say, his favorite recreation. At the drop of a hat (if this simile be permitted in this context), he will make clothes disappear, be it his own or somebody else's.

This compulsive desire to strip is, though not common, often enough associated with certain psychotic states to have acquired a technical name: Mike is denudative. Though in his case the difference may be slight, denudative is not the same as exhibitionistic: When Shakespeare presents King Lear in a climactic scene as denuditive, he does not mean to imply that his tragic hero is an exhibitionist. I should add that Mike does not have to worry about replacing vanished garments. He is a billionaire.

What is his purpose? To unveil the glorious beauty of the human body? Only at the very end (37). Communion with nature? To have water, wind, sun caress one's bare skin? Every swimmer knows of these delights, and so does Mike, but for the most part he pursues one or two other aims: His denudations are either pranks, such as stripping law enforcement officers to expose them to ridicule, or they are frankly sexual.

Heinlein does not in this book follow the old tradition of science fiction, to ignore sex. Overt sex is very much present, and indeed explicit. It is also markedly straightforward and systematized. Promiscuity would seem to be the model, but what makes promiscuity attractive is diversity and freedom of choice, and these are so far lacking that the sex life of Mike and his circle could be expressed in a simple mathematical formula: The maximum number of possible combinations are consummated. What an achievement! The only trouble is that the scheme leaves room for neither love nor spontaneity. Heinlein has succeeded in devising a system that to Romeo and to the Marquis de Sade would be equally repulsive.

It would fail to appeal to Romeo because he wouldn't be able to tell his Juliet from all the others. Panshin has rightly pointed out that Heinlein does not bother to differentiate even relatively important characters, at least as long as they are female. The reader has a hard time distinguishing Jubal's three secretaries or deciding which of them merits a place in history as the first to seduce Mike.[3]

That it wouldn't have satisfied Sade either is not because there is no sadism in it. The marquis's ambition went much beyond that. Though he showed plenty of sadism in his life, he did not emphasize such foibles in his more philosophical system.

"Sade regarded himself as the apostle of the truly revolutionary revolution, beyond mere politics and economics—the revolution in

individual men, women and children, whose bodies were hencefor-
ward to become the common sexual property of all and whose
minds were to be purged of all the natural decencies, all the labori-
ously acquired inhibitions of traditional civilization."[4] The point
has been convincingly presented in Peter Weiss's play usually known
by its shortened title *Marat/Sade*.

Monotony could be considerably relieved if homosexual acts
were permitted, and this would also sensibly increase the number of
possible matings. No higher mathematics is needed to see this. If we
have n men and n women (assuming, for the sake of simplicity,
equal representation of the sexes), then the formula for x, the number of possible heterosexual matings, is n^2; y, the number of homosexual copulations, is $n(n-1)$. If we have five males and five females we can obtain 25 heterosexual matings; but if we include
homosexual matings, the number rises to 45. It is surprising that
Heinlein allowed this opportunity to slip through his fingers.

The truth is that in spite of giving itself the air of a wild mani-
festo of wickedness, *Stranger* sticks firmly, if not to natural decencies, at least to acquired inhibitions. There is no perversion, no de-
viation; all the intercourse is "normal." Though there are titillating
hints, sexual performance does not rise to the level of anything that
could be called an orgy—except once, and then with remarkable results.

We hear about it from Ben, who appears on Jubal's front lawn
in chapter 30 and presently informs him that he needs to talk to him.
He gets to his point in chapter 33, and the conversation ends on the
last page of that chapter, having taken up more than one-ninth of
the total length of a long and complex novel. What Ben needs so
badly to confess and finds so hard to confess is this: He was sitting
with a woman, in circumstances that might briefly be described as
rather sexy. Mike joined them. After a brief conversation among the
three of them, Mike was suddenly naked; whereupon Ben, seized by
nausea, ran.

Now apart from the trick of stripping by willpower, there is
nothing unheard of about such events. In clinical practice we occasionally learn of them (I know, since I have for many years been in
practice as a psychiatric social worker). If a patient told me the story
that Ben told Jubal, I would neither be very surprised nor would I
have the slightest hesitation about interpreting it (to myself, that is:
whether I would tell the patient then and there is a different question): the man has suffered a "homosexual panic." He has been in-

vited to take part in a sexual performance to include both hetero-sexual and homosexual elements. Torn between his unconscious homosexual desires and his defense against letting them emerge into consciousness, he flees. It fits Ben's case like a glove.

This is not, however, the diagnosis that Jubal and Ben arrive at. By skillful questioning and prompting ("dig deeper," 33) Jubal gets Ben to "admit" his motive: he was jealous. Jealous indeed! Jealousy has made men do many things—shoot their rivals, for instance —but that a man in the grip of jealousy grabs his clothes and runs, this is a new one (unless, of course, we "dig deeper" and view jealousy as a derivative of homosexuality—the implication for the question of denial of homosexuality would be the same). Does this mean that if I were asked for a professional opinion I would disapprove of Jubal's handling of the case? Not at all. In psychotherapy (and Lord knows that men suffering from homosexual panic can use psychotherapy) it may be quite legitimate in certain situations to reinforce a rationalization that the patient has worked out for himself so as not to have to face a truth that would be too emotionally upsetting to him. Untruth will make you free....

II

Let us go on to another subject, one vaguely connected with nudity: the very unusual—well, let us say, funeral customs that Mike imports from Mars.

Martians don't die. They "discorporate." They do this voluntarily and with the same ease with which they annihilate other people and occasionally an entire planet (11). It doesn't hurt, and the soul lives on; assuming, in Heinlein's touching simile, an appearance somewhat like a TV picture.

It is worth noting how this makes the end of life similar for the privileged and for their victims. *Stranger* has been called a "fascist" or at least "fascistoid" book, essentially on the grounds that it celebrates inequality and that it expresses contempt for the machinery of democracy. Its disregard for human life points in the same direction. Yet there is little ill will in it, little conscious cruelty. Mike's vanishing act, bringing instantaneous death, is the most humane way of killing. Thus the Martians' enemies get the same benefit as the Martians themselves enjoy, except of course that they are not given the choice.

Quite a few works of fantasy offer comparable arrangements for making the end of life palatable, and it is almost embarrassingly easy to see why. Obviously, many people fear death, or rather dying. They find comfort in contemplating a world where its horrors are replaced by a process that is neither painful nor final. And who are we to cast the first stone? Our funeral customs and particularly our mortuary industry serve very similar purposes.

Nobody has to worry about the soul of a discorporated Martian, but the body needs to be disposed of; and this is done by the friends of the departed reverently and festively eating it. Mike hints at this delightful practice in the very first chapter of the book ("He knew that he was food"). This is undoubtedly put this way to puzzle the reader, but it becomes clearer as it is persistently mentioned again, up to the final scene when Mike has sacrificed his earthly life and a broth is brewed from part of his remains and drunk by two disciples who do not fail to appreciate both the honor and the taste: "...it was a calm happiness that did not bring tears" (38).

This is meant, I suppose, to shock the reader, and it would have so affected me, but for the fact that I happened to have been immunized. I had just seen that remarkable film, Fellini's *Satyricon*. For those who don't know the work, it ends with a rich man dying after providing in his will that the various hangers-on should share his estate if they would cut flesh from his body and eat it; whereupon after a brief debate you see those well-dressed citizens lift a leg of the corpse and unwrap it. The next shot shows them sitting there, glumly chewing.

This, as most of the film, is adapted from Petronius, a Roman writer presumably of the time of Nero. My *Encyclopaedia Britannica*, 11th edition, whence my knowledge comes, found itself in a dilemma: facts must be given, but only as they are "fit to print." The editors cut the knot with such a masterly stroke that I can't forebear quoting: "...attaches a condition to the inheritance that even Encolpius might have shrunk from fulfilling...*si corpus meum in partes conciderint et astante populo comederint*." To those who know Latin, this says plainly, "if they will cut my body into pieces and publicly eat it." As to those who don't know Latin, they are by that very fact proved to be unready to receive such choice information. They did not go to the proper schools. It serves them right.

Petronius undoubtedly wanted to pillory the *nouveaux riches* of his time by showing them stooping to anything for money. Heinlein uses the motif in a totally different context: with him, it's the "good guys'' who engage in a practice that amounts to the same as complying with the testament so lovingly detailed by Petronius. Heinlein may have intended to travesty the sacrament of communion—his choice of words tends to run to the blasphemous, and there are closer parallels such as Mike appearing to Jubal after his death just as Christ appeared to the disciples at Emmaus. It is not likely that Petronius knew or cared enough about Christianity to have any such aim. He may have simply wanted to jolt his readers by imputing to Roman gentlemen the usages of certain barbaric tribes of which they had read in Herodotus.

Such practices have survived well into the nineteenth century; indeed, in some parts of the world, to our day. In the interior of New Guinea, where it was estimated not too long ago that 10 percent of the population practiced some form of cannibalism, there is a group of tribes, totaling about thirty-five thousand persons, where a particularly terrible disease, kuru, was endemic. It was a leading cause of death, especially among children, and dying from it was prolonged and painful. These tribes used to eat their dead. They also made use of parts of the bodies, principally fatty tissues and the brain, to rub into their skin. About 1960, under government pressure, they switched to more modern methods of putting the dead to their rest. Presently kuru began to disappear. A medical team came to the conclusion that kuru was not, as had been believed, a hereditary disease but that it was caused by a virus transmitted through brain tissue smeared on the body, thus enabling the virus to enter the bloodstream through the nostrils and other mucous membranes.[5] Ghoulish behavior is not always as hygienically harmless as Heinlein's book assumes.

What these tribes in New Guinea practiced was, properly speaking, *necrophagy* (the eating of the dead). The term is not usually applied to humans—"the species of Necrophorus and Necrophaga are valuable scavengers for their habit of burying small vertebrate carcasses which may serve as food for their larvae"[6]—but the idea is the same. Whether or not we may call it cannibalism, it certainly differs sharply from cannibalism as the word is usually understood, which implies killing for the purpose of eating. Necrophagy does not involve hostility. In fact, honorific necrophagy is not a mere figment of Heinlein's imagination, but anthropologists have found it to exist: "Certain African and Australian tribes devoured their dead kinsfolk in the belief that this was the most flattering method of 'burying' them."[7] How difficult it is in our world for a writer to invent something that reality has not yet preempted!

The popular concept of cannibalism is simple, but reality is complex. There are many varieties, and each has its quite different anthropological, historical, and psychological background and implications; if they didn't there would be no point in distinguishing them. The tribes mentioned practiced endogenous necrophagy (the eaters and the eaten were members of the same tribe), in contrast to exogenous necrophagy, or exogenous cannibalism. Montaigne wrote in his famous and influential essay "Of the Cannibals," that the American Indians (of whom he had rather a distorted view) ate their prisoners, but he says that they did not do so "to nourish themselves with it, ... but to represent an extreme and inexpiable revenge." Endogenous cannibalism is in that culture evidently frowned upon, presumably in analogy to incest: A brave who is taken prisoner will brag to his captors that he has eaten men of their tribe and will taunt them that thus in eating him they will eat their own ancestors. Montaigne may have been mistaken: Much of cannibalism, especially in primitive cultures, aims at acquiring another man's virtues by incorporating his physical substance. The magic idea survives in fairy tale and folklore: By eating a lion's heart you acquire the lion's presumed stoutheartedness, and so forth.

Much of the cannibalism reported by anthropologists was ritual cannibalism, but it would not be easy to find an antonym to that term, since primitive cultures tend to ritualize all their activities. We would not expect to find ritual where we are dealing with what we might call compelled cannibalism or compelled necrophagy—the eating of human flesh in dire necessity to keep from starving, as in the grisly story of Ugolino, immortalized by Dante,[8] or in the much publicized episode of a rugby team stranded in the Andes in late 1972 when their plane crashed in a most inaccessible spot. The survivors had to subsist for two months on practically nothing but the bodies of their dead companions. They developed a rather elaborate system, but no such rituals as we find them with primitive tribes or, for that matter, in *Stranger*.[9]

The motives are as varied as the types. Endonecrophagy may serve a practical purpose, as Arthur C. Clarke implies in a remark on early hominids: "These creatures had not yet learned the useful accomplishment of burying their dead, lest they lead wild animals to the living."[10] Exogenous cannibalism is more likely to be inspired by hostility. Ritual cannibalism may be motivated by false beliefs about the structure of the world and the laws of nature, as the Aztecs presumably believed that they had to slaughter as many men as possible, tear their hearts out, and offer them on the altar of the

Sun God, or else the Sun would sicken from lack of nourishment and would no longer rise. In compelled cannibalism, hunger is of course the overriding motive.

This last type is by its nature very rare. The other types are for us very remote, either in space or in time. They are still practiced, if at all, in the most remote corners of the globe; and if there were cannibals in our ancestry, they must have lived many, many generations ago. Yet the problem is still alive in our minds. Not that we give it much thought, but it occurs with surprising frequency in literature and in jokes.

"Then there was the cannibal who was expelled from school when they caught him buttering up the teacher." Or, the not exactly pressing but somehow nagging question of how to find a rhyme to *Timbuktu* is solved by alleging that that is where they boil the missionary, and hat, and coat and *hymnbook, too*. Many are the pages of *The New Yorker* adorned with cartoons of clergymen sitting in kettles, waiting serenely for the cannibals to stop their dancing around them and get on with the job of lighting the fire.

In literature, the theme can be traced back to ancient times when fiction and myth were indistinguishable. Cronus, the father of the gods, according to Hesiod, ate them. He was later forced to "spew them out" again by his son Zeus whom his mother Rhea had saved through playing tricks on her husband. Incidentally, Cronus showed his impartiality in the struggle of the generations by castrating his father.

Later ages could no longer countenance such doings, much less impute them to gods. The crime of Tantalus consisted in slaughtering his son Pelops and serving his flesh at a banquet to which he had invited all the gods (they happened to be close relatives of his). With the exception of Demeter who because of the recent kidnapping of her daughter was too distracted to notice what she ate, the gods declined the repast, and Zeus hurled Tantalus into the netherworld to be forever tantalized. Though his crime was essentially trying to prove that gods were no smarter than men (hubris) the myth shows clearly that by that time the eating of human flesh was considered repugnant to gods.

The fairy tale of Tom Thumb which must have migrated from country to country through the centuries, as folktales will, found its classical formulation in Perrault's collection at the end of the seventeenth century. Here the intended victim is a specially small boy who with his brothers wanders into the house of an ogre. The ogre is out.

As he comes home, his wife hides the boys. The ogre "smells fresh flesh" and discovers them, but the wife prevents his killing them right away. Tom Thumb manages, through his quick wit, recklessness, and sheer effrontery to escape with his brothers, and to best the ogre. Though the tale was written down twenty-five centuries after Hesiod, the roles of the ogre, his wife, and the boy still resound with the echo of those of Cronus, Rhea, and Zeus.

Throughout the Middle Ages and beyond, cannibals were thought of as more ogreish than human, and the eating of little children was considered their specialty. There is a "Kindlifresser" (baby devourer) fountain in Berne, Switzerland. Leaflets of the Christian powers during the centuries of war with the Turks—non-Christians, hence less than human—liked to show Turkish soldiers massacring children, sometimes roasting them on spits. When after the discovery of America, Europeans began to study the natives of the New World, they paid especial attention to cannibalism, though it was no more widespread there than in the Old World. This is seen in Montaigne's work, and it has recently been beautifully demonstrated in the Bicentennial exhibition, "The European Vision of America." It is a moot question whether this preoccupation with cannibalism served mainly to offer an outlet to otherwise suppressed European fantasies, or whether its chief function was to provide a convenient excuse for the way Europeans treated the American Indians. The theme of the ogreish devourer of children reached the highest level of literary excellence in Swift's *A Modest Proposal.*

The ghoulish aspect is brought out with concise clarity in a passage in Andersen's fairy tale "The Wild Swans." The heroine is required to visit a cemetary at night. "There she saw a circle of ugly witches sitting on one of the broadest tombstones. They took their rags off as though they were going to bathe, dug with their long skinny fingers into the fresh graves, took the bodies out, and ate the flesh." It comes as a surprise that the witches are not only ghouls but also, like Mike, denudative. Andersen gives no reason why they strip. He probably didn't know himself. True creative writers seldom do.

More recent literature seems to have swung back from the idea of cannibalism as essentially inhuman to viewing it, though still with complete disapproval, as more exotic than nefarious, more or less explicable through circumstances, less horrifying than bizarre. There is a short story by Bertrand Russell that could serve as a paradigm, and a very Petronian scene in the bar of the Niniveh Hotel in *The Dog Beneath the Skin* by Auden and Isherwood. There are uncounted others.

In Kubin's *The Other Side*, one of the seminal works of surrealism, a physician is killed in a revolt of his patients ignited by a general collapse of society. He is "skewered on a gas pipe...So Lampenbogen ended his existence as a roast *en brochette*, and, what's more, badly done; his back was almost raw, barely warmed through; the belly, on the other hand, was completely charred. Only his sides were nicely crisped."[11]

In areas closer to science fiction there is Anthony Burgess's *The Wanting Seed* and, of course, H. G. Wells's *Time Machine*, where the classes diverge to the point of becoming virtually separate species, where cannibalism is not only institutionalized but newly rooted in biology. Anatole France remarked with straight-faced irony in *On the White Stone*: "Wells has in traveling into future ages discovered an end to which mankind tends that he can hardly have wished for it. To postulate a cannibalistic proletariat and an edible aristocracy is a harsh solution of the social question."

The material is too scattered to achieve a sample solid enough to establish a trend, but *Stranger* seems to mark the farthest point to which the pendulum has moved in its swing away from the condemnation of cannibalism. Though only the relatively innocuous necrophagy is within its purview, still it is the only notable work which not only registers but virtually glorifies such practices so generally felt abhorrent. And it has been eminently successful.

How could this be? Why would we have the profusion of jokes and of stories? What makes this theme, so obviously not relevant to our problems on a practical level, so relevant to our souls? I can only confess that I don't know and have to beat a retreat to the prepared defensive position that on such matters, where at the present stage of development of psychology findings tend to be either trivial or controversial, it is as important a step to raise a question as to answer it.

We generally surmise that when a topic with no visible connection to conscious interest keeps coming up, be it in conversation, literature, humor, or whatever expressive manifestation, it indicates the pressure of a repressed mental content striving to reemerge. It would be plausible then to explain the preoccupation with cannibalism as a return of the repressed. But where would the repressed content have come from originally? To have been repressed, it would have to have had some existence as conscious content at a previous stage. It could be traced back to what psychoanalysis calls the oral-aggressive phase. There is a stage, of course, in normal development when the infant, nursing, absorbs through the mouth some of the living substance of another human body—in a sense, the basic situation of cannibalism. However, the great disparity between that and a subjective experience of cannibalism constitutes a chasm that would still have to be bridged somehow.

The other possibility would be to assume that we are here encountering repression of a mental content that was conscious many generations past. But this assumption would have to rest, uneasily indeed, on two even bolder assumptions: that cannibalism is universal, or nearly so, that all branches of the human family tree have had a season of cannibalism, a hypothesis for which we do not have good evidence; and that in some way unconscious material is genetically transmitted from generation to generation. This second hypothesis is an indispensible link in the chain of reasoning that leads to some modern theories in the field of linguistics. The same is true of some of Freud's theories, but these are not part of the essential structure of psychoanalysis. In Jung's system, on the other hand, the hypothesis is central. Other schools of psychology have had little interest in the subject. Its nature makes it difficult to amass conclusive evidence. At the present stage of the science the question must be deemed moot.

The point on which there is universal agreement, though, is that civilized man feels that eating human flesh is repellent beyond any degree of which he can give an account. The revulsion becomes obvious whenever the question comes up. Any of the rare cases of cannibalism in our world becomes an immediate sensation. *Alive* has forcefully brought this out. An anthropologist has, in a standard work on the subject, stressed that usually no need is felt to account for this feeling. He begins his book with noting "the immediate abhorrence that does not need to be thought through" and ends it thus: "Man on a higher stage of development finds it hard to forgive himself for any extreme, however cogent it may have appeared in a distant past. Cannibals, therefore, as men who have drawn the ultimate consequence from an experience for which empathy is no longer possible, have from ancient days been consigned to the loathing of their contemporaries and of the generations to come."[12]

Psychoanalysis has taught us to look for a phenomenon analogous to the principle in physics that action equals reaction: An aversion for which no rational reason can be given may mask a repressed desire. Does that mean there is a possibility that our culture will revert to cannibalism if certain inhibitions are removed? Are we all, on a level so deep that it is normally never plumbed, potential cannibals?

Even to think of such a possibility seems absurd, but at least one sage whose pronouncements we would not lightly ignore has answered in the affirmative: "Oh, ages are yet to come of the confusion of free thought, of their science and cannibalism. For having begun to build the tower of Babel without us, they will end, of course, with cannibalism."[13] These are the words of Dostoyevsky's Grand Inquisitor. He does not generally speak for his author. He enters the story as the great antagonist of Christ. He embodies a force totally to be rejected; in the context of Dostoyevsky's work, however, but one force of evil: The power he here opposes, the power of "free thought," is in Dostoyevsky's system just as much an adversary of God. Hence the prophecy that it will lead to cannibalism.

However little inclination we may feel to follow Dostoyevsky's line of thought, the trend of literature that we have seen leading to *Stranger* seems too close to being a virtual illustration of what Dostoyevsky says that we could contemplate it without a feeling of unease.

III

So the great taboos of civilized man surrounding the two key areas of sex and death have been, if not shattered, dented. Mike and his cohorts have proclaimed, practiced, and glorified promiscuity. They call it free love, but it isn't very much love, and it isn't free—it is restricted to the standard pattern of heterosexual intercourse; they shy away from anything beyond. And the true believers who worship Mike as their guru and messiah have reverently engaged in ritual necrophagy, though not in cannibalism in the narrower sense of the word.

Acting with perhaps more courage than judgment, Heinlein has achieved a third breakthrough: He has endowed his hero with psi powers. In doing so, he does not overstep the boundaries of a taboo, but merely of reality. He therefore does not run up against the resistance that serves as such a strong bulwark around every taboo; he does not scandalize his readers. Though the boldest of his three innovations, it is the least conspicuous. But it may turn out to be the most important of the three. It dangles before the reader's eye the seductive image of what is scientifically known as "omnipotence," or—to give it its fuller name, the infantile idea or fantasy of the omnipotence of thought.

The concept can be defined fairly easily. The idea of the omnipotence of thought is the belief that "wishing makes it so," that thoughts have the power directly to change the external world, that the will is as effective as the deed.

The phenomenon has, of course, long been known. Much of magic is based on it, and it appears regularly enough in certain psychotic states (autism and some schizophrenic and paranoid cases) to have been noticed by psychopathology. However, since it is not part of the mental equipment of the normal adult and plays no role in "normal" life, it was long ignored by the science of psychology. Freud, with his gift of paying attention to the inconspicuous, discovered it. Still, it is not considered a cornerstone of the house that Freud built. Robert Waelder, for example, did not find room for it in the almost three hundred pages of his *Basic Theory of Psychoanalysis.*

The term "belief in the omnipotence of thoughts" was probably first used by Klemperer in the meeting of the Vienna Psychoanalytic Society of November 30, 1910. Freud spoke in the same meeting of a neurotic way of thinking "in which absolutely the same reality is attributed to thought processes as to external processes."[14] He elaborated two years later, referring to a patient of his who has since become known in the literature as "the rat-man":

> I have adopted the term "omnipotence of thoughts" from a highly intelligent man who suffered from obsessional ideas and who, after having been set right by psycho-analytic treatment, was able to give evidence of his efficiency and good sense. He had coined the phrase as an explanation of all the strange and uncanny events by which he ... seemed to be pursued. If he thought of someone, he would be sure to meet that very person immediately afterwards, as though by magic. If he suddenly asked after the health of an acquaintance whom he had not seen for a long time, he would hear that he had just died ... If ... he swore at some stranger, he might be sure that the man would die soon afterwards, so that he would feel responsible for his death. ... All obsessional neurotics are superstitious in this way, usually against their better judgment.[15]

Later in the same work Freud speaks of the omnipotence of thoughts among primitive people and in art (p. 90). It is of special interest in our context that he sees omnipotence and cannibalism linked. He returned to the subject of omnipotence repeatedly: for the last time in the book he finished just before his death.[16]

Elaboration by other psychoanalysts, notably Ferenczi, was particularly concerned with finding the place of "omnipotence" in a coherent theory of child development. A consensus was reached that the belief in the omnipotence of thought—mainly, the child's own thought—is a normal stage that children go through.[17] It is in the nature of the phenomenon that the theory so far has not been very strongly underpinned with empirical research. Conclusive data are especially hard to come by as the child is assumed to form the belief before acquiring language.[18]

A phenomenon that escapes direct observation may sometimes be inferred from the traces it leaves. In our case, they show in children's play and in jokes. Play with pretended guns is too widespread and well known to require much comment. A boy will point his toy gun (or simply a stick) in the direction of another, yell "ta-ta-ta!" and the other boy will obligingly fall to the ground, "dead." The children normally know it's "make-believe." But it is plausible to assume that the game is a vestige of a time when they did not know the difference.

An often-told joke may illustrate the same principle. A man suffers a stroke at work and dies. A colleague is chosen to go to his home and to inform the widow as tactfully as he can. He does not know how. As the woman answers the doorbell, he begins haltingly, "Your husband isn't going to be home at the usual time..."—only to be interrupted with, "Again? I wish he'd drop dead!" The messenger's face lights up. He has got his cue. He says brightly, "You'll be surprised: he did." The story makes sense only if we understand that the messenger's remark, far from being tactful, arouses guilt feeling in the woman. And this in turn depends on her accepting the idea—though rationally she knows it to be false—that her wish (which she undoubtedly has harbored before she uttered it) actually caused her husband's death.

Many more examples could be given, but it would be difficult to find illustrations from literature. Except for descriptions of psychotic states, presentation of omnipotence is rare in fiction nowadays, and has been rare for centuries. Fairy tales, however, which are to modern literature what archaeological finds are to modern cities, sometimes naively assume omnipotence.

It is quite different with cannibalism, so copiously reflected in fiction. Various observations may be adduced to account for the discrepancy. The alternatives are not as clearly opposed: You either eat human flesh or you don't, but with regard to omnipotence there are infinite gradations. Furthermore, the idea that anybody would *really* believe in the magic power of his thoughts is too absurd to be a good subject for literature; or so it seemed until *Stranger* came along.

It is a factor of probably much greater importance that the belief we are here dealing with is primarily a cognitive rather than an emotional stage, or deficiency. It is not so much repressed in normal development as it is overcome. The child does not overcome it in an internal struggle, but outgrows it, discards the idea, albeit reluctantly, when he reaches the "age of reason"—the term is appropriate here—when experience teaches him. As fantasy, the idea of omnipotence may persist. It lingers in such art forms as the comic strip, it regains a lease on life in paranoid delusions. It retains its grip on those who are so discouraged by the conflicts of later childhood that they take refuge in their earlier beliefs (which they have learned are not valid) and "refuse to grow up."

The "witty" effect of a story like that of the woman who wished her husband dead depends on the punch line acting like a spark jumping from one wire to another. It illuminates, and thereby relieves, the tension between truth and pretense, between the repressed and the conscious. But what is repressed in this story is the woman's death wish, not her concept of how the wish would come true.

This analysis is only seemingly contradicted by the observation that much of literature, especially "lowbrow" literature, caters to the reader's desire to see his power magnified. The hero offers him a chance to identify with a figure much more powerful, glorious, successful, and enviable than he is himself. The story gives him a trellis on which his daydreams can climb to heights he could not otherwise reach.

But that is different. To be more potent is one thing, to be omnipotent another. The difference between the conventional hero's enhanced power and the omnipotent hero's unlimited power is not merely one of quantity. They are the answer to different yearnings. They stem from different layers of the personality, different past stages of development. The normal person will daydream of great fame, fortune, glamour, but not of more. He makes up for what he missed in the later years of his childhood. He does not see himself in his daydreams as omnipotent, an idea going back to far earlier times.

In technical terms, fantasies of great power and glory are oedipal, fantasies of omnipotence preoedipal. To labor still under oedipal problems is rather common; but most normal grown persons have come to terms with preoedipal problems. They have discarded omnipotence altogether, or have relegated it to a level where it is too far from consciousness even to fashion daydreams from it. So there are many Walter Mittys in literature, but rarely a Valentine Michael Smith.

Mike Smith is a transcendent hero. He is enviable. Having accomplished the breakup of the sexual taboo, he has what we might wish to have. He embodies the breaking of the taboo against cannibalism, where it is far less obvious that the deed realizes a widespread wish, but where we are led to believe that on some submerged level this is likewise true.

Above all, he has those powers that stern reality ungraciously denies man: He can be instantly wherever he wants to be; he can make his body obey him, or absent himself from it. He can remove any obstacle and kill anybody: he simply wishes them to disappear and they "are not"; he does not even have to bother to eat them. He is the fulfillment of the most cherished and most primitive of our desires, of the hidden and unacknowledged longing for omnipotence. That this is rare in modern literature indicates that few readers feel the need. That the devotees of *Stranger* do seem to get gratification from the vicarious fulfillment of a wish usually more deeply buried might make us wonder what sort of people they are.

Stranger has achieved a considerable reputation, though not unmixed with notoriety. While scoffers have not been lacking, it has soared to great popularity with readers. The book has a large, enthusiastic following. Phrases from it—"grok," "share water"—have become part of the American language. How has Heinlein wrought the miracle? What makes the novel work?

It is easier to see how it does not work. It obviously doesn't work as science fiction is supposed to, by capturing the reader's imagination through offering exciting, intriguing innovations in the realms of technology and science. What the book presents in these areas is, as we have seen, either trivial or indistinct. Nobody has paid any attention to the space wizardry and gadgetry.

Nobody would even be tempted to pay attention to them were it not for the fact that *Stranger* is usually thought of as science fiction. But that it is generally so perceived is not due to its intrinsic qualities, but to an almost coincidental external factor: *Stranger* is considered science fiction because in our American culture that is, or was at the time of the book's publication, the catchall under which such works were classified.

In France it would be called *utopie phantastique*, in Germany *phantastische Utopie*: terms fitting very much better, for they point up the strong sides of the book and they stress that it consists of two rather heterogenous elements. Fantastic literature is in a sense a literature of indulgence. While in genuine utopia and genuine science fiction the author comes to grips with problems of the outside world, fantasy works on problems inside himself. In *Stranger* the rift runs through the entire work.

There are, on the one hand, Heinlein's ideas about religion and politics. He treats religion sardonically and does his best to demolish established religion. He does not make too clear what he would prefer to it. His treatment of politics is equally sardonic. He shows little love for the welfare state or democracy, but none whatsoever for a police state. His government, however constituted, should be a government of laws not of men, and above all it should leave the citizen severely alone—this is the book's utopian, or ideological content.

On the other hand, there is the celebration of the three breakthroughs—sex, cannibalism, omnipotence. Let us call this the fantastic, or emotional content.

Which of the two is it that "makes" the book?

Literature can be precious to its readers in various ways. Words can entrance by the sheer beauty of their sounds; this mainly distinguishes poetry from prose. Literature can also supply useful information. But its chief value—and that's particularly true of the novel—is that it provides vicarious experience. *Stranger* does this abundantly.

Putting it in a somewhat oversimplified manner, vicarious experience is one of three ways of gratifying a desire. For example, a man wants a drink. He can go and get one—direct gratification. He can spin a daydream wherein he takes a drink—gratification through fantasy. Or, third, he can find pleasurable release of his longing in reading about a man taking a drink (or seeing it in a movie, and so forth; the same truth holds for various media)—vicarious gratification.

Why would a person resort to vicarious gratification through literature instead of aiming at more direct gratification, in daydream or deed? Well, wish fulfillment in fantasy may lag from failure of the imagination. Most of us are unable to conjure up images of women as beautiful and sexually stimulating as the images on the screen. The possibilities of wish fulfillment through acting out are even more limited. Such attempts are likely to run head-on against the hard wall of reality. For instance, for a man to go around shooting people as liberally as he might want to is not practical (though some try); but it *is* practical to watch the Western where the "good guys" can do so with impunity, or on a more sophisticated level to read Hermann Hesse's *Steppenwolf* where the "Magic Theatre" at last sets the hero free to massacre those people whose attitudes he does not approve.

It is very much of a commonplace by now, and a very common complaint, that the development of our civilization, at least in the last eighty years or so (since the "closing of the frontier" according to some historians), has been marked by our lives getting increasingly organized. As we become more "civilized," the sphere of our spontaneity and individual action gets more and more restricted. This may be the reason why vicarious experience tends to grow in importance. The "entertainment industry," of which literature is, alas, in a sense a part, plays an increasing role.

Note that our hypothetical man who wants a drink will not be satisfied reading about a man who wants a drink—that would be realistic (mimetic) literature; it offers its gratifications but we do not need to concern ourselves with them here since *Stranger*, whatever it is, is certainly not realistic in this sense—but he wants to read about a man who *gets* a drink. This could in itself also be realistic literature; but as a growing disparity develops between inflated individual wishes and deflated societal possibility of getting them fulfilled, realistic literature has less opportunity for depicting wishes granted. This may go some way toward explaining the ascendancy of fantasy and other nonmimetic literature in our present culture.

The desires that literature vicariously satisfies aim normally at sensual, chiefly sexual, pleasure, and at self-aggrandizement. Their specific form and content vary with the individual's emotional makeup and with the stage of his development. Therefore, different books appeal to different personality types and different ages.

Stranger addresses itself primarily to the fantasy of omnipotence. Keen-eyed observers have seen this—well, at least some of it. For example (I apologize for the style; it is Time's, not mine): "Heinlein's Valentine Michael Smith...descends to earth, where Heinlein puts him through a Voltairian gavotte full of broad satire at the expense of organized religion, and teaches him strychnic cynicism about human nature. But what makes V. Michael so groovy, outasight, oh wow! etc., is his powers of clairvoyance and telekinesis."[19]

Next in importance is the fantasy of promiscuity, of indiscriminate, effortless, repetitive sexual intercourse with an unlimited number of agreeable, healthy, unindividualized members of the opposite sex. Anthony Burgess—and the author of The Wanting Seed and A Clockwork Orange knows what he is talking about when he ponders sex and science fiction—has borrowed the term "pornotopia" to characterize this noble vision: "...pornography depersonalizes, creating an abstract paradise Steven Marcus called Pornotopia, in which the only emotion is lust and the only inhabitants animated phalluses and vulvae."[20]

This is not quite as primitive a fantasy as the fantasy of omnipotence, but its emotional emptiness reveals its childishness. It is hard to imagine a man who has not been tempted by these fantasies. It is just as hard to bestow the name man on a person who has not overcome these temptations. The nature of the third fantasy, necrophagy, is less clear; if it appeals by awakening long slumbering strivings in the reader's mind, they must have come from a very ancient, primitive level.

Some works of literature are content to embody the reader's fantasies. They are often called lowbrow, and sometimes bad books. Then there are books that transcend the reader's fantasy. They embody it, but they lead further. Not satisfied with depicting the events that embody the fantasy which cried for vicarious gratification in the first place, they present experiences befalling the hero that point beyond them. They show a way toward solving the problem of the unsatiability of the fantasy by an accommodation with other forces within the individual's character, and with the demands of reality. They are known as good books.

Good books help the reader to grow. Heinlein's book embodies primitive fantasies. There is no evidence in it of any attempt to transcend them.

So much for the novel's main emotional thrust. How does it look from the angle of what earlier in this section we have called the ideo-logical content? Before tackling this somewhat thorny question, let us consider on a more practical level what the book may be worth as a source of information.

Instructional value may redeem a bad book. A story that em-bodies nothing but primitive sexual fantasies may yet convey valu-able information on the life-style of the people it has chosen to em-body the fantasies. A crime story may teach police methods. Etc. However, when a writer casts his lot with science fiction, fantasy, or any genre removed from realism, he largely renounces his chance to instruct. The teaching value of *Stranger* is limited, though you may want to turn to it if you wish to know what the proper table manners are when you consume the body of a departed friend.

I have just spoken of "experiences befalling the hero." Now that raises the question, who is the hero? It's a simple matter with short stories or even some longer works that clearly concentrate on one figure. Rhysling, the "Singer of the Spaceways," blind like Homer, is clearly the hero of Heinlein's "The Green Hills of Earth" (the short story, not the anthology). He has no competition for the honor. With more complex works it may or may not be more diffi-cult. Nobody will wonder who the hero of *Hamlet* might be. But whom would you call the hero of *The Brothers Karamazov*?

It has been said in many discussions of *Stranger* that its "real" hero is not Mike but Jubal. To me the assertion has always sounded peculiar, but it depends on what criteria you use for calling a char-acter in a work its hero. When it comes to applying them to a speci-fic work, there may be disagreement. In theory there is, I think, good consensus. We call a character the hero if these conditions are met: (a) He occupies the center of the stage, literally or figuratively. He is a participant in most of the action. (b) We identify with him. When he wins, we rejoice; his ebbing fortunes sadden us. This dis-tinguishes him from the villain, who may be a principal figure like the hero, and this is the prerequisite for the work becoming a vicar-ious experience. (c) His personality or fate undergoes changes through the action of the work. In tragedy this is likely to go to the extreme—the hero's death, and in some instances, his apotheosis, as in *Stranger.* (d) The work's message, if it has one, is embodied in the hero.

If that seems a futile exercise in semantics, consider this: Condi-tions (a) and (b) are fulfilled by Mike, and to a large extent by Jubal also. Mike, however, fulfills condition (c), while Jubal does not. As to condition (d), it depends on what you think is the message of

Stranger. This is the crux of the matter. That Jubal is the real hero can only be maintained, in defiance of the fact that he fails to meet condition (c), if a certain message is read into the book. To call Jubal the hero begs the question.

To wit, the question is: What in *Stranger* is essential? Is it the emotional or the ideological content? Or, if it is the combination of both, what is the relation of these two elements to each other?

To come to an answer, we must penetrate into a different layer of personality. Technically speaking, we must move from id psychology to ego psychology. To an extent we have already done so, almost inadvertently, in speaking of the characteristics of "good" books. We must now make it explicit. One thing that the development of psychology has achieved is to establish a scheme of psychologic dynamics. We can assume that the force of the rather elemental drives which power the daydreams that seek vicarious fulfillment in literature is not unopposed, does not have free play; that the emotional life of the individual consists in interaction of a variety of forces, and that some of them hem in and counteract the basic driving force. As the individual matures, he acquires his "superego" —a chorus of voices, as we might call them, within him (though originally they have come from the outside) which tell him that it is forbidden, detrimental, shameful to seek the unhampered fulfillment of his basic drives, be it directly or vicariously, especially if the basic drives are still in a childish state or tend to regress to it.

A burglar who wants to get by a watchdog may throw him a piece of poisoned meat, or in our more humane age, meat saturated with tranquilizers. A writer who wants to get a hearing for his embodiment of a primitive fantasy may lull the countervailing forces into inactivity by throwing them the meat of the loftier, more realistic, less primitive aspects of his work. He may say, in substance, to the distrustful superego: Look, I am not pandering to omnipotence or promiscuity. What I really want is to present a picture of the science of the future and of the workings of supranational government, and to demonstrate the shortcomings of Christianity. If I also discuss necrophagy, well, it's an interesting subject and good clean fun, and so remote that it can't do harm! You do not seriously think that I could corrupt your pupil, seeing that he isn't going to become a cannibal whatever I say, is he? This would be the function of the ideological content in works that do not want truly to transcend the fantasies they embody.

On the face of it, I admit, the argument may look just as good the other way around. When I published a much shorter and simpler version of this essay in *Riverside Quarterly*, correspondents came back at me thus: You say that the real meaning of *Stranger* is that it presents the id with the sweet gratification of its desires, getting license to do so by bribing the superego with pretended interest in loftier things. But I say that the author's real aim is to offer to the ego a harangue on Christianity, and that to get a hearing he had to bribe the id by throwing it that tranquilizing meat of omnipotence and promiscuity.[21]

If we were dealing with a problem in abstract logics, this would be unassailable. Both sides of the coin are genuine—except for one thing: It may be true that one part of the reader's personality has to be sedated to enable the other part to hear the author, but the two parts are not equal. Only one will respond; only the effect on the id can generate the emotional involvement, the enthusiastic acceptance. The ideological material, destined for the superego, would at best get a respectful hearing. If it were true that the id had to be bribed to allow the superego to get Heinlein's message, the result would be quite different from what it has been. The message would be received politely, with all the joy and excitement you get from a textbook on religion or on world government that you read because you have to.

It must be stressed here that we are talking about the way the book works, not about Heinlein's intent. Let us not fall prey to the "intentional fallacy." Once a work is completed and released, it is a thing in its own right. What the author intends is one thing; how the work achieves its effect, another. Whether Heinlein's heart was in the ideological or in the emotional content of *Stranger* may be an interesting question, but hardly as interesting as what the book actually conveys, and certainly irrelevant to this latter question.

My aim has been to analyze *Stranger*, not to criticize Heinlein. I am not insensitive to his writings. I have a feeling for "The Green Hills of Earth," though Panshin calls it "a very pretty, sentimental narrative" marking a "comparative low point."[22] I even think Rhysling's song is fine poetry, and I believe that fine poetry is rare and precious. None of this affects my opinion that *Stranger* presents the id with the sweet gratification of its desires, getting license to do so by bribing the superego with pretended interest in nobler thoughts.

5. Variations on a Theme: Human Sexuality in the Work of Robert A. Heinlein

RONALD SARTI

BY THE END of the 1950s, Robert Heinlein had established himself as the Dean of science fiction, a beloved storyteller whose ways had grown familiar after twenty years of pleasurable reading. Few would have wanted him to change, and fewer still would have expected it. And yet, abruptly, Heinlein's work did change. With the arrival of the new decade, Heinlein's stories took a startling new direction, the reason for which remained a mystery to his readers. Perhaps most surprising was Heinlein's sudden concern for the theme of sexuality. He seemed to have become fascinated with the subject and began exploring such explicit sexual topics as promiscuity, incest, and narcissism. The avant-garde discovered Heinlein's new work and hailed his vision of the sexual future. At the same time, they generally ignored his earlier works, regarding them as adventure stories devoid of meaningful sexual content. They were wrong.

Heinlein's concern with sexuality did not suddenly leap into existence with the Sixties. Throughout the 1940s and 1950s, Heinlein had dealt with aspects of sexuality as peripheral themes in his work, and subtly developed a consistent sexual viewpoint through the creation of many unique characters and relationships. With these characters and relationships, Heinlein demonstrated a sexual objectivity and vision almost unseen in science fiction, and rarely matched in contemporary American literature. The importance for the genre is that Heinlein—throughout his career—has always been in the vanguard of sexual honesty in science fiction.

This is not to say that Heinlein has always been successful, nor that his own creations have been as sexually honest as he might have wished. Unfortunately, for all that he accomplished, Heinlein has experienced severe problems in his treatment of the sexual theme. These problems have limited his success and caused failure, most dramatically in the later part of his career when the sexual theme had become central to much of his work. Heinlein has never been able to overcome these problems totally.

Heinlein's whole career must be considered in order to understand the nature of his success and failure, but a study of his work is most easily accomplished by dividing his career into the two most obvious periods: a first period, consisting of the twenty years in which Heinlein developed sexual topics as peripheral themes; and a second period, in which some aspect of sexuality is an important theme in almost every work. In this way, it is hoped that we will arrive at an understanding not only of Heinlein's success or failure with individual themes, but also of those sexual elements common to his work and essential to the philosophy which inspires them.

First Period (1939-1958)

From his first story in 1939 through his excellent *Have Space Suit—Will Travel* in 1958, Robert Heinlein was the master storyteller of science fiction. As storyteller, his themes were neatly developed in the context of his work through action and characterization, with only minor commentary by the narrator. Many of the themes were familiar to science fiction: the ability of Man to survive and conquer, the evil of slavery and dictatorship, and the need for individual freedom and responsibility. The theme of individual freedom was usually applied to political expression, but Heinlein developed it much further. By logical extension, the concept of freedom had to include sexual freedom, and this freedom underlies Heinlein's intellectual attitudes about sexuality.

However, in the stories of Heinlein's first period, the theme of sexuality was developed only as a peripheral interest rather than as a central theme. There were a number of factors which might account for this lesser interest. For one, Heinlein was more concerned with other themes, other freedoms more directly threatened by the shadow of political dictatorship. For another, the sexless purity of science fiction in the 1940s and 1950s was jealously guarded by editors and publishers. When asked why in the 1960s he had suddenly started writing so freely about sex, Heinlein replied, "Because there was no market for sex in science fiction before then."[1] This was especially true for the dozen juvenile novels he produced in his first period. The readers were assumed to be adolescents, and therefore restrictions were even more severe than in ostensibly adult science fiction.

In spite of all these restrictions, Heinlein accomplished a great deal with the theme of sexuality. Even in his juveniles, various aspects of sexuality were subtly developed and woven into the fringe of the story line. Through the creation of unique character types and healthy relationships, Heinlein entertained and enlightened his readers with both a fresh look at their own sexual conventions and mores, and a suggestion of the possible alternatives that lay before them.

Heinlein, of course, does not always succeed. He uses techniques which are inherently weak when dealing with a complex subject like sexuality. Yet, he overcomes these weaknesses enough times to have an important effect upon the reader, and to advance the artistic and thematic legitimacy of sexuality in science fiction. Because of these accomplishments, the male and female characters, their relationships, and Heinlein's techniques deserve to be studied separately.

Basically, Heinlein's male characters may be divided into two categories: the competent and the incompetent. The incompetents are of little use in the practical world. They function mainly as caricatures for purposes of contrast, satire, and humor, and include such types as the spoiled brat, the jellyfish father, the pompous blowhard, and the bungling meddler. The competent male characters are divided into two types: the stock competent and the Heinlein hero. The competents are the pragmatic, realistic, capable men who keep the wheels turning. One might be a scientist, teacher, pilot, cop, bartender, whatever. He is a nice guy, sometimes harassed, but doing his job and doing it well. Often a stock competent will have a large enough role to rank as a secondary hero and serve as mentor or partner to the hero. The competent are members of the composite that Alexei Panshin has correctly analyzed as the Heinlein Individual.[2] This Heinlein Individual may appear in an early, middle, or late stage of life, but he is the same character—losing innocence and growing older and more worldly-wise at each stage, though just as competent as ever.

The Heinlein hero is merely the Heinlein Individual whom the story is about. But the typical Heinlein hero has some peculiarities that make him sexually interesting to the reader. Although he is smart, talented, and able to learn, the young version of the hero is grossly naive about women and sex. In "'If This Goes On—'" the young hero, John Lyle, begins his narration by implying that he had never even talked to a woman other than his mother.[3] And this is an adult story.

A level of ignorance and naiveté might be excused in Heinlein's juvenile novels due to editorial requirements. Yet even in these the ignorance transcends the need. In *Tunnel in the Sky*, the hero cannot guess that the person he shares a cave with is a girl. And in *Citizen of the Galaxy*, the adolescent hero—an ex-slave raised in a gutter environment—still has no sexual knowledge or experience, and does not recognize the situation when girls are clearly interested in him.

This ignorance must make us wary of what the naive young hero feels or tells us about women and sex. He is still learning, still losing his innocence. His attitudes (those of twentieth-century America) serve a purpose, since they allow Heinlein to inject our own sexual conventions and mores into the story where they can be criticized. In *Starman Jones*, the young hero, Max Jones, feels that the heroine Ellie is not too bad a person—considering she's a girl. She can even play a game of three-dimensional chess, which Max feels is beyond the intelligence of most girls. It is only after Ellie has proved her bravery, and admitted that she is a chess champion, that she corrects Max: "Mr. Jones, has it ever occurred to you, the world being what it is, that women sometimes prefer not to appear too bright?"[4] The hero can learn; it just takes a few gentle taps with a sledgehammer. The reader too has been shown that his own assumption—if sympathetic to the hero's—was similarly incorrect, and that there are alternatives to his preconceived notions. Thus, because of the young hero's inexperience (not to mention Heinlein's purpose), we must be wary of his pronouncements.

In contrast, the sexual statements of the respected, knowledgeable, older heroes can usually be taken as representative of Heinlein's own view. Still, the older heroes have their sexual "oddity," perhaps left over from their former romantic youth. Seen again and again is the hero's insistence upon marriage (or at least, vows) before having sexual relations with the woman he loves—and this after the heroine has offered herself free of charge. In "The Year of the Jackpot," the hero, Potiphar Breen, pops the question to his heroine outside an isolated cabin:

> After a time he pushed her gently away and said, "My dear, my very dear, uh—we could drive down and find a minister in some little town?"
> She looked at him steadily. "That wouldn't be very bright, would it? I mean, nobody knows we're here and that's the way we want it. And besides, your car might not make it back up that road."

"No, it wouldn't be very bright. But I want to do the right thing."

"It's all right, Potty. It's *all right.*"

"Well, then . . . kneel down here with me. We'll say them together."

"Yes, Potiphar." She knelt and he took her hand. He closed his eyes and prayed wordlessly.

When he opened them he said, "What's the matter?"

"Uh, the gravel hurts my knees."[5]

Besides the opportunity for humor, there are several possible explanations for this characteristic, all equally valid. First, the scene is a case of ego gratification for the hero. The Heinlein hero never has to grovel for sex—it is always offered free of charge. In Heinlein's second period, the hero Lazarus Long comments upon this tendency: "'I never risk being turned down; I wait to be asked. Always.'"[6] A second probable explanation is that much as Heinlein criticizes our restrictive sexual conventions, he cannot entirely overcome them himself. There is still the recognition that vows will make it morally right in some way. A final explanation for this characteristic of his heroes is that Heinlein actually believes that a special relationship between a man and a woman can exist and deserves to be marked and differentiated from the common affair. That this is the case will be seen in our discussion of relationships.

However, before discussing relationships, Heinlein's women deserve consideration. More important to science fiction than Heinlein's male characters are his female characters. Because of their importance, they have drawn more attention and been roundly praised and condemned. Anne McCaffrey feels that "Robert Heinlein's women are horrors: excuseless caricatures of 'females,'"[7] while Pamela Sargent admits that they "may represent an advance over much previous sf."[8] We will see that they contribute greatly to Heinlein's early accomplishments with the theme of sexuality.

Heinlein's female characters closely follow the male categories. The major division is between the competent and the incompetent, with the incompetent again being caricatures such as the hysterical parent, or the snobbish lady. Fittingly, Heinlein matches male and female incompetents into couples, as in "'And He Built a Crooked House,'" where they provide much of the comic effect.

The competent female characters compose the equivalent of a female Heinlein Individual, and are used both as stock competents and as heroines. The stock competents are of a type rarely seen in previous science fiction and important for the assumptions which they imply. They appear in the background of many stories, functioning as space pilots, military officers, medical doctors, scientists, and mathematicians. They are professional in their duties and respected for their competency. Theirs is a society in which women have proved themselves and are judged according to their ability rather than their sex. In the 1940s and 1950s, this vision of the future must have had a great effect. A whole generation of young readers— conditioned to a male-dominated society where women airline pilots were nonexistent, and a woman doctor the exception—saw that women might be capable of more than their traditional roles.

This effect was intensified with the extraordinary Heinlein heroine, a female remarkable for her competence and achievement, and almost unknown in American literature and society. Damon Knight tells us that Heinlein's wife was the model for many of these heroines:

> Heinlein's red-headed wife Ginny is a chemist, biochemist, aviation test engineer, experimental horticulturist; she earned varsity letters at N.Y.U. in swimming, diving, basketball and field hockey, and became a competitive figure skater after graduation; she speaks seven languages so far, and is starting on an eighth.[9]

The Heinlein heroine may not have all the skills Ginny has mastered, but whether child, adolescent girl, or adult woman, she is interesting for the unusual qualities she does exhibit. All Heinlein's heroines are brave and intelligent, the adult heroine often a skilled professional in a scientific or military field. And these qualities are more important than the size of a bustline. Ignoring that unkillable stereotype, the Heinlein heroine is not necessarily beautiful, nor even pretty. Physical beauty, while occasionally noted, is not emphasized.

Even more startling for a literary heroine is the fact that she is sometimes faster-acting and more rational than the hero, and able to kill ruthlessly when he is endangered. While fleeing catastrophe in "The Year of the Jackpot," the hero, Breen, stops his car and finds a pistol thrust against his head by a stranger. The heroine, Meade, responds in typical Heinlein fashion:

> Meade reached across Breen, stuck her little lady's gun in the man's face, pulled the trigger. Breen could feel the flash on his own face, never noticed the report. The man looked puzzled, with a neat, not-yet-bloody hole in his upper lip—then slowly sagged away from the car.
> "Drive on!" Meade said in a high voice.
> Breen caught his breath. "Good girl—"
> "Drive on! *Get rolling!*" (2)

This is refreshing. Too long have storybook heroines screamed and fainted while some poor slob gets stomped on by Igor the Monster. Wounded, pregnant, even slug-ridden, the Heinlein heroine remains dedicated to the survival of her hero and herself.

Intelligent and courageous, the Heinlein heroine embodied a positive new image of womanhood, an image that was not lost upon the readers. The Heinlein heroine was exciting. She was a woman they had never imagined, and she presented possibilities that were strangely appealing. To a generation of impressionable minds, she was Woman as capable human being.

Yet, there is one flaw to the remarkable Heinlein heroine. The adult heroine—strong-willed, competent, well-adjusted—becomes a meek and obedient kitten when the hero commands. In *The Puppet Masters*, the hero, Sam, and the heroine, Mary, find themselves in the middle of a battle:

> Mary had walked west on the highway with the downy young naval officer while I was examining the corpse. The notion of a slug, possibly still alive, being around caused me to hurry to her. "Get back into the car," I said.
>
> She continued to look west along the road. "I thought I might get in a shot or two," she answered, her eyes bright.
>
> "She's safe here," the youngster assured me. "We're holding them, well down the road."
>
> I ignored him. "Listen, you bloodthirsty little hellion," I snapped, "get back in the car before I break every bone in your body!"
>
> "Yes, Sam." She turned and did so.[10]

Yes, Sam. Yes, Potiphar. Yes, master. When the hero puts his foot down, that's it. Me man. You woman. Obey.

So much for pilot training and karate lessons. The skills and intelligence of the heroine—and her individual freedom—are subordinated to the ego of the hero. Of course, in each case he just happens to be right (odd coincidence that, no?), but the total obedience of the heroine is unexpected. It becomes incomprehensible when, in *The Puppet Masters*, the same hero later insists upon the individual rights of his wife as a human being:

> "...Those records were snitched out of my wife's head and they belong to *her*. I'm sick of you people trying to play God. I don't like it in a slug and I don't like it any better in a human being. She'll make up her own mind. Now *ask her*!" (30)

In effect, what the hero wants for a heroine is a liberated woman who knows her place.

Anyone have a bigger sledgehammer?

The Heinlein heroine's inconsistent behavior cannot be explained away, nor excused. It stands as a—pardon the expression—male chauvinist tribute to the hero, implying that women—even such as the heroine—enjoy being dominated. The image of the Heinlein heroine is thus not the ideal that it might have been. Heinlein himself could not break away from his own emotional attachment to the obedient female.

Nevertheless, on the whole the standing of the heroine and of the female competent must be judged highly. Rather than being condemned for this single fault, they should be applauded for the stereotypes they broke and the progressive outlook they embodied. In their time, they were a great advance both for science fiction and for literature in general.

Following close behind Heinlein's female characters in importance are the relationships between heroes and heroines. For convenience, we may classify them into four basic sets: (1) the young hero and young heroine, as in *The Star Beast*; (2) the adult hero and young heroine, as in *Have Space Suit—Will Travel*; (3) the adult hero and adult heroine, as in *The Puppet Masters*; and (4) the adult married couple, either as hero and heroine as in "The Unpleasant Profession of Jonathan Hoag," or as competent parents (actually secondary heroes and heroines) as in *The Rolling Stones*. With these four sets, Heinlein is able to highlight patterns of sexual behavior, such as love, romance, marriage, and role-playing; to demonstrate the effects of environmental conditioning and sex discrimination; and to promote intersexual need and partnership.

The basic assumption in all of these relationships is that the heroine—in spite of her occasional obeisance—is as capable as the hero. Promoted is the idea that women are the equal of men in courage, intelligence, and skill. At least, they have the potential for such equality. That they had not fulfilled (or been denied) their potential during Heinlein's lifetime was obvious: no women were piloting *his* flights. Yet able women such as his wife, Ginny, did indeed exist, and so there had to be reasons for the status of women in twentieth-century America. One reason is given in *Magic, Inc.*, when a competent, worldly-wise male character observes:

"It's like this: Most women in the United States have a shortsighted, peasant individualism resulting from the male-created romantic tradition of the last century. They were told that they were superior creatures, a little nearer to the angels than their menfolks. They were not encouraged to think, nor to assume social responsibility. It takes a strong mind to break out of that sort of conditioning, and most minds simply aren't up to it, male or female...."[11]

But more than just this type of environmental conditioning is at work. For those who overcome the restrictive conditioning of their society, there is also sexual discrimination to contend with. Heinlein tears down the banners of discrimination with a romantic but effective little story symbolically entitled "Delilah and the Space-Rigger." A competent female radio technician arrives to work on a space station under construction by an all-male crew. She is frustrated by the stubborn engineer in charge who doesn't think much of her and refuses to accept her ability:

> Then he called her in. "Go to the radio shack and start makee-learnee, so that Hammond can go off watch soon. Mind what he tells you. He's a good man."
> "I know," she said briskly. "I trained him."[12]

In a microcosm of our own society, the heroine is not allowed to learn the rules, but then is blamed when she breaks them.

In many of the stories of his first period, Heinlein creates a different sort of society in which women are accepted—at least to some degree—on talent rather than sex. In other stories, as we have just seen, the futuristic society is not so very different from our own. Ellie in *Starman Jones* has to hide her abilities to be "feminine," and Maggie in "'If This Goes On—'" has been trained for nothing except the position of domestic and mistress. In both works, the heroines reflect twentieth-century limitations on womanhood, and it is clear that Heinlein dislikes these limitations upon the freedom of women. His works echo the opinion that women are potentially capable, and that in a possible future society they will assume a rightful, integral place in the professional world, with the same freedom as men to develop themselves into competent individuals. But Heinlein's work also implies that in our own type of society, the majority of women—due to environmental conditioning and sexual discrimination—have been forced into an artificial mold of incompetence. Denied the chance to develop herself, it is only an outstanding woman who overcomes her environment, and even she may be forced to hide her capabilities in order to fit a romantic role of womanhood.

Perhaps this is why so many of Heinlein's adult heroes are matched with adolescent or preadolescent heroines. Heinlein may like younger heroines because he considers them unspoiled by cultural conditioning. There is evidence for this in a novel from Heinlein's second period, *Glory Road*, in which the hero's mentor explains that the typical American woman is sure of her domestic genius, in bed and out. The mentor adds that it is impossible to convince her otherwise "'Unless you can catch one not over twelve and segregate her, especially from her mother—and even that may be too late....'"[13] In another novel from Heinlein's second period, *Time Enough for Love*, the hero does literally "catch one" and then raises her on a pioneer planet with the help of his mistress, who "was born on Earth but had shucked off her bad background when she migrated; she did not pass on...the sick standards of a dying culture."[14] When the child is grown, the hero marries her.

This marriage follows logically. The Heinlein hero—in order to find a heroine worthy of him—must raise her himself, in his image. By early contact, he will mitigate the cultural conditioning which the child-heroine will later encounter. This may explain some of the brief, puzzling relationships we see in *The Door into Summer* and *Time for the Stars*. In these instances, brief contact between adult hero and young heroine results in a later marriage.

In any case, where a relationship is developed between competent characters of different sexes, the characters are fundamentally equal, regardless of their ages. This equality is inherent in the interdependence of hero and heroine which is necessary in order to survive and succeed. It is suggested in the relationships of "The Unpleasant Profession of Jonathan Hoag" and *The Puppet Masters*, but it is shown most clearly in the last work of Heinlein's first period, *Have Space Suit—Will Travel*. Kip, the hero, and the eleven-year-old heroine, Peewee, accomplish things together. But they do so only after each has persuaded the other to act in the most prudent and competent manner. Their relationship is complementary. He reins in her impetuosity and she gets him to ignore his male ego. For example, Kip and Peewee are climbing a mountain on the Moon in a desperate attempt to escape danger. Kip (the hero) narrates:

> I wanted to be a hero and belay for her—we had a brisk argument. "Oh, quit being big and male and gallantly stupid, Kip! You've got four big bottles and the Mother Thing and you're topheavy and I climb like a goat."
> I shut up.[15]

Each partner encourages the other to do what is necessary for survival, rather than letting their particular masculine or feminine nature —and their romantic conceptions of the proper behavior—take control and ruin them. They function as a team to which each brings different skills and talents, and it is a team in which each has an equal share, an equal responsibility in the struggle. Alone, either would have failed to overcome the odds.

With a relationship established on such equal and solid footing, respect and affection follow naturally. And where the hero and heroine are of suitable age, the partnership will also develop into a deeper emotional relationship. The expression of their love is a total commitment to each other which is romantic in its idealism. There is a total need for the other person, as Kip in *Have Space Suit—Will Travel* recognizes in his parents' relationship:

> I have talked more about my father but that doesn't mean that Mother is less important—just different. Dad is active, Mother is passive; Dad talks, Mother doesn't. But if she died, Dad would wither like an uprooted tree. (5)

In *Farmer in the Sky*, the hero's mother has died, and his father must flee all the way to the moon Ganymede in order to start life over again. Lifelong permanency and fidelity are implicit in the unwavering devotion of each partner for the other.

Fortunately, these ideal relationships are not allowed to become overly romantic. Heinlein recognizes the problems of marriage, and he always recalls the difficulty of such relationships, as with the various marriage contracts ("term, renewable, or lifetime") offered the hero in *The Puppet Masters*.[16] And in *Methuselah's Children*, Heinlein suggests that people could not or would not live out relationships which lasted longer than a normal lifetime.

Even the characters temper their own romanticism with realistic observations about the limits of love. The Heinlein hero, knowing life for what it is, does not expect his heroine to be a virgin. In "'If This Goes On—'" the heroine Maggie readily admits her sexual past to the hero, who shrugs it off and marries her anyway. And in *The Puppet Masters*, the hero casually dismisses any worries about the heroine's sexual experience as "her business" because "marriage is not ownership and wives are not property" (21). Heinlein may indulge in romantic notions, but he is not ruled by them. The ideal relationship is held possible in spite of a hard look at the reality in which it must exist.

That the relationships should lead to a family would be expected, and great store is placed in family life. This fact, strangely enough, has earned Heinlein some criticism. Representative of several Heinlein females, one of his characters has voiced an explicit desire for nothing more than a man, "six babies and a farm."[17] This attitude has been interpreted as an attempt by Heinlein to put women "back in the kitchen where they belong." It is overlooked that male characters are also devoted to the family, and that the quality of this domestic life is more important that professional careers. Several sets of married couples seem to have given up hectic careers in order to devote themselves to the profession of parenthood. In *The Rolling Stones*, Edith Stone is an M.D., and Roger Stone is an engineer and retired mayor of Luna City. She stays home—and so does he, by writing space opera serials in his living room with his family around him for inspiration. In *Have Space Suit—Will Travel*, the hero's parents, a former mathematician and his most promising student, have established a quiet life in a small town, providing a permanent home rather than the hotel rooms the hero remembers from his boyhood when his parents pursued their glamorous careers. The message is that parenthood is more important than anything else. Not to be forgotten is the fact that characters—male and female—choose domesticity as a mode of personal fulfillment; they are not forced into it by conditioning or discrimination. Pamela Sargent makes note that:

> As a matter of fact, Heinlein's female characters *choose* their fates to a certain extent. They are generally not passive creatures but strong-willed sorts who make up their own minds about what they want.... It seems that Heinlein genuinely believes that parenthood is an exciting occupation and as fulfilling as anything else might be. This is a good and defensible position.[18]

If Heinlein advocates parenthood and domesticity in his first period, it is not that he wishes to restrict either sex to a subordinate role, or reinforce society's conventions. Rather, it is his own appraisal of each sex voluntarily finding fulfillment in important roles for which they are biologically suited, forming a complementary partnership between competent equals.

Obviously, Heinlein's relationships are relatively complex, and it is difficult to squeeze them into a rigid mold. There are elements which might be criticized as uninspired repetitions of society's romantic conventions and traditional mores. Certainly, Heinlein is a victim of his own environment and his own emotional nature. He could not sluff off all the mores and all the conventions. Some are too appealing and enjoyable, sentimental and clichéd and irrational and chauvinistic as they might be. But Heinlein was able to discard many conventional notions, and his intellectual honesty and love of freedom resulted in a progressive view of the relationships between the sexes. The partnership of man and woman, their interdependence, their equality and individual freedom, and their free choice of life-style connote a vision far removed from romantic or sentimental tradition. Like the Heinlein heroine, these relationships rank as one of Heinlein's real accomplishments with the sexual theme during the first period of his career. Their importance—both to the artistic and sexual development of science fiction, and to the sexual philosophy of Heinlein's readers—must not be underestimated.

As successful as Heinlein's characters and relationships are on the whole, the ability of any single character or relationship to promote the sexual theme is dependent upon the techniques used to portray that character or relationship. Unfortunately, Heinlein uses two techniques which are badly suited to the development of this theme, and the result has been occasional mediocrity and failure.

Heinlein's first technique is to use a highly selective point of view, in which he "ignores completely the pain, jealousy and uncertainty that are the ordinary stuff of human experience."[19] We rarely see doubt or worry or fear at work upon a character. He or she may be experiencing intense jealousy or pain over a relationship, but we will not see the restless days or sleepless nights. The character might mention the fact at some point, or state that he has gotten over it; but we will rarely see the emotion at work upon the individual. Sam in *The Puppet Masters* rationalizes away jealousy ("her business"), and that is that: no twinges, no doubt, no curiosity. The result is that there is little emotional development with which the reader can identify.

The second technique Heinlein uses is the distancing of himself and the reader from those moments when intimacy and emotion are required. He often accomplishes this distancing by employing conversation to convey the scene. The conversation itself often consists of a continuous banter which attempts to be casual and relaxed, but is actually artificial and uncomfortable. In one scene from *Beyond This Horizon*, the hero (upon their first meeting in his apartment) disarms the heroine, wrestles her into submission, and then kisses her:

> ...."That," he observed conversationally, "was practically a waste of time. You 'independent' girls don't know anything about the art."

"What's wrong with the way I kiss?" she asked darkly.
"Everything. I'd as lief kiss a twelve-year-old."
"I can kiss all right if I want to."
"I doubt it. I doubt if you've ever been kissed before. Men seldom make passes at girls that wear guns."
"That's not true."
"Caught you on the raw, didn't I?..."[20]

The action, when it is described, can be horribly romantic and clichéd, and Heinlein's attempts to portray the emotional side of a feminine nature often are simply trite mannerisms such as the liberal use of "dear" in conversation, or bursting into tears at touching moments. Again, going to *Beyond This Horizon* for an example (Heinlein really was out of sorts with this one), we have this sentimental little exchange between another hero and heroine:

"I—But...Oh, Marion, Marion!" He stumbled forward toward her, and half fell. His head was in her lap. He shook with the racking sobs of one who has not learned how to cry.
She patted his shoulder. "My dear. My dear."
He looked up at last and found that her face was wet...(12)

What we are deprived of is a close look at the complex psychological and emotional elements common to humanity, and a realistic translation of those elements into action and expression. Heinlein strips his stories of the distractions and crosscurrents that make up a human being and a human relationship. And this omission is due, simply, to Heinlein's uneasiness about portraying such intimate matters of human experience.

This is a particularly important failure, because for all their originality, Heinlein's characters are only two- or three-dimensional, and the success of a character depends upon the close, careful development of those dimensions. If those dimensions are not developed, the character fails to come alive. For example, in *Methuselah's Children*, Mary Sperling has the usual heroine competency. But she also fears death. These are the two dimensions of her personality. We are told often enough of her fear, but we never really see her wrestling with this problem. It just sits on top of her, weighing her down, making her dull, and never changing. Mary is thus relatively uninteresting to a reader accustomed to the Heinlein heroine's competence.

Similar problems apply to Heinlein's relationships. In *The Door into Summer* there is a love affair between an adult hero and a twelve-year-old heroine who remains one-dimensional throughout. Suspended animation and time travel even out their ages so that they can have a conventional marriage, supposedly after the heroine has spent her entire adolescence without seeing the hero (he's in cold sleep), but still loving him enough thereafter to go into cold storage herself for twenty years. As sketchily drawn as the heroine-child is, she is an essential element of the plot, the motivating factor behind much that the thirty-year-old hero does:

> She would not look up and her voice was so low that I could barely hear her. But I did hear her. "If I do... will you marry me?"
> My ears roared and the lights flickered. But I answered steadily and much louder than she had spoken. "Yes, Ricky. That's what I want. That's why I'm doing this."[21]

It is understood that the hero needs to know the heroine as a child in order to save her from her environment. But *why* the hero loves this particular child is never shown to us. Heinlein does not reveal the process by which this attraction has been reached. We would like to be happy for them in the end, but the question of why always comes back to haunt us.

There are a goodly share of failures due to Heinlein's discomfort, and his subsequent exclusion of emotions and arm's-length distancing of the intimate. Yet, in a substantial number of works he is able to overcome this discomfort and enjoy a more relaxed handling of characters and relationships. He does not abandon his techniques entirely, and the situations remain romantic, but he achieves a more intimate tone, and we get to see brief, revealing glimpses of the vulnerable, human side of his characters. The result is those stories which are most successful and do the most to advance the sexual themes with which Heinlein is concerned. One success is " 'If This Goes On—.' " Heinlein gives us some well-paced, well-developed scenes in which we see the emotional confusion of hero and heroine. For example, John Lyle is struggling against his own sexual impulses as he watches the heroine swimming nude:

> Again I could not take my eyes away if my eternal soul had depended on it. What is it about the body of a human woman that makes it the most terribly beautiful sight on earth? Is it, as some claim, simply a necessary instinct to make sure that we comply with God's will and replenish the earth? Or is it some stranger, more wonderful thing?
> I found myself quoting: "How fair and how pleasant art thou, O love, for delights!

"This thy stature is like to a palm tree, and thy breasts to clusters of grapes."

Then I broke off, ashamed, remembering that the Song of Songs which is Solomon's was a chaste and holy allegory having nothing to do with such things.[22]

Here, the character comes alive as a vulnerable human being, subject to the doubts and fears which chain us all.

A like achievement is found in "The Unpleasant Profession of Jonathan Hoag," where the hero and heroine are a married couple who grow more confused and frightened as they delve deeper into supernatural mystery. Heinlein allows us to see these emotions at work, acting upon them, and they come alive as characters. And in *Have Space Suit—Will Travel*, the hero and heroine's understanding of each other develops throughout the novel, as does their mutual respect and affection.

In all these stories, our sympathetic interest and understanding of the characters and of their relationships make us receptive to the points Heinlein is making. In "'If This Goes On—'" Heinlein scorns a society where women are either virgins or whores, and blind sexual repression is the norm. With "The Unpleasant Profession of Jonathan Hoag," he shows us that a married couple can be friends as well as lovers, partners against a harsh and threatening life. And in *Have Space Suit—Will Travel*, the interdependence of man and woman is exemplified again and again. The points are well made—as well made as the characters and relationships are drawn. They have all been given the care and attention they deserve. Heinlein is at his best here, relaxed and comfortable. And so is the reader.

In retrospect, the development of sexual themes in Heinlein's first period was an important achievement and success. For science fiction, Heinlein created characters and relationships far more honest than the stereotypes previously used, and touched upon subjects that the genre had hitherto ignored. For his readers, he had presented observations and alternatives that were different and exciting. If his techniques implied discomfort and resulted in occasional failure, he was able to overcome his deficiencies in many works.

Thematically, by its distinctiveness and merit, this first period in Heinlein's long career must be regarded in its own right and evaluated by its own accomplishments and failures. Yet, this period may also be kept in mind as the essential foundation for Heinlein's second period. Early sexual themes, and the philosophies they embodied, would undergo development and manifest themselves in the sexually preoccupied novels of Heinlein's second period. More ominously, the deficiencies that lurked in his techniques would become crucial as he gained interest in the many variations of the sexual theme, and pursued them not as peripheral interests, but as themes central to the purpose of his work.

Second Period (1959-)

In 1959, after twenty years of enjoyable continuity, Heinlein began the second period of his career in which he changes from Heinlein the storyteller to Heinlein the moralist. This change is marked by three principal characteristics: first, Heinlein becomes increasingly didactic, subordinating story, plot, and character to the development of his theme; second, his work becomes implicitly pessimistic and defeatist; and third, the theme of sexuality becomes central to much of his work. Although we are only concerned with sexuality, all three characteristics are closely associated with each other in a tangle of cause and effect, and thus their interaction must be considered. By so doing, it may be possible to understand the overall sexual philosophy and psychological viewpoint from which Heinlein is writing. But before we can adopt this approach, we must first study some of the individual works of this period, analyzing the sexual theme of each, deciding upon its success or failure, and familiarizing ourselves with those elements which repeat themselves and form the expression of Heinlein's sexual beliefs.

Based upon his original belief in individual freedom, Heinlein's toleration of sexual activity broadens throughout his second period. With this toleration comes an impatience with subtlety. His stories slow to an agonizing crawl as elaborate views and ideas are put forth for the reader's consumption. Long, involved discussions between characters allow Heinlein to lecture upon every aspect of sexuality, and the result is that Heinlein enters all the sexual worlds forbidden to science fiction, such as emasculation, promiscuity, group sex, incest, narcissism, and the nature of hetero- and homosexuality. However, with the sexual theme foremost, the discomfort and ineffective techniques which earlier plagued Heinlein's work also come to the front and limit his study of each sexual theme.

Heinlein continues to express interest in the same aspects of sexuality which concerned him during his first period. The family—extended beyond the conventional nuclear unit—plays a major role in his novels, as does parenthood. And stripped of such notions as fidelity and permanency, love remains as a powerful force in Heinlein's work. All of these appear time and again as critical elements in his second period.

As with everything else in his work, some aspects of sexuality do change. For instance, the Heinlein heroine experiences a sad degeneration in many novels. Heinlein no longer bothers to develop his heroines, and they usually devolve into vaguely drawn sex objects. Perhaps Heinlein's basic attitudes toward women remain the same, but the patience required to create an enjoyable heroine is lacking. The heroine's only new characteristic is the urgent desire to be impregnated by the hero, some even going to the extremes of artificial insemination (against the hero's will) in order to bear the child of the Heinlein hero.

Another change from his first period is Heinlein's direct concern with specific aspects of sexual behavior. Sex in all its permutations has become a thing of endless wonder to Heinlein, as evidenced by the sexual variety of the stories which Heinlein has written in this period. "'All You Zombies—'" is an unusual short story utilizing time travel and a sex-change operation to create a solipsist's nightmare. With *Podkayne of Mars*, Heinlein attempts a feminine point of view (an exception to the heroine degeneration) by having a female narrator. *Glory Road* is a parody in which Heinlein creates the ultimate Heinlein heroine, (the second exception) in order to satirize the romantic notions implicit in his long line of characters and relationships. Besides this, he tosses in a reversal of conventional sex roles, and flirts briefly with a situation conveying tones of bestiality. And *Farnham's Freehold* is a novel in which all the male characters are emasculated and rendered impotent in one way or another, while *The Moon Is a Harsh Mistress* provides a detailed picture of life in a "line family" with multiple wives and husbands.

Individually, these works are less important to our study and must be set aside in order to consider the three novels in which Heinlein is most concerned with sexuality: *Stranger in a Strange Land*, *I Will Fear No Evil*, and *Time Enough for Love*. These three novels not only provide specific examples of Heinlein's success and failure, but also most clearly illustrate the philosophy which Heinlein has adopted in his second period.

Stranger in a Strange Land (published in 1961) is the first sexually important work of Heinlein's second period. It is a conglomeration of many things, including religion, satire, and adventure, but is most interesting to us for its development of the sexual themes of promiscuity and group sex.

It is the story of Valentine Michael Smith, a human who is raised by Martians and learns superhuman powers. He returns to Earth humanly inexperienced, is educated, and then forms a sexually active church in which he teaches "grokking" to those who are qualified to understand the nature of existence and thus share in the superpowers. He is killed by a mob at the end of the novel because of his rejection of all conventions and mores of a hypocritical society.

Robert Plank has criticized the novel as a series of "primitive sexual fantasies" with no informative value,[23] and Alexei Panshin mentions that "the sexual relations are beyond criticism, self-justified,"[24] because Heinlein gives them as being right, and either a character can see this truth and "grok," or he cannot. Both observations are valid. The novel seems to be a long and loud bugle call for a perfect sexual freedom between all the spiritually beautiful people in the world. The dastardly villains preventing this dream from becoming a reality are human jealousy and the Judeo-Christian moral code.

The hero Michael Smith feels that sexual union should be a merging of bodies and souls in shared ecstasy, but that:

> "... Instead it was indifference and acts mechanically performed and rape and seduction as a game no better than roulette but less honest and prostitution and celibacy by choice and by no choice and fear and guilt and hatred and violence and children brought up to think that sex was 'bad' and 'shameful' and 'animal' and something to be hidden and always distrusted. This lovely perfect thing, male-femaleness, turned upside down and inside out and made horrible.
>
> "And everyone of those wrong things is a corollary of 'jealousy.' ..."[25]

Linked to this human emotion of jealousy, and possibly growing out of it, is our religious code of sexual morality. This time Mike's mentor, Jubal, has his say:

> "...the ethics of sex is a thorny problem. Each of us is forced to grope for a solution he can live with—in the face of a preposterous, unworkable, and *evil* code of so-called 'Morals.' Most of us know the code is wrong, almost everybody breaks it. But we pay Danegeld by feeling guilty and giving lip service. Willy-nilly, the code rides us, dead and stinking, an albatross around the neck." (33)

As we see, Heinlein is not blind to the emotional and environmental factors ordering our existence. He succeeds in clearly putting his ideas about them before us. The only thing needed is the evidence to validate these ideas—but this we never get. Instead of showing us how we might throw off "constraints" and achieve these heights of emotional and sexual freedom, Heinlein simply gives us a finished product, a perfect community free of restrictions such as jealousy and morality. Promiscuity and group sex are given as the natural order, and the solution for everything from job dissatisfaction to menstrual cramps.

Such a community is possible because Michael and company have the ability to grok those who are worthy. Only the good of heart are able to grok and enjoy the delights of sexual and spiritual union. The rest will never make it through the door. Mike states:

> "... I had no slightest wish to attempt this miracle with anyone I did not already cherish and trust—Jubal, I am physically unable even to attempt love with a female who has not shared water with me. And this runs all through the Nest. Psychic impotence—unless spirits blend as flesh blends." (36)

Even Jubal recognizes that "it was a fine system—for angels" (36).

This is the problem with *Stranger in a Strange Land*: The novel creates a sexual utopia that does not apply to the common lot of humanity. Heinlein again ignores the "common stuff of human experience." For example, we are told that a character, Ben, suffers from jealousy, while a heroine, Jill, is intolerant of a "waterbrother" who likes to collect pictures of nudes. Ben and Jill come closest to displaying the emotional elements that make up ordinary human existence. But in both cases, Heinlein keeps their problems at arm's length and solves them with a little superpower, so that suddenly the characters grok. No more problems.

What Heinlein is doing, of course, is utilizing his old techniques, and now as before they fail him. Only now, their weakness betrays his sexual argument and threatens the success of the novel itself. How are we to know who is worthy to share water, and who should be discorporated? How can we tell if another is able to achieve spiritual union as well as physical union? Heinlein ignores this reality. He raises arguments, but offers no proof. He suggests change, but offers no workable alternatives. Heinlein's satire is excellent, and his ideas are thought provoking. But no meaningful discussion can be found of the value and place of the promiscuity which is so highly touted.

I Will Fear No Evil (1970) is the most ambitious of Heinlein's novels, and perhaps that accounts for the fact that it is his worst failure. The novel fails as a satire—if it was meant to be one—because it satirizes very little. It fails as a story because the narration is tedious and the plot dull. It might have succeeded as an exploration of the nature of sexuality, for it is certainly concerned with that subject. Highlighted would have been such important topics as the heterosexual and homosexual drives, and the interrelationship between the physiological and psychological processes in a sexual being. But here, too, it fails.

Instead, *I Will Fear No Evil* succeeds as nothing more than a long catalog of naughty stories, including: the young secretary and the older executive; the young boy and the housewife next door; the cuckolded husband (three wives—three children—three horns); the high school cheerleader impregnated by the basketball team; the scantily dressed maid; the spanking; the nurse and the seven interns, the society lady and her two servants, and so on. Between these revelations of the life histories of the characters, we are told the story of Johann Smith, an old billionaire in a state of infirmity and kept alive with tubes, wires, and shoestrings. A once-vigorous man, his old age is a living death, and he prefers either to live or to die. The escape is to have his brain transplanted into the first body that becomes available—which turns out to be that of his female secretary Eunice, who has been killed by a mugger. The story recounts the experience of Johann's adjustment to being a woman.

The concept is fascinating, and a host of questions arise. Johann has a man's psychology, but his body is a woman's. How will Johann feel when a man touches him? Or a woman touches him? How will the mind adjust? Which is the homosexual act? When will Johann be sexually aroused—and when *should* he be? Which will predominate, psychological conditioning or physiological drives? And how will others relate to the change? What about those who loved the hero as a man—or loved Eunice, to whom the body belonged? How will these others respond?

Heinlein raises these questions himself. For example, Jake, a friend of Johann's and the lover of Eunice, breaks down and has to be sedated when Johann proposes a toast to the dead woman whose body he is occupying. And the hero, who finds himself attracted to both men and women, realizes that:

> "...I'm in the damnedest situation a man ever found himself in. I'm not the ordinary sex change of a homo who gets surgery and hormone

shots to tailor his male body into fake female. I'm not even a mixed up XXY or an XYY. This body is a normal female XX. But the brain in it has had a man's canalization and many years of enthusiastic male sex experience. So tell me, Jake, which time am I being normal, and which time perverse?"[26]

The hero answers his own question, and makes what seems to be a major point of the book:

> "...From my unique experience, embracing both physiological sexes directly and not by hearsay, I say there is just *one* sex. Sex. *SEX*! ..." (14)

This is an unusual point to make, and we might expect an author to use every page to prove his thesis by showing the hero adjusting, and explaining how he responded physiologically and emotionally to each sexual step. This does not happen.

Again, as in *Stranger in a Strange Land*, the rightness of Heinlein's premise is self-justified. Johann experiences *no* problems adjusting because there is only one sex, and he has done nothing but change the vehicle of his pleasure. An irascible old man before the transplant, Johann becomes an agreeable, charming personality in Eunice's body. He finds himself thinking about sexual relations with his doctors even before he has recovered from the operation. Oh, he *says* he has trouble adjusting: "The time I'll feel like a queer is the first time some *man* kisses [me]. I'll probably faint" (10). Johann does not faint, he just enjoys. And this is all we see.

The simplicity of adjustment extends to the hero's acquaintances. Jake, who knew the hero and loved Eunice, should be having gigantic problems adjusting, considering the promising scene in which he broke down earlier. But no, he, too, regains his composure and becomes the perfect gentlemen with Johann (and Eunice's body) out of deference to old friend and buddy Johann. Later, he ends up marrying the hero.

Even if we credit the self-justified point of the story with some validity, it is fatally compromised by plot and technique. First of all, Johann is not alone in the body of Eunice! When he awakens from the transplant operation, he discovers that the consciousness of Eunice still resides in the body, right along with his own consciousness. Eunice becomes Johann's sexual mentor and the heroine of the story, helping Johann adjust to being a woman, not that he really needs much help (later in the novel, Jake dies and they haul *his* consciousness into their body with them). This circumstance immediately destroys any chance for a viable consideration of the situation, and renders meaningless the many questions that are begging to be answered.

Also, since the point is self-justified and there is no need to deal with the messy, complex development of human sexuality, we are left free to consider such truly profound matters as the quality of different kisses, the difficulty in buying women's clothes, and the erotic histories of the characters (all those naughty stories).

More tiresome than these matters are the endless conversations. Heinlein has the ability to write witty and informative dialogue. Here, he is merely trite and repetitive. The following passage is an example of a conversation between Johann and Eunice (supposedly occurring mentally within Johann's brain inside Eunice's body— got that straight?). Johann has just kissed his female nurse, Winifred:

> Winifred left about sixty seconds later. (Well, Eunice? How did that one stack up?) (Quite well, Butch. Say eighty percent as well as Jake can do.) (You're teasing.) (You'll find out. Winnie is sweet—but Jake has had years more practice. I'm not chucking asparagus at Winnie. I thought you were going to drag her right in with us.) (With Mrs. Sloan outside and watching our heart rate? What do you think I am? A fool?) (Yes.) (Oh, go to sleep!) (11)

This banter fills up page after page in the novel, and we might almost consider it part of a grand parody if Heinlein did not treat it so seriously, and with such repetitious detail.

This type of conversation is also utilized to narrate Johann's reactions to the kisses he receives and bestows. Johann gets to kiss almost every character in the book (Heinlein is fascinated with kissing), and we get to hear about every experience. Yet, for all that Heinlein is constantly suggesting sexual arousal, he never delivers the real thing. As with previous works, no sexual coupling is ever actually described. We are told about Johann's first sexual experience the morning after, and it turns out that Johann was drunk and everything was fuzzy. Convenient.

Why Heinlein should tease us all through the novel and then avoid the moment of truth may only be explained by those old problems, his inhibitions. He is still not comfortable with intimate scenes of human emotion, and he falls back on the same techniques he used before, and then some. The naughty stories, Eunice's consciousness, the worthless conversations, and the kissing are all devices to avoid coming to grips with a subject that Heinlein does not know how to handle.

Yet, Heinlein does overcome one inhibition, when for the first time in his work he introduces a sexual four-letter word. He uses it twice, both times in the same paragraph at the very end of the novel and just before Johann-Eunice-Jake die giving birth:

> "Everything always hurts, Roberto—everything. Always. But some things are worth all the hurts . . . It is good to touch—to fuck—be fucked. It's—not good—to be—too much alone. . . ." (29)

It is too bad that for all his effort, this is all Heinlein had to say. The sexual themes which are mishandled so badly do need to be explored. But Heinlein's methods are not the ones to use.

In his most recent novel, *Time Enough for Love* (1973), Heinlein is more successful because he takes care to be a storyteller—and an artist—rather than just a moralist or sexual adventurer. The novel is ostensibly about love, but actually deals with the sexual themes of incest and narcissism, which are given as manifestations of that love.

Time Enough for Love is a rambling, picaresque account of the past life of Lazarus Long. After two thousand years the hero is tired of life, but is prevented from committing suicide by the long-lived Howard Families. They convince Lazarus that he should live long enough to relate his experiences for their benefit, and so he does. Meanwhile, the people he has met form a family around him, and many of the females have themselves impregnated by Lazarus in one way or another, some even serving as host mothers to cloned versions (female reproductions) of the hero. His interest in life revived, but still seeking something new in the way of adventure, Lazarus goes into the past, ends up having an affair with his own mother, and then gets himself killed in World War I. The novel ends with his family of the future snatching Lazarus off the battlefield and reviving him.

Throughout the novel, the emphasis is upon the sexual aspects of his adventures, as signaled in the title of the novel. The key to the title may be found in one of the excerpts from Lazarus Long's Notebooks:

> The more you love, the more you *can* love—and the more intensely you love. Nor is there any limit on how *many* you can love. If a person had time enough, he could love all of that majority who are decent and just. ("Intermission")

It is also made clear that "whatever 'love' is, it's not sex" ("Variations on a Theme IV"). We find love to be much more, as Lazarus explains:

> The longer I was privileged to live with Dora, the more I loved her. She taught me to love by loving me, and I learned...Learned that supreme happiness lies in wanting to keep another person safe and warm and happy, and being privileged to try ("Variations on a Theme XII").

So, love is defined as being the supreme happiness of the one who loves, and is achieved by caring most deeply for another human being. Simple enough, and the definition is applied consistently throughout the novel. But the definition is a narcissistic one. Love is supreme happiness. We want to make ourselves happy, and so we love others, and take care of others—not for their sake, but for our own. The principle extends to everything we do:

> ...once you pick up a stray cat and feed it, you cannot abandon it. Self-love forbids it. The cat's welfare becomes essential to your own peace of mind—even when it's a bloody nuisance not to break faith with the cat ("Variations on a Theme VI").

With this narcissistic interpretation, almost every chapter may be (and is intended to be) interpreted as a variation upon this theme. All of Lazarus Long's sexual and emotional relationships thus become expressions of self-love. The narcissism becomes quite literal at times, as when Lazarus makes love to the two cloned female versions of himself whom he has helped raise:

> "...Coupling with us might be masturbation, but it *can't* be incest because we *aren't* your sisters. We aren't your kin in *any* normal sense; we're *you*. Every gene of us comes from *you*. If we love you—and we do—and if you love us—and you do, some, in your own chinchy and cautious fashion—it's Narcissus loving himself. But this time, if you could only see it, that Narcissist love could be consummated" ("Variations on a Theme XVII").

Similarly, the theme of incest runs just as deeply through the novel, and is considered in the same type of unique variations. At one point, Lazarus explores in scientific detail the relationship of a set of mirror twins whom he buys out of slavery. They are diploid brother and sister having the same mother and father, sharing the same host womb, growing up together as brother and sister, but with no genetic reason to prevent their mating, as they wish. The result of the investigation is a new understanding by the reader of the nature of incest. It becomes clear that:

" 'Incest' is a legal term, not a biological one. It designates sexual union between persons forbidden by law to marry. The act itself is forbidden; whether such union results in progeny is irrelevant. The prohibitions vary widely among cultures and are usually, but not always, based on degrees of consanguinity" ("Variations on a Theme IX").

The basic message is that incest is a cultural taboo imposed because of genetic dangers, but often of no logical relation to the genetic dangers which it is meant to avoid. Whether or not one agrees with Heinlein's ideas, his consideration of incest does leave the reader with enough information and knowledge to apply such investigative methods to the cultural and genetic validity of his own incest taboos. In this way, Heinlein has succeeded with his theme.

The theme of incest is carried to fruition when Lazarus Long goes back in time and has a sexual and emotional love affair with his mother. Heinlein overcomes his own sexual inhibitions by finally including a sex scene, the one in which this relationship is consummated. Yes, Heinlein is still uncomfortable, and the dialogue is still artificial, but somehow the scene works, perhaps because of the reader's amazement at seeing such a thing in a Heinlein novel.

Time Enough for Love succeeds in many ways, and it will probably be ranked as Heinlein's most complex and interesting work. The primary accomplishment of the novel is Heinlein's masterful intertwining of the themes of incest and narcissism into each chapter and each example. For instance, one of the most romantic chapters concerns Lazarus and Dora, a child he has saved and raised as his own. When she comes of age, she wants to have a baby by Lazarus. After having raised Dora as his daughter, the incestuous element is clear in the emotional relationship. Lazarus is changing from father to husband. Then, Lazarus himself raises the issue of narcissistic self-love for this act. He has married Dora because she is a stray kitten he must take care of out of self-love. Thus, the relationship has both its incestuous and narcissistic elements. Both themes are also inherent in his relations with his cloned selves, with the mirror twins, with his family, and with his mother. The intricate plotting of these sexual themes is the work of a master craftsman.

By the elaborate repetition of the two themes, the novel is also a success for the manner in which it raises questions and suggests alternatives. Through the numerous variations of each theme, the reader is familiarized with the subject and begins to see the complexities of the theme, and to consider it outside the narrow bias of his own cultural point of view. This is an accomplishment.

However, with the novel's success comes its failure. As entertaining as the novel may be, and as many questions as it may raise and as much thought as it may stir, there is little real human substance to apply to our own situation. The mirror twins are not really normal brother and sister; Dora is not Lazarus' biological daughter; and his cloned female selves are neither sisters nor daughters. Even his mother is no longer his mother. She is a "lovely young matron, just his 'own' age" ("DaCapo III"), a woman who happens to be the mother of the child that Lazarus was two thousand years before. In too many cases, scientific manipulation accounts for a sexual improbability. Scientifically, the examples work, and the novel is good science fiction. But these examples fail to offer insights into the human factors that make up so many of these problems. Again, as in *Stranger in a Strange Land* and *I Will Fear No Evil*, the complex psychological and emotional elements that make up sexuality are ignored.

None of Heinlein's work in his second period is as successful as it might have been, and the fault is mainly with his inadequate handling of the sexual theme. The variations on this theme are cleverly presented and effective within limits—but these limits are disappointing. Heinlein's persistent reluctance to deal with the human condition of emotional vulnerability forbids any true application of the sexual studies he has undertaken. For this reason, Heinlein's second period must be looked upon as one of unfulfilled promise. Our consolation is that if Heinlein did not provide any answers, at least he asked the needed questions.

Having completed an evaluation of some works of this period in terms of the success or failure of each, it is now possible to consider the philosophy and psychology which have dictated Heinlein's extensive interest in the theme of sexuality.

Heinlein has always put great store in physical survival, and in his first period optimistically showed us the ability of the competent man to succeed against the odds. Heinlein himself was the archetype of competency and success. By the end of his first period he had already written a massive body of literature, carved out an inestimable niche for himself in science fiction, and was regarded with adulation by a large body of fans. Most would view such a life as a great success.

However, by the beginning of his second period in 1959, Heinlein was fifty-two years old and reaching the age when one's own mortality becomes obvious. A man might realize that for all his competence and for all his victories he could not escape the eventual defeat of death. Old age would strip him of his abilities and leave him powerless before this fate.

Heinlein's writing in his second period seems to reflect this type of thinking. For all their competence, his heroes are strangely unable to alter circumstances, are emasculated, and rendered impotent against the forces of the universe. The realities of old age and death also figure more prominently in Heinlein's work. In *Stranger in a Strange Land*, Michael is killed by the mob. The novel *I Will Fear No Evil* is about one man's desperate attempt to escape old age and death. And *Time Enough for Love* is about a man who cannot die. Heinlein was in his sixties when he wrote *Time Enough for Love*, an aging man writing about an ageless man. The attraction of the fantasy is obvious.

But if a man is not a Lazarus Long, if he cannot affect his fate, if he can no longer find importance in his temporary victories against the universe, where can he seek purpose? How can he give life meaning?

Religion is one answer, but Heinlein seems to have rejected that. If ever a believer in a God, Heinlein implies throughout his second period that he is atheistic. He rejects the Judeo-Christian code in *Stranger in a Strange Land*, and later makes it clear in *Time Enough for Love* that "Religion is a crutch for people not strong enough to stand up to the unknown without help" ("Intermission"). Denying himself this comfort, it is indeed a gloomy realization that death is the end of everything, without either physical or spiritual immortality.

Yet, there is another way to gain a measure of physical immortality. The answer is genetic survival, and it is this answer that Heinlein has grasped in order to give meaning and purpose to life. If a man cannot live forever, at least he can ensure the survival of a part of himself in his children. This attitude is reflected in his novels. Michael Smith impregnates at least half a dozen women by the time of his death. Johann Smith takes great care to have his female body impregnated with his own seed, and far into Heinlein's Future History, Lazarus Long is literally the genetic forefather of an important segment of the human race, and propounds that "racial survival is the *only* universal morality."[27]

To ensure this type of survival, the *family* is essential. Not only does it protect and educate the children, but it also provides comfort and holds off the grim thoughts of that ultimate fate. The love and adoration of the family, and the careful education of the children in the image of the father (hero) are essential to his psychological well-being, and far overreach any temporary interests in a professional career or adventure to the stars. This is why so many of Heinlein's stories at this time are domesticated, either utilizing the family scene as an essential story element like the "Nest" in *Stranger in a Strange Land*, or in providing a warm sanctuary from which the hero may venture forth upon occasion as Lazarus does. For lack of this family, Lazarus—having been kicked around the universe for a few centuries—even welcomes death until a new family has built up around him and provided a "home" to return to. It is the family that rescues Lazarus from the battlefield and brings him back to life, in symbolic manifestation of the physical immortality that the family allows.

What the hero gives in return is *love*. There is that special love for *the* woman, the tender love for many women, and the warm, asexual love for "that majority who are decent and just," both men and women. The hero must love all these because it is good to love, as Michael Smith and Johann Smith and Lazarus Long all know. This is why their "families" grow so large. The more one loves, and the more there are to love, the happier one is, and it is this happiness which will deny the Fates and push back the heavy knowledge that weighs down the human spirit.

Thus, parenthood, the family, and love—always important in Heinlein's early work—evolve into essential elements of his later philosophy by forming a consistent denial of one's own purposeless mortality. However, there is another element perhaps just as essential, one that Heinlein has newly turned to in his second period. The "icing on the cake,"[28] the bountiful gift which spices up human existence, is sex. In denying death, in making a family, in loving others, "this lovely perfect thing, male-femaleness" plays an essential role that fascinates Heinlein. If all conventional adventures have shrunken in importance, the sexual adventure looms in their place. Sex can provide a first step toward love by encouraging intimacy ("growing closer"), so why not have sex often, with many people, in order to hasten the love ("spiritual union") in which happiness and comfort can be found? Besides, sex is fun, so why limit it in any way? Why let jealousy create inhibitions? Why let illogical taboos and morals interfere with this innocent pleasure that does so much to deny the reality of our own demise? Why not explore the different types of sexual love and see how we have limited ourselves and denied ourselves this great comfort?

Having evolved this philosophy, having discovered the purpose and pattern by which to live, Heinlein must preach the gospel of his new revelation, perhaps to himself as much as to others. Family! Sex! Love! These are the weapons with which to challenge the universe and deny death. These are the important things in life, the essential elements of a desperate happiness. In our pitifully short lives, there must always be time enough for these.

6. The Evolution of Politics and the Politics of Evolution: Social Darwinism in Heinlein's Fiction

PHILIP E. SMITH II

IN HIS RECENT history of science fiction, James Gunn tries to account for the success of Robert Heinlein's early works: "He seemed capable of coming up with ideas that never had been thought before or of revitalizing old ideas with new treatments. He would write the definitive treatment of more science fiction themes than any writer since H. G. Wells, and perhaps because—unlike Wells—he had no apparent philosophy to promote, his stories seemed to exhaust the possibilities implicit in their concepts."[1] I believe that Gunn's evaluation is incorrect in one important respect: since the beginning of his career as a writer, Heinlein has based his most important fictions on a very apparent philosophy: social Darwinism.

The application of Darwin's theory of evolution through natural selection to the realm of human activities characterized much nineteenth- and early twentieth-century thought. Darwin himself gave a brief formulation of his theory's social application in *The Descent of Man*:

> Man, like every other animal, has no doubt advanced to his present high condition through a struggle for existence consequent on his rapid multiplication; and if he is to advance still higher, it is to be feared that he must remain subject to a severe struggle. Otherwise he would sink into indolence, and the more gifted men would not be more successful in the battle of life than the less gifted. Hence our natural rate of increase, though leading to many and obvious evils, must not be greatly diminished by any means. There should be open competition for all men; and the most able should not be prevented by laws or customs from succeeding best and rearing the largest number of offspring.[2]

Formulations such as "struggle for existence" and "battle of life," along with Herbert Spencer's phrase, "survival of the fittest," were used to explain and justify all kinds of human activities, from the successes of capitalist entrepreneurs to the victories of warring countries. The specifically American expressions of this mode have been discussed in Richard Hofstadter's *Social Darwinism in American Thought*. Hofstadter shows that "There was nothing in Darwinism that inevitably made it an apology for competition or force"; but, he continues:

> How, then, can one account for the ascendency, until the 1890s of the rugged individualist's interpretation of Darwinism?
> The answer is that American society saw its own image in the toothand-claw version of natural selection, and that its dominant groups were therefore able to dramatize this version of competition as a thing good in itself. Ruthless business rivalry and unprincipled politics seemed to be justified by the survival philosophy. As long as the dream of personal conquest and individual assertion motivated the middle class, this philosophy seemed tenable, and its critics remained a minority.[3]

The doctrines of social Darwinism are still alive in American culture, especially in such popular forms of expression as "genre" fiction: spy thrillers, Westerns, and, of course, science fiction. Since the nineteenth century, American science fiction has thrived on social Darwinistic speculations; Heinlein's philosophy is squarely in the tradition of thought manifested by writers such as Edgar Rice Burroughs and E. E. Smith.

Heinlein's social Darwinism combines a grim, Hobbesian vision of the nature of man together with a reductive and tautologically self-justifying belief in the survival of the fittest through natural selection. In Heinlein's political fantasies, as in his version of biology, the fittest survive because they are the fittest. An inspection of the development of Heinlein's fiction over his more than thirty years of writing reveals that while the imagined forms of its application are various, the basic social Darwinistic idea remains a constant.

Beyond This Horizon (serialized 1942, published in book form 1948) is the most complete early expression of Heinlein's views on the evolutionary process as a determinant both of human nature and of the political system most appropriate to it. Heinlein's eugenic utopia continues a tradition of speculative fiction which has its roots in Plato's *Republic*. However, the most influential antecedents of this novel appear to be H. G. Wells and Aldous Huxley. Just as Huxley's pessimistic *Brave New World* answers Wells's hopeful and visionary *A Modern Utopia*, so Heinlein's *Beyond This Horizon* contradicts Huxley and reasserts the evolutionary dynamism and progressive spirit characteristic of Wells's utopias.

In *A Modern Utopia* Wells stipulates that since Darwin "quickened the thought of the world," the modern utopia "must not be static but kinetic, must shape not as a permanent state but as a hopeful stage, leading to a long ascent of stages."[4] Wells describes a World State which attempts to reconcile individualism and human liberty with the demands of social organization to attain "the maximum general freedom" (MU p.34). He recognizes that in such a state, the "way of Nature," natural selection, can be palliated but not denied: "if it can be so contrived that every human being shall live in a state of reasonable physical and mental comfort, without the reproduction of inferior types, there is no reason whatever why that should not be secured. But there must be a competition in life of some sort to determine who are to be pushed to the edge, and who are to prevail and multiply. Whatever we do, man will remain a competitive creature..." (MU p.137).

Heinlein also takes a dynamic and optimistic social Darwinist position in regard to the reconciliation of the need for political order and the progressive improvement of the human race. While Aldous Huxley imagines a socially static world governed absolutely by Controllers whose duty is to suppress individual liberty and breed functionalized beings, Heinlein's Moderators for Genetics act on their belief in the libertarian, republican, and dynamic ideals of a benevolent world government. In chapter 2 of *Beyond This Horizon*, Moderator Mordan explains to Heinlein's hero, Hamilton Felix, "'the responsibility of improving the race under the doctrines of our republic is not a simple one. We can advise but not coerce. The private life and free action of every individual must be scrupulously respected. We have no weapon but cool reason and the appeal to every man's wish that the next generation be better than the last.'"[5]

Heinlein's plot calls for Hamilton Felix, a member of the genetic "star line," to resist the master plan for racial improvement. At the beginning of the novel he finds himself, in contrast to his name, unhappy; further, he can see "'no reason why the human race *should* survive...other than the fact that their make-up insures that they will'" (BTH 2).[6] It becomes Mordan's task to convince Hamilton Felix of the worth of human progress through eugenics. Heinlein provides Mordan with lectures on human nature, genetics, and social theory. Felix, in turn, gets involved in defending Mordan against a revolutionary plot; falls in love, marries, and has children with the genetically "right" person; and by the end of the novel has found satisfaction and new hope in research into parapsychology and immortality. Felix's children, Theobald and Justina, are living proof of reincarnation and telepathy as well as man's ability to use and improve upon natural selection.

Heinlein's central message, however, concerns the interaction of nature and humanity and the survival of the race: "Natural selection—the dying out of the poorly equipped—goes on day in and day out, inexorable and automatic. It is as tireless, as inescapable, as entropy" (BTH 14). But in Heinlein's utopian future, nature's bloody tooth and claw operate slowly; Mordan must explain to Felix why eugenic selection aids the natural process: " 'Easy times for individuals are bad times for the race. Adversity is a strainer which refuses to pass the ill equipped. But we have no adversity nowadays. To keep the race as strong as it is and to make it stronger requires careful planning. The genetic technician eliminates in the laboratory the strains which formerly were eliminated by simple natural selection' " (BTH 2). Mordan points out that there are limits to what artificial selection can accomplish: most importantly, it cannot change what Heinlein sees as an essential quality of human nature, the fighting spirit. Mordan relates the history of the Genetic Wars to illustrate that experiments which tampered with that quality were unsuccessful. When pacifists tried to create a nonviolent human, "to get rid of war by stamping it out of the human spirit," the resulting "sheep" did not survive. The lesson is: "The 'wolves' ate the 'sheep.' Not physically in the sense of complete extermination, but genetically speaking, we are descended from 'wolves,' not 'sheep' " (BTH 2).[7]

Mordan adds two other basic survival characteristics to the essential qualitites of human nature: " 'cool self-interest' " and " 'general adaptability' " (BTH 2). During the Genetic Wars, the attempts of the Empire of the Great Khans to " 'monkey with the balance of human characteristics resulting from a billion years of natural selection' " (BTH 2) proved failures: "...the true men won. Won because they fought and continued to fight, as individuals and guerilla groups" (BTH 2). But even in Heinlein's eugenic utopia of true men there are those who have not learned the lessons of the Genetic Wars, and would attempt to establish a tyranny based on selective breeding of "leader types" and repression of the rest of humanity. Felix helps quash the rebellion by the Survivors Club against the society of true men; after the victory, Mordan explains why defeat of the rebels was inevitable: " '...it would be simplest to state that they never did have what it takes. The leaders were, in most cases, genetically poor types, with conceit far exceeding their abilities'" (BTH 10).

Heinlein characteristically creates fictional situations in which conflicts are resolved unambiguously, and, as many readers have observed, his fiction also manifests his delight in imaginative description of process. In *Beyond This Horizon*, biology explains behavior. There are no tough conflicts of opposing legitimate interests; in Heinlein's fictional future, although men may combat with one another or against nature, there is no doubt where right resides. Despite Felix's temporary malaise and the minor inconvenience of a revolution, the system works. For Heinlein, biology also explains politics: A political system allowing a maximum of personal freedom and a minimum of government interference will best accomplish the advancement of the race. Heinlein's world is run efficiently by an elected, representative oligarchy called the Board of Policy; the superintelligent members, or Planners, debate and decide issues such as eugenic programming and allocation of money for scientific research. Their dedication and intelligence place them above suspicion; they recall the "voluntary nobility," or "Samurai," who perform similar services in Wells's *A Modern Utopia*.

Even the social custom of carrying weapons (Felix wears an antique .45-caliber Colt automatic) and challenging any discourteous person to duel has its biological place in Heinlein's society. Mordan again explains: "'Well, in the first place an armed society is a polite society. . . . But gunfighting has a strong biological use. We do not have enough things to kill off the weak and the stupid these days. But to stay alive as an armed citizen a man has to be either quick with his wits or with his hands, preferably both. It's a good thing'" (BTH 15).

The underlying fantasy-wish of *Beyond This Horizon* involves a justification of life and politics based on libertarian and competitive principles which are derived from a social Darwinistic interpretation of evolution. Heinlein's fictional utopia exhibits the author's vision of such a society—but it also includes his fantasy of transcending the biological limitations of evolutionary development as we know it by endowing the best specimens of the human race with telepathic powers and the certainty of reincarnation. The soul of Carvala, an aged female member of the Board of Policy, does not die with her body, but turns up in Felix's newborn daughter, Justina. This double fantasy, survival of the fittest humans coupled with the award to that elite group of telepathy and immortality, is a common one in Heinlein's fiction. Even in fictions where such transcendence is not provided, the happy endings usually affirm that the hero and the elite will be able to cope successfully with their problems.

In other early fictions Heinlein also portrays optimistically political systems which reconcile the need for social order with what he sees as the optimum condition for evolutionary advancement: maximum personal freedom and competition for the individual. In some cases, such as *The Day After Tomorrow* and "'If This Goes On—'" elite revolutionary groups are depicted successfully overturning oppressive authoritarian regimes in order to reestablish the original political freedoms of the vanquished United States.

In *The Day After Tomorrow* (serialized 1941, published as a book 1949, originally titled *Sixth Column*) the United States has been conquered by the PanAsian hordes. A small band, or "sixth column," of patriots routs the yellow peril with racial rayguns which are able to "'knock over all the Asiatics in a group and not touch the white men.'"[8] People of other colors do not figure in this novel —America is made safe for the return of the white man's government. Heinlein's hero, Whitey Ardmore, plans that after the defeat of the invaders he will "'locate all the old officials left alive and get them back on the job to arrange for a national election'" (DAT 11). Except for stopping the plot of a crazed American scientist who wants to establish a dictatorship, Ardmore shows no further concern for postwar politics. But he does make clear that the United States' original error consisted in not heeding a biological/political law: "'We got into this jam by thinking we could settle things once and for always.... Life is a dynamic process and can't be made static'" (DAT 11).

Similarly, "'If This Goes On—'" (serialized 1940, revised for book publication 1953) demonstrates Heinlein's acceptance and endorsement in his early fiction of the eighteenth-century republican principles of the American Revolution. In the novella, part of the Future History series, the United States has fallen under the rule of a religious and military tyranny claiming divine sanction through a now-dead evangelist called the First Prophet. Heinlein, perhaps inspired by Kipling's "The Man Who Would Be King," describes the revolt of a Cabal, united by Masonic ritual and trappings, against the authoritarian regime. After joining the Cabal, Heinlein's young hero, John Lyle, overcomes his religious indoctrination by unrestricted reading of Tom Paine, Patrick Henry, and Thomas Jefferson. Lyle discovers that the "first republic" of these patriots had been "a community of free men, deciding their own affairs by peaceful consent."[9]

Characteristically, Heinlein portrays an elite group of free men in " 'If This Goes On—.' " Late in the novella, John Lyle differentiates himself from the leaders of the Cabal: "I am typical, perhaps, of the vast majority, the sort of person who has to have his nose rubbed in a thing before he recognizes it, while Zeb and Maggie and General Huxley were of the elite minority of naturally free souls... the original thinkers, the leaders" (ITGO 11). Heinlein's distinction between ordinary men and this elite minority of "naturally free souls" is an important one. Earlier in the narrative Lyle comes to realize a Heinlein axiom (repeated in other fictions by other characters): "...no amount of force can control a free man, a man whose mind is free. No, not the rack, not fission bombs, not anything— you can't conquer a free man; the most you can do is kill him" (ITGO 6).[10] In Heinlein's fiction the elite of "naturally free souls" (whether born into this condition, or educated into it as John Lyle eventually is) remains the best hope for the maintenance of political freedoms and the advancement of the race. As the Cabal's revolution nears its successful conclusion, its leaders establish a provisional constitutional convention which has as its "single purpose" the working out of "orderly methods of restoring the old free democratic processes; any permanent changes in the constitution, if needed, would have to wait until after free elections" (ITGO 14).

In "Coventry" (1940), the companion piece to " 'If This Goes On—' " in the Future History series, Heinlein imagines another utopian society which accomodates maximum personal freedom with a stable social order. In the U.S.A. after the Second Revolution, all social interactions are governed by the principles of the Covenant, "the first scientific social document ever drawn up by man..." The Covenant provides for a libertarian system which any person may freely accept or reject. Those who accept it are permitted to engage in any kind of action or mode of conduct which does not physically or economically damage another human. Those who reject the Covenant and do not wish to volunteer for psychological readjustment are (in a realization of the social exile described by the phrase, "to send to Coventry") ostracized to Coventry, a large reservation of exiles within the United States. This system, while it encourages peaceful existence and compromise, does so at the expense of violent competition, both economic and physical. However, Heinlein provides that those who seek danger and adventure may find it (as they were able to in *Beyond This Horizon*) in experimental laboratories or in the exploration and colonization of the planets.

Heinlein's "Coventry" concerns a young literary critic, David MacKinnon, who, in a moment of "atavistic violence" punched someone in the nose. MacKinnon, motivated by his reading of Jack London and Zane Grey, chooses to leave the safety of the United States for the frontier anarchy of Coventry. What he finds there causes him to reassess his rejection of the Covenant and eventually to return to the United States to warn of the danger of a revolt by the outcasts. In Coventry MacKinnon meets "Fader" Magee, a member of Heinlein's self-reliant, naturally free elite, who is really a secret agent for U.S. Army Intelligence named Captain Randall. Magee and Doc, Coventry's only physician, help the naive literary critic come to terms with his own personality and by the end of the story MacKinnon has achieved the self-confidence and belief in libertarian social order characteristic of the other elite males in Heinlein's early fiction. MacKinnon's final goal is to emulate Fader by joining the Army's secret service.

If the social Darwinistic ideas prominent in *Beyond This Horizon* are not specifically referred to in "Coventry," they continue to be basic to Heinlein's political and social thought. The dissatisfaction of MacKinnon (who is described before his condemnation of the American social contract as having "the noble dignity of a wild animal at bay") with the safe and orderly life under the Covenant reflects Heinlein's own ambivalence about the issue of social order versus racial survival, that is, that the race progresses best where severe conditions increase the efficiency of natural selection. The Future History sequence embodies the continual struggle of humanity to improve and change in the face of natural and artificial barriers.[11] For example, in "Logic of Empire" (1941), set about fifty years earlier than " 'If This Goes On—' " Heinlein's hero, Humphrey Wingate, discovers under the pressure of life on a Venusian slave plantation that he must develop the determination to resist the possibility of easy accommodation with bondage. Wingate escapes to a community of runaway slaves where he finds a "culture and a government. True, it was a rough frontier culture and a simple government with few laws and an unwritten constitution, but a framework of customs was in actual operation and its gross offenders were punished—with no higher degree of injustice than one finds anywhere." There Wingate enjoys freedom and self-fulfillment such as he had never known on Earth. His decision at the end of the story to return to his home planet is shown to be a bad one—no one will pay serious attention to his exposé of slavery on Venus, and the political and social freedoms of Americans are shrinking with the onset of nationwide religious hysteria.

Two other early stories not written as part of the Future History series are notable because they represent variant interpretations of the utopian ideas of freedom for all humanity, evolutionary progress, and the role of the elite. In "Lost Legacy" (1941), a parapsychology fantasy, Heinlein's heroic trio of university researchers discovers humanity's forgotten power to read minds, fly, and compress a villain into a twenty-inch sphere, "like a deepsea diver caught in an implosion, like an orange in a squeezer."[12] The unsuspected existence of mental powers such as these disproves the commonly hypothesized origins of mankind, but not the theory of evolution through natural selection. The secrets of human origins and superpowers are revealed when the heroic trio finds Ambrose Bierce living in a cave on Mount Shasta with a small band of people who have discovered how to use their psychic potential. It is revealed to the three researchers that parapsychological powers are unknown to the rest of mankind because in the distant past they were reserved especially to an elite called the New Men, the founders and rulers of Atlantis and Mu. When those ancient civilizations collapsed, only a few priests escaped with the knowledge, which was transcribed and left at the tops of mountains such as Shasta. Now the three heroes feel they have a mission: "*'As we see it, in order to make men free, free so that they may develop as men and not as animals; it is necessary that we undo what the Young Men did. The Young Men refused to permit any but their own select few to share in the racial heritage of ancient knowledge. For men again to become free and strong and independent it is necessary to return to each man his ancient knowledge and his ancient powers'*" (LL 9).

To combat the evil forces which continue to encroach upon human freedom, the heroes establish a Boy Scout camp on Mount Shasta and show the youthful campers how to use their superpowers. In reaction, "all over the country the antagonists of human liberty, of human dignity—the racketeers, the crooked political figures, the shysters, the dealers in phony religions, the sweat-shoppers, the petty authoritarians, all of the key figures among the traffickers in human misery and human oppression, themselves somewhat adept in the arts of the mind and acutely aware of the danger of free knowledge—all of this unholy breed stirred uneasily and wondered what was taking place" (LL 12). At the conclusion of the story, the forces of evil are in retreat and the forces of good are contemplating the future evolution of man: " 'When we have done what there is for us to do here, we move on to where there is more to do. The human race was not meant to stay here forever' " (LL 12). In a brief coda Heinlein describes Earth deserted by humanity; but evolution will continue, and instructions have been left on mountaintops to aid the progress of the great apes toward intelligence.

Like the conquest of the PanAsians in *The Day After Tomorrow*, the defeat of the forces of evil in "Lost Legacy" is the very stuff of adolescent power-fantasy; but even so, Heinlein insists on the maintenance of human liberties—no forceful mass indoctrinations will be allowed: " 'Every step must be voluntary, accomplished by reason and persuasion. Each human being must free himself; freedom cannot be thrust on him' " (LL 11). These libertarian principles of the benevolent elite in "Lost Legacy" disappear in "Gulf" (1949), another power fantasy about the evolution of supermen (also included in *Assignment in Eternity*). Heinlein combines a secret agent/adventure plot with a description of " 'New Man, *homo novis*, who must displace *homo sapiens—is* displacing him—because he is better able to survive than is homo sap.' " After the chief New Man, Kettle Belly Baldwin, convinces the secret agent, Joe Gilead, that an evolutionary "gulf" exists between the supermen and common men, he explains that New Men (geniuses) have existed throughout history. They finally organized themselves in order to fight communism, and after defeating that " 'totalitarian political religion, . . . We helped to see to it that the new constitution was liberal and—we thought—workable. But the new Republic turned out to be an even poorer thing than the old. The evil ethic of communism had corrupted, even after the form was gone. We held off. Now we know that we must hold off until we can revise the whole society.' "

Heinlein describes the New Men's method of social reform as secretive manipulation of the common men by any means necessary, including assassination: " 'We keep a "Better Dead" list; when a man is clearly morally bankrupt we close his account at the first opportunity.' " Joe Gilead argues feebly against this scheme as antithetical to democracy, human dignity, and freedom; Baldwin replies that democracy is outmoded and inefficient: " 'For a hundred and fifty years or so democracy, or something like it, could flourish safely. The issues were such as to be settled without disaster by the votes of common men, befogged and ignorant as they were. But now, if the race is simply to stay alive, political decisions depend on real knowledge of such things as nuclear physics, planetary ecology, genetic theory, even system mechanics. They aren't up to it, Joe.' "

Joe, disturbed by Baldwin's conclusions, finally accedes to them but Heinlein puts in a claim for Joe's sympathy with the common folk: "... this issue upset him; his brain followed Baldwin's argument and assured him that it was true; his inclinations fought it. He was confronted with the sharpest of all tragedy: two equally noble and valid rights, utterly opposed." Joe, brushing tragedy aside, happily undergoes the training necessary to become a fully proficient New Man, and before leaving on an assassination mission (successful in stopping the evil enemy, but unfortunately fatal to both Joe and his New Woman bride), Heinlein provides Baldwin with a peroration justifying the New Men's policies:

> "Damn it, Joe, face up to it. This world is run the way my great aunt Susie flies a 'copter... common man *can't* learn to cope with modern problems. No use to talk about the unused potential of his brain, he has not got the *will* to learn what he would have to know. We can't fit him out with new genes, so we have to lead him by the hand to keep him from killing himself—and us. We can give him personal liberty, we can give him autonomy in most things, we can give him a great measure of personal dignity—and we will, because we believe that individual freedom, at all levels, is the direction of evolution, of maximum survival value. But we can't let him fiddle with issues of racial life and death; he ain't up to it."

Despite Joe Gilead's show of ambivalence toward Baldwin's elitism and the sop to the reader of calling the situation a tragedy of two opposed rights, "Gulf" presents a positive case for transferring the inequalities produced through natural selection to the right-wing politics of authoritarian control. "Gulf" inverts the values of "Lost Legacy"—the New Men of the later story are analogous to the Young Men of the first, except that the New Men are exalted and the Young Men condemned. In "Lost Legacy" the principle of equalitarian access to the knowledge and power of the elite is defended; in "Gulf" the story premise calls for the elite to keep inviolate its mysteries, and to administer secretly the affairs of the great herd of inferior common men.

s major difference between the two stories suggests the po-
of Heinlein's political fantasies. While he extrapolates fic-
alternatives from a basic idea of human nature determined
by evolution, Heinlein also endows his stories with various kinds of
conservative, libertarian visions ranging from the optimistic and
utopian individualism of *Beyond This Horizon* or "Lost Legacy"
to the pessimistic, anticommunist elitism of "Gulf." Thomas
Hobbes also based his politically conservative idea of covenant on
man's brutish nature: "man surpasseth in rapacity and cruelty the
wolves, bears, and snakes that are not rapacious unless hungry and
not cruel unless provoked, whereas man is famished even by future
hunger."[13] Heinlein's political sympathies have many affinities
with Hobbes's—it is no surprise, then, to find in Hobbes a phrase
which accurately sums up the polarities of Heinlein's conserva-
tivism: "To speak impartially, both sayings are very true: that *man
to man is a kind of God;* and that *man to man is an errant wolf.*"[14]

Nor should it surprise anyone that some of Heinlein's fictions,
like "Gulf," which envision rule by an elite, come dangerously close
to fascism. Gertrude Himmelfarb has described the development of
fascism from right-wing social Darwinistic thought:

From the "preservation of favoured races in the struggle for life" [the
subtitle of Darwin's *The Origin of Species*], it was a short step to the
preservation of favored individuals, classes, or nations—and from their
preservation to their glorification. Social Darwinism has often been understood in this sense: as a philosophy exalting competition, power,
and violence over convention, ethics, and religion. Thus it has become
a portmanteau of nationalism, imperialism, militarism, and dictatorship, of the cults of the hero, the superman, and the master race.
The hero or superman, most recently translated as *Führer*, is assumed to
be the epitome of the fittest, the best specimen of his breed, the natural
ruler who exercises his rule by right of might. As he is the instrument of
providence to lead his nation to victory, so the nation is the instrument
that will raise civilization to a more sublime state. And as he made his
way by struggle and force, so the nation must make its way in the world
by war and conquest.[15]

Heinlein is certainly not a fascist—he is too committed to individualism, and one of his favorite plot premises is the revolt of freedom-
loving individuals against an authoritarian regime. Yet one cannot
escape the disturbing fact that his political fantasies occasionally
treat approvingly the social Darwinistic idea of elitist, militaristic,
or authoritarian rule.

Another expression of Heinlein's right-wing political stance is his opposition to communism (which is itself a left-wing form of social Darwinism).[16] Heinlein studs his fiction and occasional non-fiction with sentiments such as the following, taken from his "Concerning Stories Never Written: Postscript": "Remember Karl Marx and note how close that unscientific piece of nonsense called *Das Kapital* has come to smothering out all freedom of thought on half a planet, without—mind you—the emotional advantage of calling it a religion. The capacity of the human mind for swallowing non-sense and spewing it forth in violent and repressive action has never yet been plumbed."[17] Heinlein's expressions of his attitude toward communism changed with the onset of the Cold War from a be-mused tolerance in the early 1940s to a virulent hatred seen in "Gulf" and the passage quoted above. Heinlein's earlier, more tolerant point of view is seen in *Beyond This Horizon* where the hu-man colony on Pluto is described as communal (BTH 4) and Hein-lein pokes fun at American socialism by means of a time traveler from the twentieth century who relates an argument with a "parlor bolshevik" (BTH 6). Also, in *The Day After Tomorrow* Heinlein briefly includes an old anarchist comrade as a loyal American and an opponent of the PanAsians, but dispenses with the anarchist's "philosophy" as "confused, confusing, and impractical" (DAT 2).

Heinlein's anticommunist position is apparent beneath the invaders-from-outer-space plot of *The Puppet Masters* (1951). An elite group of American secret agents stops the menace of parasitic, communally aware slugs from Titan, Saturn's sixth satellite. The "titans" dominate the minds of their human hosts, and as they work ever closer to the corridors of national power by subverting lower- and middle-rank officials and finally members of Congress, the slugs' advance recalls Cold War propaganda scenarios of the early 1950s designed to warn the United States against creeping communism. Heinlein makes sure the allegory does not escape the reader; his narrator, Elihu Nivens, comments: "I wondered why the titans had not attacked Russia first; the place seemed tailor-made for them. On second thought, I wondered if they had. On third thought, I wondered what difference it would make."[18] In fact, Heinlein has it both ways: the slugs represent communists for readers in the present, and in his future world Russian Communism has already been defeated but not destroyed by the United States in World War III: "Too big to occupy and too big to ignore, World War III had not settled the Russian problem, and no war ever would. The parasites might feel right at home there" (PM 15).

The Puppet Masters also repeats the racial war premise of The Day After Tomorrow: "this was a fight for racial survival against an outside invader" (PM 3); "homo sapiens would be as extinct as the dodo if we did not move" (PM 12). After much excitement and adventure, and with a little help from H. G. Wells's The War of the Worlds, the titan slugs, like Wells's Martians, are killed by a disease. In The Puppet Masters, however, Heinlein goes Wells one better by having the humans think of using bacteriological warfare in the cause of racial survival. The novel concludes with a "report" written by the narrator before the human expedition takes off to "clean up Titan" (PM 35). In it Heinlein spells out for the human race the Hobbesian and Darwinistic moral of its first contact with alien beings: "This is for keeps and we intend to show those slugs that they made the mistake of tangling with the toughest, meanest, deadliest, most unrelenting—and ablest—form of life in this section of space, a critter that can be killed but can't be tamed. . . . Whether we make it or not, the human race has got to keep up its well-earned reputation for ferocity. The price of freedom is the willingness to do sudden battle, anywhere, any time, and with utter recklessness" (PM 35). Once the slugs are eliminated, humanity cannot relax its vigilance nor abandon its military might. There may be other races on more distant planets with which man must contend. "Well, if Man wants to be top dog—or even a respected neighbor—he'll have to fight for it. Beat the plowshares back into swords; the other was a maiden aunt's fancy" (PM 35).

Compared with the xenophobic fantasy of The Puppet Masters, Heinlein's next novel for adults, Double Star (1956), seems positively benign. Here Heinlein imagines that humans may try to get along peacefully with nonthreatening aliens. He dramatizes the necessity of interspecies tolerance by having his protagonist, Lorenzo Smythe, cured through hypnotism of acute anti-Martian racial prejudice. Smythe, an actor, is hired to impersonate a kidnapped statesman, Joseph Bonforte (that is, "good strength"), just in time to participate in a Martian family's ceremony of adoption. As the novel develops Smythe gradually takes on more responsibilities because Bonforte, though rescued from captivity, is too debilitated to resume public life. Finally, when the great man dies, Smythe "becomes" Bonforte completely with the aid of Bonforte's staff and his own acting talents. Accepting the ideas of Bonforte and gaining confidence in his own potential as politician, Smythe, like John Lyle of " 'If This Goes On—' " earns full admission to an elite group: " 'Look, Chief, you've learned that a political personality is not one man; it's a team—it's a team bound together by common purposes and common beliefs. We've lost our team captain and we've got to have another one. But the team is still there.' "[19]

The common purposes and beliefs of the Expansionist Party are "founded on the notion that free trade, free travel, common citizenship, common currency, and a minimum of Imperial laws and restrictions are good not only for the citizens of the Empire but for the Empire itself" (DS 8). Heinlein has transferred the ideals of nineteenth-century British hegemony to an interplanetary setting; the political system is parliamentarian, and Bonforte himself is reminiscent of Disraeli and Gladstone. Just as nineteenth-century British imperial rule had its pseudoscientific justification in Walter Bagehot's *Physics and Politics* (1869), so also Bonforte provides a social Darwinistic rationale for the Expansionists' imperialistic program: "Expansionism had hardly been more than a 'Manifest Destiny' movement when the party was founded, a rabble coalition of groups who had one thing in common: the belief that the frontiers in the sky were the most important issue in the emerging future of the human race. Bonforte had given the party a rationale and an ethic, the theme that freedom and equal rights must run with the Imperial banner; he kept harping on the notion that the human race must never again make the mistakes that the white subrace had made in Africa and Asia" (DS p. 85). Bonforte's belief in freedom and equal rights is as much pragmatic as principled—he realizes the practical benefits of plain dealing: it fosters competition and therefore aids survival. Further, "if the human race did not behave accordingly they weren't ever going to win to the stars because some better race would slap them down for double-dealing" (DS 7). But double-dealing is permitted when Heinlein's right-thinking elite needs to deceive the electorate with a bogus Bonforte—*Double Star* thus demonstrates again the polarity of Heinlein's political fantasies. Despite Bonfortean rhetoric about the price of expansion being virtue (DS 7), there is another principle at work: the end (when defined, *a priori*, as right by the author) justifies the means.

Heinlein's *The Door into Summer* (1957), a potboiler which, he fondly recalls, took only thirteen days to write,[20] continues *Double Star*'s social Darwinistic theme of human progress through free enterprise. Here the center of attraction is Daniel Boone Davis, an inventor and entrepreneur who believes in "Bicycle-shop engineering with peanuts for capital, the way Ford and the Wright brothers had started."[21] The explanation of Davis's name allows Heinlein the chance to make a familiar political statement: "My old man named me Daniel Boone Davis, which was his way of declaring for personal liberty and self-reliance. I was born in 1940, a year when everybody was saying that the individual was on the skids and the future belonged to mass man. Dad refused to believe it; naming me was a note of defiance. He died under brainwashing in North Korea, trying to the last to prove his thesis" (DIS 2). In the fictional setting of 1970, Davis, Sr.'s dying wish (and Heinlein's fantasy) has come true —communism has been defeated. But even without the Marxist menace to worry about, one cannot be too careful, Davis learns. Unable to detect in time the "underlying predatory animal" (DIS 3) in his business partners, he finds himself swindled, but later gains his revenge through an elaborate scheme dependent on time travel. The novel closes as Davis, now a millionaire, settles into a happy life in the year 2000. His parting sermon to the reader extols progress with unabashed social Darwinistic boosterism, and it gives away the secret of how to manage a conglomerate of two corporations: "I don't run them and they compete. Competition is a good idea— Darwin thought well of it" (DIS 12).

Darwin also thought well of the possibility of improving the human race through selective breeding—in *The Descent of Man* he remarks, "Man scans with scrupulous care the character and pedigree of his horses, cattle, and dogs before he matches them; but when he comes to his own marriage he rarely, or never, takes any such care. ...Yet he might by selection do something not only for the bodily constitution and frame of his offspring, but for their intellectual and moral qualities."[22] Heinlein returned to the subject of eugenics in 1958 with the publication of *Methuselah's Children* in a form revised and expanded from its original appearance as a serial in *Astounding Science Fiction* in 1941. The novel chronicles the adventures of the Howard Families, Americans who have participated in a program of voluntary selective breeding designed to increase life expectancy. Heinlein imagines that the Howard Foundation began to select participants in 1874 (coincidentally, three years after the publication of *The Descent of Man*). Heinlein's protagonist, Lazarus Long, born in 1912 and christened Woodrow Wilson Smith, is the oldest living human when the novel begins in 2136.

Heinlein divides *Methuselah's Children* into two sections. The first, set in the familiar framework of the Future History series, chronicles the exodus of the Howard Families from the United

States. Even the libertarian guarantees of the Covenant are unable to save them from the envy of short-lived humans and the threat of genocide when the existence of the long-lived Families is made public. Lazarus Long has never accepted the "present gentle custom against personal weapons";[23] thus armed in atavistic defiance of the Covenant, he contrives to hijack a starship and transport the Families out of the solar system.

In Part Two Heinlein describes the Families' attempts to settle on two different planets inhabited by aliens. In each case, humans cannot adapt or do not choose to because they would be forced to sacrifice their individuality. On the first planet, the humanoid Jockaira seem to be the dominant race, but they turn out to be domestic animals, servants of their "gods," who are the true dominant race. These superintelligent beings gratifyingly endorse Heinlein's view of human nature: "'The gods have spoken. Your kind can never be civilized(?).... The gods require that you leave'" (MC pt. 2, chap. 3).

The Jockaira's gods transport the Families to another planet, this one inhabited by furry, telepathic "Little People" the size of human children. Welcomed by the Little People, the Families partake of a "lotus-land" existence: "indeed there was little government of any sort; the Families lived in cheerful easy-going anarchy on this favored planet" (MC pt. 2, chap. 4). Further, the Little People offer to teach humans how to overcome their individuality, to achieve the state of mental immortality in which individual bodies might die, but the group mind lives on. This fantasy recalls the "Homo Gestalt" imagined by Theodore Sturgeon in *More Than Human*; but it is also reminiscent of the communally-minded slugs from *The Puppet Masters*. As far as Heinlein and Lazarus Long are concerned, "to form any such group identities...would be, Lazarus felt very sure, to give up whatever it was that made them *men*" (MC pt. 2, chap. 4). When one woman does join the Little People's group ego, her loss of identity confirms Lazarus' "firm unreasoned conviction that he was not intended for, or not ready for, this timeless snug harbor of ease" (MC pt. 2, chap. 4).

Lazarus persuades the Families to return to Earth, where they find that during their seventy-four-year odyssey the short-lived humans have met the evolutionary challenge of the Families' genetic advantage and learned how to achieve longevity through rejuvenation processes. This triumph, however, has created an overpopulation problem. The solution, Lazarus quickly suggests, is survival through emigration—he proposes to enhance his life span with the new rejuvenation techniques and then " 'go into the real estate business ... We'll stake out this corner of the Galaxy and see what it has to offer' " (MC pt. 2, chap. 8). More importantly, however, Heinlein has Lazarus planning to reassert the dynamism, combativeness, and intellect of humanity in the face of the Jockaira's gods. " 'We'll have a showdown, anyway. I've never been satisfied with the outcome there. There ought not to be anything in the whole universe that man can't poke his nose into—that's the way we're built and I assume that there's some reason for it' " (MC pt. 2, chap. 8). Lazarus may not know the reason, but Heinlein does—it is the same Darwinistic conviction about the nature of man as the fittest survivor which underlies all of his fantasies. The survival of the race depends on individuals like Lazarus Long who believe that "whatever the answers are, here's one monkey that's going to keep on climbing, and looking around him to see what he can see, as long as the tree holds out" (MC pt. 2, chap. 8).

Heinlein's next two novels, *Starship Troopers* (1959) and *Stranger in a Strange Land* (1961), repeat the conservative and Darwinistic Heinleinian themes of human nature, social and political structures, and racial necessity to expand outward to the stars. In a 1972 interview Heinlein confirmed the ideational kinship of the two novels: "Effectively, the two books were written simultaneously. In my mind, there was never any conflict between the two books—*both* books were quite savage comments on the present state of our society and *both* books have the same basic theme: That a man, to be truly human, must be unhesitatingly willing at all times to lay down his life for his fellow man. Both are based on the twin concepts of love and duty—and how they are related to the survival of our race."[24] While racial survival remains the constant fantasy wish and individual sacrifice its agency, the sociopolitical environments vary between the novels. Even so, the variance fits an observed pattern in Heinlein's fiction. *Starship Troopers* continues the bellicose elitist tradition of *The Day After Tomorrow* and *The Puppet Masters. Stranger in a Strange Land* stems from *Beyond This Horizon*, "Lost Legacy," and *Methuselah's Children*, all somewhat gentler fictions which do not exclude conflict and competition, but which also emphasize individualism and imagine the possibility of many humans gradually learning or inheriting the superior traits of the elite.

Starship Troopers and *Stranger in a Strange Land* also resemble one another because in both novels Heinlein has overindulged his tendency to lecture the reader. In *Starship Troopers* Heinlein uses the device of classes in "History and Moral Philosophy" attended by the protagonist, Johnnie Rico. Heinlein's pedagogy is closer to hectoring than instruction, but Johnnie absorbs and accepts social Darwinistic justifications for a militaristic, libertarian, and anti-democratic political system in which only discharged veterans of two years' Federal Service are citizens, voters, and officeholders.

Dennis E. Showalter chastises the authors of "vehement, virtually unanimous criticism"[25] of *Starship Troopers* as a fascistic and militaristic polemic. Although he notes the similarity between Heinlein's "crude Social Darwinism" and Hitler's *Mein Kampf*, Showalter argues, with abundant reference to historical analogs, that Heinlein's society is "neither militarist nor fascist in the scholarly sense of these concepts" (p. 120). He suggests that "Rome in the second or third centuries C.E." (p. 120) is a better historical parallel than twentieth-century fascist regimes. This seems like special pleading, however, since Rome provided much of the inspiration for modern fascism and since Showalter waffles unconvincingly about the distinction between the scholarly and general uses of "militarism." Finally, Showalter bases much of his case on the dubious supposition that "to the end of his story, Rico remains virtually untouched by any motives, any ideals beyond the appeal of comradeship, the sense of belonging. He repeats loftier ideas, but does not accept them emotionally" (p. 117). I disagree, and contend that Heinlein justifies Rico's growing sense of duty and his proficience as a professional soldier by describing the naive youth's education into both an intellectual and an emotional acceptance of social Darwinism. In this way, Rico achieves the state of being "truly human" which Heinlein mentions in the 1972 interview—the concept recalls the "true men" of *Beyond This Horizon* and the "free souls" of "'If This Goes On—,'" suggesting again the continuity of Heinlein's thought.

As Alexei Panshin observes, *Starship Troopers* resembles "the sort of recruiting film that purports to show the life of a typical soldier, with a soundtrack commentary by earnest, sincere Private Jones who interprets what we see for us."[26] Johnnie Rico's interpretation of events begins, after a flash-forward action sequence in chapter 1, as a retrospective narration of his advancement from recruit to officer in the Mobile Infantry, the toughest, most elite force in the Army. The key action demonstrating Rico's commitment to "truly human" duty is his gradual replacement of the values of his parents with the social Darwinistic creed of Heinlein's "veteranocracy." The final endorsement of this change in values comes when Rico's father also accepts them, abandoning his comfortable life as a businessman in order to enlist in the Mobile Infantry—he is reunited with his son and by the end of the novel has become Johnnie's platoon sergeant. Heinlein dramatizes the process of Rico's change by interspersing four segments of lectures on History and Moral Philosophy at significant points in the narrative.

The first lecture follows an argument between Rico and his father over Johnnie's wish to enlist for Federal Service. Rico, Sr.'s criticism of military life contrasts with the Darwinistic arguments of Dubois, Johnnie's instructor, that " 'Violence, naked force, has settled more issues in history than has any other factor, and the contrary opinion is wishful thinking at its worst. Breeds that forget this basic truth have always paid for it with their lives and freedoms.' "²⁷ When called on to recite the difference between civilian and soldier, Johnnie responds with the textbook definition (" 'A soldier accepts personal responsibility for the safety of the body politic of which he is a member, defending it, if need be, with his life. The civilian does not' " [ST 2]), but cannot say if he believes in it or not.

Nevertheless, Johnnie enlists, partly out of peer group pressure and partly to define his own life differently than his parents had planned for him. His next crisis occurs near the end of basic training —nearly ready to resign over what he considers the injustice of a flogging, Johnnie receives two letters, one from his mother, offering the easy solace of home ("Little boys never get over needing their mother's laps—do they, darling?" [ST 6]), the second from Dubois (who turns out to be a retired lieutenant colonel in the Mobile Infantry). Dubois, keeping tabs on Johnnie's progress through service friends, encourages the recruit to pass successfully over the spiritual "hump," by which he means the "soul-turning readjustments and re-evaluations necessary to metamorphose a potential citizen into one in being" (ST 6). Dubois suggests that this experience of a "basic truth" may occur so completely on the emotional level that Johnnie has felt something he could not put into words—Dubois supplies the missing formulation: "The noblest fate that a man can endure is to place his own mortal body between his loved home and the war's desolation" (ST 6).

Ironically, Johnnie has not yet passed his hump—but the letter spurs a memory of Dubois's lecture disproving the Marxist work theory of value and also condemning the democracies of the twentieth century because both systems neglected the true index of value: individualistic struggle. " 'The best things in life are beyond money; their price is agony and sweat and devotion...and the price demanded for the most precious of all things in life is life itself—ultimate cost for perfect value' " (ST 6). This memory and a few strains of martial music bring forth Johnnie's realization that he *does* accept on the emotional level the values of Dubois and the entire system: "I suddenly realized I felt good.... Then I knew. *I had passed my hump!*" (ST 6).

Rico's convictions are soon tested and found strong—because of negligence which could have cost a life, he must endure a flogging. He also witnesses the hanging of a murderer, and he justifies both corporal and capital punishment to himself and the reader by recalling Dubois's lecture on evolutionary ethics and justice. Since pain functions as a survival mechanism perfected by evolution, Dubois argues that it should be used on criminals to warn of threatened survival. Humans have no innate moral sense nor any natural rights; rather "moral sense" is " 'an elaboration of the instinct to survive. The instinct to survive is human nature itself, and every aspect of our personalities derives from it. Anything that conflicts with the survival instinct acts sooner or later to eliminate the individual and thereby fails to show up in future generations. This truth is mathematically demonstrable, everywhere verifiable; it is the single eternal imperative controlling everything we do' " (ST 8). Dubois points out that there are stronger imperatives than personal survival, however, and the reconciling principle is duty: " 'we can solve any moral problem, on any level. Self-interest, love of family, duty to country, responsibility toward the human race—we are even developing an exact ethic for extra-human relations.... The basis of all morality is duty, a concept with the same relation to group that self-interest has to individual' " (ST 8). Heinlein, speaking through Dubois, specifically condemns twentieth-century Americans for taking their "rights" for granted and neglecting their duties: " 'No nation, so constituted, can endure' " (ST 8).

The climactic sequence in Rico's process of value absorption comes after he has proven himself in combat. On his way to Officer Candidate School, Johnnie meets his father, now a corporal in the Mobile Infantry. They discuss his reasons for joining—partly the death of Johnnie's mother in a bombing attack, partly the example of Johnnie himself—but overall, the strongest reason compelling his decision was the realization that there was a real difference between a "civilian" and a "man": " 'I had to perform an act of faith. I had to prove to myself that I was a man. Not just a producing-consuming economic animal...but a *man*'" (ST 12).

This demonstration of parental acceptance of Darwinistic values precedes the final section of lectures about History and Moral Philosophy. Therein Heinlein describes the history of the founding of the veterans' government as the twentieth-century democracies collapsed, and gives the practical justification for its survival: it works. Its success he attributes to the proven values of those who are enfranchised: " 'Under our system every voter and officeholder is a man who has demonstrated through voluntary and difficult service that he places the welfare of the group ahead of personal advantage'" (ST 12). At the end of this section, Heinlein returns to the basis of his system and to the final proof of Rico's conversion. Rico sketches the answer to "one of those master's-thesis assignments" required for the course: "prove that war and moral perfection derive from the same genetic inheritance" (ST 12). His response is a reprise of the doctrine Heinlein has preached not only in this novel but throughout his fiction: "moral behavior is survival behavior above the individual level—as in a father who dies to save his children" (ST 12). The logical extension of this principle to the war against the "Bugs" already under way confirms the "why" of combat as cited by Johnnie's father: it is in the nature of man. Johnnie closes his meditation on history and moral philosophy with an elaboration of his own and his father's reasoning about racial war:

> Either we spread and wipe out the Bugs, or they spread and wipe us out—because both races are tough and smart and want the same real estate....
> But does man have any "right" to spread through the universe?
> Man is what he is, a wild animal with the will to survive, and (so far) the ability, against all competition. Unless one accepts that, anything one says about morals, war, politics—you name it—is nonsense. Correct morals arise from knowing what Man *is*—not what do-gooders and well-meaning old Aunt Nellies would like him to be. (ST 12)

Not only is the rhetoric similar to the closing statement of *The Puppet Masters*, but also the racial enemies of mankind have much in common. The Bugs are, predictably, type-cast villains in Heinlein's war-as-state-of-nature. They provide the antithesis of Heinlein's insistence on individuality as basic to human nature and politics because the Bugs, like the slugs, are communists: "We were learning, expensively, just how efficient a total communism can be when used by a people actually adapted to it by evolution; the Bug commissars didn't care any more about expending soldiers than we cared about expending ammo. Perhaps we could have figured this out about the Bugs by noting the grief the Chinese Hegemony gave the Russo-Anglo-American Alliance; however the trouble with the 'lessons from history' is that we usually read them best after falling flat on our chins" (ST 11).

The course of education in anticommunist social Darwinism presented in *Starship Troopers* is the most concentrated and complete single expression of Heinlein's views on the politics of evolution anywhere in his fiction. This novel is also the last one in which he provides a utopian social system for all of humanity. Since *Starship Troopers* Heinlein's political fantasies have focused increasingly on the dealings of individuals and small groups with less than cosmic governments, such as the revolt of the Lunarites in *The Moon Is a Harsh Mistress* or the plans for governing Secundus and Tertius in *Time Enough for Love.*

Even though its setting is an Earth governed by a planetary Federation, *Stranger in a Strange Land* deals with individual rather than political ways of achieving racial survival. As in "Lost Legacy" and *Beyond This Horizon*, Heinlein imagines that humans will learn to use latent parapsychological powers; he also supposes it possible to achieve immortality, or at least a continued psychic existence after bodily death. Heinlein optimistically fantasizes that humanity, equipped with such superhuman attributes, will be able to hold its own in competition with other intelligent races.

The existence of human superpowers is revealed through Valentine Michael ("Mike") Smith, a child born to members of the first expedition to Mars. Mike, raised to young manhood by Martians after his parents' death, brings back to Earth the mental "discipline" of that older and more advanced race. With the aid of Gillian, his nurse, and a journalist named Ben Caxton, Mike escapes from governmental protective custody and finds refuge at Freedom Hall, the home of Jubal Harshaw. Harshaw, an author, doctor, and lawyer, "'is so rugged an individualist that he would fight the whole Federation with just a pocket knife if it suited him....'"[28] Harshaw aids Mike in gaining freedom from interference and special recognition from the planetary government, plus a sizable inheritance.

Mike begins to learn about human beings from his companions at Harshaw's; his most important discovery is human sexuality.

Conversely, Mike gradually instructs his human friends in the techniques of Martian mental discipline, " 'simply a method of efficient functioning in anything'" (SSL 36). The more he learns, the more ignorance and culturally imposed blindness he detects. Mike's remedy is to found a religion, the Church of All Worlds, as a means of teaching the Martian language and through it, mental discipline sufficient both to free the individual from culturally imposed untruths and also to permit the best use of man's latent superpowers. " 'Mike is like the first man to discover fire. Fire was there all along —after he showed them how, anybody could use it... anybody with sense enough not to get burned with it'" (SSL 35). An elite group of humans who have passed through the educational stages of the Church of All Worlds (like the Boy Scouts in "Lost Legacy") carries on Mike's mission when he decides to prove the power of his discipline by accepting physical death. He maintains a beatific serenity while being murdered by an angry mob. After his bodily death Mike's spirit, as "Archangel Michael," joins the group of discorporated human entities, analogous to the Martian "Old Ones," who serve as guardian angels for the destiny of the race.

The novel's Darwinistic lesson is taught just before Mike's martyrdom. While still in his body, he has discovered cause for alarm about the survival of the human race—he has been used as a "spy" without being conscious of it. The Martian Old Ones, wishing to learn about Earth, have telepathically lifted all of Mike's knowledge. He fears that they will decide to destroy Earth, leaving only the rubble of an asteroid belt behind—this was the fate of the planet in orbit between Mars and Jupiter. But Mike has also learned that there is cause for hope about the future of humanity. First, he notes, " 'Male-femaleness is the greatest gift we have—romantic physical love may be unique to this planet'" (SSL 36). Second, Mike has had to learn the most significant difference between humans and Martians, the way in which members of each race compete for survival: " 'here babies do not compete but adults do; on Mars adults never compete, they've been weeded out as babies. But one way or another, competing and weeding takes [sic] place... or a race goes downhill. But whether or not I was wrong in trying to take the competition out at both ends, I have lately begun to grok that the human race won't let me, no matter what'" (SSL 36).

Mike pessimistically concludes that he has been on " 'the wrong track—that *this* race *must* be split up, hating each other, fighting, constantly unhappy and at war even with their own individual selves

...simply to have that weeding out that every race must have'"
(SSL 36). Jubal Harshaw listens to Mike's opinions and corrobo-
rates them encouragingly in terms of the familiar Heinleinian social
Darwinistic view of man:[29]

> "You've been fretting that since you failed to hook ninety-nine out of
> a hundred, the race couldn't get along without its present evils, had to
> have them for weeding out. But damn it, lad, you've been *doing* the
> weeding—or rather, the failures have been doing it by not listening to
> you"

> "If all you say is true—and I'm not judging; I'm asking, you're answer-
> ing—then competition, far from being eliminated, is rougher than ever.
> If one tenth of one percent of the population is capable of getting the
> news, then all you have to do is *show* them—and in a matter of some
> generations the stupid ones will die out and those with your discipline
> will inherit the Earth." (SSL 36).

Heinlein puts to rest any further doubts about man's ability to
foil the Martian inclination to eradicate Earth and the human race.
First, Heinlein informs the reader on the concluding page of the
novel: "But, by the time they would slowly get around to it, it would
be highly improbable approaching impossible that the Old Ones
would be able to destroy this weirdly complex race. The hazard was
so slight that those concerned with the third planet did not waste a
split eon on it" (SSL 39).

Second, Heinlein borrows from Ruth Benedict's *Patterns of
Culture* the idea of Apollonian and Dionysian cultures to confirm
the basic difference between Martian and human nature. Benedict
describes the Apollonian culture of the Zuni as an anomaly among
North American Indians in that it kept the middle of the road, de-
emphasized sexuality, distrusted individualists, delighted in formal-
ity, sobriety, and the way of measure: "In the pueblos, therefore,
there is no courting of excess in any form, no tolerance of violence,
no indulgence in the exercise of authority, or delight in any situation
in which the individual stands alone."[30]

Benedict notes that the majority of North American Indians
"were passionately Dionysian. They valued all violent experience,
all means by which human beings may break through the usual sen-
sory routine, and to all such experiences they attributed the highest
value" (PC p. 81). Benedict's example of the Dionysian culture, the
Kwakiutls, provides an antithesis to the Zunis. The Kwakiutls cele-
brate individual power, violence, property, dislocation of the senses,
and even cannibalism in religious ceremonies (PC pp. 156-95). Hein-

lein's use of Benedict to differentiate between Martians and humans occurs during a discussion of whether or not Martians would invade Earth:

> "I see another objection. You know the classification of cultures into 'Apollonian' and 'Dionysian.'"
> "I know in general."
> "Well, it seems to me that even Zuni culture would be called 'Dionysian' on Mars. You've been there—but I've been talking with Mike. That boy was raised in an Apollonian culture—such cultures are not aggressive."
> "Mmm...I wouldn't count on it."
> Mahmoud said suddenly, "Skipper, there's evidence to support Jubal. You can analyse a culture from its language—and there isn't any Martian word for 'war.' At least, I don't think there is. Nor for 'weapon'...nor 'fighting.' If a word isn't in a language, then its culture never has the referent." (SSL 21)

Mike's Apollonian, Martian cultural traits, and their failure to attract new disciples, are demonstrated in the carnival magic show where he performs under the significant name, "Dr. Apollo." The carnival boss explains to Mike that his act is a bore because he does not cater to the desires of the ordinary human "chump" onlooker who "'wants sex and blood and money....What else does a chump want? Mystery! He wants to think the world is a romantic place when it damn well ain't. That's *your* job...only you ain't learned how'" (SSL 26).

Mike successfully combines the Apollonian, Martian mental discipline with a medium which caters to Dionysian human desires in his "religious" service; Ben Caxton describes it to Jubal Harshaw as similar to a seance:

> "But it wasn't mild; it packed terrific wallop."
> "The word is 'Apollonian.' [replies Jubal] ... As opposed to 'Dionysian.' People simplify 'Apollonian' into 'mild,' and 'calm,' and 'cool.' But 'Apollonian' and 'Dionysian' are two sides of one coin—a nun kneeling in her cell, holding perfectly still, can be in ecstasy more frenzied than any priestess of Pan Priapus celebrating the vernal equinox....Another error is to identify 'Apollonian' with 'good'—merely because our most respectable sects are Apollonian in ritual and precept. Mere prejudice." (SSL 31)

Heinlein shows that the success of Mike's religion in attracting suitable "fit" converts who can safely be made part of the elite depends on an accommodation of the mental discipline derived from the extremely Apollonian, Martian culture with the comparatively

Dionysian behavior patterns of human culture. Thus, in *Stranger in a Strange Land*, Heinlein imagines that the probable success of humanity in coping with not only Martians, but other extraterrestrial species, depends on the evolutionary survival in human nature of Dionysian individualism tempered by Apollonian discipline of mind. Instead of considering seriously Benedict's cultural explanations of human nature, which would be a new and interesting departure for Heinlein, he merely adopts her categories and twists them to coincide with his own. *Stranger in a Strange Land* presents no more than the description of human nature as combativeness modified by self-interest given by Mordan in *Beyond This Horizon* and repeated or assumed in the rest of Heinlein's fiction.

The two lackluster novels written after *Stranger in a Strange Land* offer considerably less in the way of ideas than their predecessors. *Glory Road* (1963) and *Farnham's Freehold* (1964) are perfunctorily written individualistic fantasies, the first a sword-and-sorcery excursion into alternate universes, the second a postatomic holocaust time-travel novel. Both fantasies define themselves as worlds which offer an escape from the realities of life in mid-twentieth-century America; both novels condemn the state and practice of politics in the United States; both draw support from social Darwinistic views of human nature and evolution.

In consonance with the increasing exaltation of rugged individualism in his later fiction, Heinlein's fantasies about political systems seem to favor those which govern least. In *Glory Road*, for example, a "distinguished comparative culturologist" explains to the hero that "every human race tries every political form and that democracy is used in many primitive societies . . . but he didn't know of any civilized planet using it, as *Vox Populi, Vox Dei* translates as: 'My God! How did we get in *this* mess.'"[31] When the hero asks how advanced human societies *do* run things, the learned response is "'Mostly they don't'" (GR 17).

In *Farnham's Freehold* the hard-hat, right-wing hero, Hugh Farnham, decides that, given the state of affairs in mid-twentieth-century America, the atomic war in progress above his bomb shelter "'might be good for us. . . . I mean our country.'"[32] Farnham feels that the war will aid natural selection: "'This war may be the first war in history which kills the stupid rather than the bright and able —where it makes any distinction. . . . This time the boys in service are as safe or safer than civilians. And of civilians those who used their heads and made preparations stand a far better chance. Not every case, but on the average, and that will improve the breed. When it's over, things will be tough, and that will improve the breed still more' " (FF 2).

Instead of immediate participation in the great and purifying postatomic new frontier, however, Farnham and company must endure temporary slavery. The atomic blast transports them into the far future, where they are eventually captured by black aristocrats. Farnham and his second wife and children finally are shipped back in time to the day of the original atomic war, and changes in small details of their surroundings convince them that " 'If the future can change the past . . . maybe the past can change the future, too. Maybe the United States won't be wholly destroyed' " (FF 22). Heinlein leaves the readers with a happy ending—the Farnhams live through the second atomic attack, and the disorders and epidemics which follow. Their survival as American flag-waving, gun-toting owners of a mom-and-pop grocery store and trading post surrounded by a minefield further demonstrates Heinlein's fantasy that the self-reliant, individualistic, natural elite of free people will inherit the earth.

Precisely this kind of elite inherits the Moon in Heinlein's next novel, *The Moon Is a Harsh Mistress* (1966). Heinlein imagines that the "Loonies," a population of transported convicts, political exiles, and their descendants, revolt successfully against the administration of the mother planet. The parallel with the American Revolution is emphasized throughout the novel, including even the date of the declaration of Lunar independence, July 4, 2076. Because of their origins and environment, the Loonies are portrayed as a society of survivors: "a society adapts to fact, or doesn't survive. Loonies adapted to harsh facts—or failed and died."[33] Even so, only the fittest of these survivors can be trusted with the efficient direction of a revolution, and even then only with the aid of a *deus ex machina*, a computer with a personality and a conscience.

The novel is short on the usual social Darwinistic justifications but lengthy nevertheless owing to Heinlein's fascination with process—he describes in sometimes excruciating detail all aspects of the organization and operation of the revolution.[34] But the basic goals and methods of the revolution are founded on familiar individualistic tenets. Professor Bernardo de la Paz, the theoretician of the elite cell of revolutionaries, describes himself as a "rational anarchist" in the tradition of Thomas Jefferson and Ayn Rand; but his theories and methods of manipulation resemble those of Kettle Belly

Baldwin, the leader of the elite New Men in "Gulf." The "Prof" explains his political stance as an extension of his individualism:

> "...A rational anarchist believes that concepts such as 'state' and 'society' and 'government' have no existence save as physically exemplified in the acts of self-responsible individuals...."

> "...My point is that one person *is* responsible. Always. If H-bombs exist—and they do—some *man* controls them. In terms of morals *there is no such thing as 'state.'* Just men. Individuals. Each responsible for his own acts."

> "...I will accept any rules that *you* feel necessary to *your* freedom. *I* am free, no matter what rules surround me. If I find them tolerable, I tolerate them; if I find them too obnoxious, I break them. I am free because I know that *I alone* am morally responsible for everything I do." (MIHM 6)

David Ketterer, in *New Worlds for Old*, has argued an overly ingenious interpretation of "rational anarchist," claiming that the phrase's "second meaning"—"an anarchist who disrupts a reasoned response"—is most important.[35] This wrench of meaning fits Ketterer's thesis because it allows him to claim the necessity "for the Loonies to develop a new world of mind based upon the conception that successful existence on the moon must take the form of a closed system exclusive of Earth" (NWO p. 152). But Ketterer does not successfully reconcile his perception of a radically altered state of consciousness among Loonies ("the concept that revolution is a matter of re-education") with the problem of what he euphemistically calls "the controlling intellect" (NWO pp. 155 and 154). It is hard to believe his claim for a liberating revolution in consciousness or a meaningful new world of mind since the Loonies' consciousnesses are manipulated with a skill to be envied by the most dedicated Inner Party directors of the Ministry of Truth in Orwell's *1984*.

Not only does Prof believe that one man is always responsible, he takes upon himself the responsibility for directing the revolution: "'...revolutions are not won by enlisting the masses. Revolution is a science only a few are competent to practice'" (MIHM 5). Competence means also the management of political processes after the revolution by the same elite group with the same elitist theory. Prof points out that "'parliamentary bodies all through history, when they accomplished anything, owed it to a few strong men who dominated the rest'" (MIHM 14). Therefore it becomes necessary to pay lip service to "the myth" of "the will of the people" by seeming to run an honest election while in fact manipulating the nominations so that the candidates of the elite group will be opposed as often as possible by "yammerheads" (MIHM 21). As always in Heinlein, the success of any process functions tautologously as its own justi-fication, and the operation of the "free" political system in *The Moon Is a Harsh Mistress* is no exception.

In *I Will Fear No Evil* (1970), Heinlein continues his late ten-dency to indulge in overlong works of individualistic fantasy, this time focusing on the efforts of an old man to prolong his life. As George Slusser points out, "Its actual story line, once all the accre-tions are pared away, is hardly more substantial than the early Hein-lein story it most resembles, 'Requiem' (1940)."[36] That story, the third Heinlein published, borrowed its title and premise from R.L. Stevenson's well-known sentimental poem. The novel's title, re-calling the hopeful counsel of the Twenty-third Psalm, refers not to spiritual affirmation, but rather to the sentimental consolation of immortality through one's descendants and through the survival of humanity. According to one of Heinlein's spokesmen, " 'a baby has a unique virtue. It is always the hope of our race. Its *only* hope.' "[37] But, as depicted in the novel, life on Earth in the late twen-tieth century offers little cause for optimism—the way to solve its problems, Heinlein suggests, is to avoid them by migration. At the end of *Methuselah's Children* Lazarus Long prepares to migrate to the stars; here the pregnant multiple-being named "Joan" goes to the Moon to bear her child. She/he dies in childbirth, but her/his baby lives as a testament to Heinlein's social Darwinistic belief in survival through continual competition and through the expansion of frontiers. His familiar prognosis is expressed near the end of *I Will Fear No Evil*: " 'We've reached an impasse; we can't go on the way we're headed—and we can't go back—and we're dying in our own poisons. That's why the little Lunar colony has *got* to survive. Because *we* can't. It isn't the threat of war, or crime in the streets, or corruption in high places, or pesticides, or smog, or "education" that doesn't teach; those things are just symptoms of the underlying cancer. It's too many people....So anyone who can ought to go to the Moon as fast as he can manage it' " (IWFNE 26).

In an interview granted in 1972, Heinlein elaborates on the same idea in the context of a plea for recognition of the priority of the American space program. The nation's and mankind's best interests will be served if the "space race" with Russia continues: "Mankind needs this competition; it needs it very badly, in order to escape ultimate disaster. All of us, all mankind, face a situation that is simultaneously the most dismaying and the most hopeful in all our history. We are at a cusp, a decision point. We can decide to go one way, to the stars, and enjoy unlimited opportunities, unimagined possibilities, endless evolution and eternal racial life. Or we can refuse the challange, stay where we are—and die."[38]

The language of unlimited opportunities and unimagined possibilities captures the strain of hopeful fantasy which has run continuously for over thirty years through the grim fabric of Hobbesian human nature and social Darwinistic thought in the fiction of Robert Heinlein. His most recent novel, *Time Enough for Love* (1973), carries on this interwoven theme of hope and social Darwinism for over six hundred pages in the hardbound edition. Again the focus of one character's survival and immortality as emblematic of racial survival and immortality confirms the tendency in Heinlein's later work to avoid imagining utopian social and political systems. Heinlein's fictions have evolved away from the early influence of Wellsian utopianism and toward the model of another kind of fantasy altogether, that peculiarly American expression of Horatio Algeresque success in the world of childish social Darwinistic dreams, L. Frank Baum's Oz books.

The Land of Oz has received occasional glancing mention in Heinlein's fiction: John Lyle compares the Cabal's limestone caverns to the Gnome King's palace in "'If This Goes On—'" (ITGO 9), and in *Time Enough for Love*, Lazarus Long returns to the Kansas City Public Library (where Heinlein probably spent many days as a boy) to reacquaint himself with some of his "oldest friends," including H. G. Wells and "the Marvelous Land of Oz as described by the Royal Historian and portrayed in color by John R. Neill ..."[39] Heinlein mentions the dichotomy between the vision of Wells and that of the Oz books in "Pandora's Box," the introductory essay to the collection, *The Worlds of Robert A. Heinlein*. There he describes one of his stories, "Solution Unsatisfactory," as "consciously Wellsian," that is, "written by the method which Wells spelled out for the speculative story" (p. 10). But after some further discussion, he concludes that present advances in the development of doomsday weapons make "the grimness of 'Solution Unsatisfactory' seem more like an Oz book in which the most harrowing adventures always turn out happily" (p. 11). Similarly, in *Time Enough for Love*, the grimness of Heinlein's social Darwinism turns

out to lead to an Oz-book happy ending for Lazarus Long and his
"nest," a godlike elite of Heinleinian long-lived superhumans,
some of them—his cloned selves—literally created in Lazarus' own
image.

The self-indulgent fantasy of *Time Enough for Love* may constitute the longest happy ending ever written, since it finishes off the
Future History series, that group of stories and novels which Heinlein began to write in the 1940s. Heinlein's resurrection of Lazarus
Long takes the form of an archivist's collection of recorded anecdotes and stories, complete with introduction and notes. This mode
suspends Heinlein's responsibility for providing a plot—he arranges
the sections of the novel in imitation of the themes and variations of
a musical composition. Instead of the typical structure in which actions are interspersed with their justifications as the narrative moves
to a climax (for example, *Starship Troopers* or *Strangers in a
Strange Land*), narratives themselves sometimes are used to illustrate the aphorisms and lessons which drop regularly from Lazarus
Long's lips. There are more maxims than stories to accomodate
them, so the novel includes two separate sections of wise saws from
the "notebooks" of Lazarus Long.

Long's accumulated wisdom reflects the familiar Heinleinian
social Darwinistic point of view. The one difference between this
and previous versions lies in the finality of the proof—twenty-three
hundred years from now, man has still "encountered not one race
as mean, as nasty, as deadly as our own" (TEL Introduction), and
the race has expanded across the Galaxy while increasing in population to over five hundred billion people. Should some benighted individual members of the race not yet have learned the lesson of its
successes, however, Lazarus Long is still qualified to lecture on
"that aggressive self-reliance necessary to a free human" (TEL
"Variations on a Theme VI"). Or, he will recall with affection his
"temporary mental aberrance during which he had sought a political solution to what he saw as a great danger: reproduction by de-
fectives" (TEL "Variations on a Theme VI").

Long, then known as "Dr. 'Genocide,'" wished to deny medical
treatment to any defective who would not submit to sterilization;
but having regained his "emotional detachment," he shortly realized that "grim old Mother Nature, red of tooth and claw, invar-
iably punished damfools who tried to ignore Her or to repeal Her
ordinances; he need not interfere" (TEL "Variations on a Theme
VI"). Long later characterizes such political behavior in one of the

excerpts from his Notebooks: "Political tags—such as royalist, communist, democrat, populist, fascist, liberal, conservative, and so forth—are never basic criteria. The Human race divides politically into those who want people to be controlled and those who have no such desire. The former are idealists acting from highest motives for the greatest good of the greatest number. The latter are surly curmudgeons, suspicious and lacking in altruism. But they are more comfortable neighbors than the other sort" (TEL "Second Intermission"). The polarities of Heinlein's conservatism are finally contained, if not reconciled as different aspects of the same character: the "idealist" and elitist Dr. Genocide is another identity of the individualistic, comfortable curmudgeon, Lazarus Long.

Long's idea of a government which ensures comfortable neighbors is again one which governs least. The government which Long established and Ira Weatheral administers on Secundus is antidemocratic, cheap, and simple: " '—a constitutional tyranny. One in which the government was forbidden to do most things... and the dear people, bless their black flabby little hearts, were given no voice at all' " (TEL "Variations on a Theme III"). The governments and societies of Tertius and Happy Valley (on New Beginnings) come even closer to a Heinleinian version of Oz for the elite: only the hardiest survivors belong, and in Happy Valley, "...the only law we had was the Golden Rule" (TEL "Variations on a Theme XII").

In writing the fairy tale of *Time Enough for Love*, Heinlein has exhausted the accumulated wind of his fantasies; practically any situation, social, political, sexual, which has appeared in his previous novels, recurs in *Time Enough for Love*. The basically reductive nature of Heinlein's thought appears here also: Ultimately, everything relates only to the physical individual and to those governing biological laws which have ruled Heinlein's individuals throughout his fiction. The suspension of death and time for the sake of the fantasy only make these absolutes loom larger in fact. Lazarus Long may be able to live forever, clone further copies of himself, and even travel back in time and copulate with his mother; but the fairy-tale ease with which these feats are accomplished makes his cry of "Carpe diem!" a hollow banality just as unsatisfactory and reductive as his social Darwinistic political fantasies are.

On April 5, 1973, Robert A. Heinlein performed in fact what some of his characters accomplished in fiction: he lectured on history and moral philosophy. His audience, the brigade of midshipmen at his alma mater, Annapolis, heard Lieutenant Heinlein (retired) give an address that would have done credit to Colonel Dubois of the Mobile Infantry. Later printed in *Analog*, it contains and elaborates Heinlein's (and the colonel's) standard definition of moral behavior as survival behavior; then Heinlein tries to show that patriotism is a human refinement of baboon tribal custom:

> I don't think baboon language is complex enough to permit them to discuss such abstract notions as "morality" or "duty" or "loyalty"—but it is evident that baboons *do* operate morally and *do* exhibit the traits of duty and loyalty; we see them in action.... But that baboon behavior can be explained in evolutionary terms.... Baboons who fail to exhibit moral behavior do not survive; they wind up as meat for leopards....
>
> The next level in moral behavior higher than that exhibited by the baboon is that in which duty and loyalty are shown toward a group of your own kind too large for an individual to know all of them. We have a name for that. It is called "patriotism."[40]

Another author, Ursula K. LeGuin, has recently described her reactions to the baboon ideology of nineteenth-century social Darwinism advocated not only in Heinleinian history and moral philosophy, but generally in American science fiction:

> The only social change presented by most [American] SF has been towards authoritarianism, the domination of ignorant masses by a powerful elite—sometimes presented as a warning, but often quite complacently. Socialism is never considered as an alternative, and democracy is quite forgotten. Military virtues are taken as ethical ones. Wealth is assumed to be a righteous goal and a personal virtue. Competitive free-enterprise capitalism is the economic destiny of the entire Galaxy. In general, American SF has assumed a permanent hierarchy of superiors and inferiors, with rich, ambitious, aggressive males at the top, then a great gap, and then at the bottom the poor, the uneducated, the faceless masses, and all the women. The whole picture is, if I may say so, curiously "un-American." It is a perfect baboon patriarchy, with the Alpha Male on top, being respectfully groomed, from time to time, by his inferiors.
>
> Is this speculation? is this imagination? is this extrapolation? I call it brainless regressivism.
>
> I think it's time SF writers—and their readers!—stopped daydreaming about a return to the Age of Queen Victoria, and started thinking about the future. I would like to see the Baboon Ideal replaced by a little human idealism, and some serious consideration of such deeply radical, futuristic concepts as Liberty, Equality, and Fraternity. And remember that about 53% of the Brotherhood of Man is the Sisterhood of Woman.[41]

The model of baboon patriarchy is also rejected by social philosophers as a fossil of nineteenth-century thinking. Richard Hofstadter summarizes the conclusions "now accepted by most humanists":

> that such biological ideas as the "survival of the fittest," whatever their doubtful value in natural science, are utterly useless in attempting to understand society; that the life of man in society, while it is incidentally a biological fact, has characteristics that are not reducible to biology and must be explained in the distinctive terms of a cultural analysis; that the physical well-being of men is a result of their social organization and not vice-versa; that social improvement is a product of advances in technology and social organization, not of breeding or selective elimination; that judgments as to the value of competition between men or enterprises or nations must be based upon social and not allegedly biological consequences; and, finally, that there is nothing in nature or a naturalistic philosophy of life to make impossible the acceptance of moral sanctions that can be employed for the common good.[42]

Some science fiction writers have attempted to go beyond the baboon patriarchy toward the humanist conclusions Hofstadter describes. Ursula LeGuin has produced two distinguished novels, *The Left Hand of Darkness* and *The Dispossessed*, both of which undertake the reexamination of assumptions necessary for American science fiction's progress into the mainstream of twentieth-century thought. But it is hard to imagine that Heinlein will bring his ideas of human nature up to date with current evolutionary science and moral philosophy. If he writes more fiction, it is to be expected that thirty years' survival as a writer of social Darwinistic fiction have convinced him not to challenge his own basic assumptions or to argue with success, since, as he believes, success is its own justification, sanctioned by the laws of evolution.

7. Major Political and Social Elements in Heinlein's Fiction

FRANK H. TUCKER

In DISCUSSING the principal political and social ideas which are expressed or reflected in the Heinlein literature, it is best to begin by observing that these are in no sense tract novels and stories, and the political content is secondary or even incidental to the narratives. One should also note that the usual uncertainty regarding fictional material applies here, as to whether or not the statements of various characters reflect the author's views. However, we are obliged to rely on such statements usually as our primary source, and where they recur or are emphasized, they can be considered as significant.

First let us look at elements which are essentially individual matters. There are several ways in which the author's concepts of the "proper individual," the hero and the leader, shed light upon our subject. There are many strong characters, functioning in the stories as exemplary figures, even acting as leaders of their people or as guides to younger, less experienced characters. These leaders often seem to reflect an outlook which is typical of the intelligent, fairly conservative achievers of the author's own generation in the United States. They are go-getters, and are often ready to dedicate their efforts to the common causes of exploration, liberation, and other forms of service to mankind, or at least to their own segment of mankind.

The author is a realist, but he is rather optimistic about human destiny. In *The Door into Summer* we read, "Despite the crape-hangers, romanticists, and anti-intellectuals, the world steadily grows better because the human mind, applying itself to environment, *makes* it better."[1] This progress is seen as having been facilitated, during the past history of man, by competition and by the process to which the name of Charles Darwin is attached, natural selection and survival of the fittest—a tendency in nature toward the proliferation of mutated types which are more able to cope with their en-

172

vironment, accompanied by the tendency of the less fit types to die out. During the forthcoming development of mankind, in addition to these trends in nature, the author sometimes contemplates the use of genetic planning, and even genetic engineering—alteration of germ cell material—to enhance these tendencies.

Franz Rottensteiner has termed Heinlein's stories "an endorsement of social Darwinism." Fittingly, he says also that the characters in these stories "personify an ethic of success."[2] Although Heinlein accepts the Darwinian label, the phrase "social Darwinism" should be used cautiously because it has come to include a thoroughly ruthless approach to human affairs, dignifying the abuse of colonial populations and the extermination of supposedly inferior races as natural, ultimately beneficial processes.

In *Farnham's Freehold* we find an estimate that a twentieth-century atomic war might actually have the long-range effect of improving the stock of the human race. After such a holocaust, that is, the survival of individuals would be a real struggle, and the survivors of that competition for sustenance would tend to be the most fit persons. World Wars I and II, on the other hand, brought death mostly to the fighting forces, in which the fitter individuals were concentrated, sparing the poorer specimens who were not at the front. This concept is perhaps meant to apply only to the United States, since at the time in question there were many deaths elsewhere from starvation and genocide, not directed particularly toward the fighting forces.

At any rate, another appreciation of the racial value of hard times appears in *Beyond This Horizon*, where the sage District Moderator for Genetics, Mordan Claude, says, "Easy times for individuals are bad times for the race,'" and the corollary is that when there is not enough adversity there must be compensatory governmental intervention and planning. There is much more in this latter novel about genetics. The character Hamilton Felix is described as a genetic superman, highly fitted for survival. We also read about the aftermath of an atomic war in 1970. The survivors used genetics to breed people who would be more peaceable, more like sheep than wolves, but the experiment failed because the nation was attacked by more wolflike peoples, who won.[3]

There is much more discussion of genetics in *Farnham's Freehold*, but not on the part of the heroes; rather it is the overlords of the arrogant superrace of the time who refer to the matter most often. A more decent reference to Darwinism occurs in *Starship Troopers* with some worried musing that because a certain planet lacks radiation in its atmosphere there will be no mutation, thence no zoologic competition and no progress in life forms. The musing extends to the observation that people don't worry about future generations as they should.[4] This sounds a little like Edmund Burke's dictum that our responsibility as human beings extends not only to the living but also to the past generations and the yet unborn generations of the human community.

The application of Darwinian thought to the new situations created by the discovery and development of new frontier lands was made by Charles Darwin himself, in *The Descent of Man*, where he pointed out that a kind of selection process operated when people made the choice to go out to the New World of the Western Hemisphere during the era of settlement: those who went tended to be those who had more courage, initative, or innovativeness. Heinlein also is mindful of this factor in his anticipation that space travel might ruin the Earth by draining its best minds away. He certainly thinks of space exploration as being akin to the old eras of colonization and the Westward Movement on Earth. One of his Moon ships is called the *Pioneer*, and its sister ships have the equally significant names of *Mayflower* and *Colonial*. In another story, a group of fugitive settlers on Venus are described as having their own "rough frontier culture," under the guidance of a headman who handles justice like Judge Roy Bean. The formerly soft lawyer who is settled there notes the virtues of frontier life, harsh though it is, and he wonders if he should return to his former, sterile life as a fat, prosperous Earthling. In another narrative, the frontier of Western Americana is reenacted even in such details as a Conestoga wagon, on a remote planet, and the protagonist remarks that the frontiers have a wholesome, "culling" effect on mankind.[5]

The frontier as a safety valve for an overcrowded land and a stultified culture, one of the elements in the "Frontier Thesis" of the famous American historian, Frederick Jackson Turner, seems to be what Damon Knight has in mind when he remarks that even the somewhat wild Heinlein juvenile-story plots, about high school kids being sent in a survival test to remote and savage planets, are not unlikely in the context of an Earth grossly overcrowded by its population explosion.[6]

One further introductory note is needed here regarding archetypal images, those very widespread and ancient modes through which the human mind brings to its surface its deepest conceptions of problems and solutions, including the human figures which, as archetypal images, may represent our chief hopes and hazards. The reader is not asked to accept Carl Jung's interpretations of these phenomena, and it would be unwise to assert that Heinlein has done so. Such archetypal images as savior figures, whether young or old, male or female, earthbound or heaven-sent, are often found in the Heinlein stories. They may have been put there simply because such figures were natural and needful for the story. Or perhaps, as Damon Knight believes about Heinlein's Freudian probings, he has mortared some of them in, without conviction, thinking that they improve his product (p. 86).

Certainly it is evident that Heinlein at some point had become familiar with quite a mass of archaic, occult, and psychoanalytic information. In *Waldo*, for example, we find a certain defense of the accomplishments of magic. In *Magic, Inc.* there is reference to a full set of demons—Lucifugé, Sataniacha, Ashtoreth, Mammon, and Beelzebub.[7] There is much magic and fantasy in *Glory Road*, in which the character Star, for instance, represents the archetypes of the Terrible Mother, witch, and so forth. More pertinent to our political interests here would be the inclination of Heinlein to have a senior guiding figure in his stories, a "wise old man," as the Jungians would say. Examples of this include Mordan Claude in *Beyond This Horizon*, Dr. Jefferson in *Between Planets*, Jubal Harshaw in *Stranger in a Strange Land*, Sam Anderson in *Starman Jones*, Professor Bernardo de la Paz in *The Moon Is a Harsh Mistress*, and Lazarus Long in *Methuselah's Children* and *Time Enough for Love*. Lazarus, living to be thousands of years old, is surely the epitome of this figure. He also represents the type who is specially endowed with a marvelous quality, as are many of the savior and hero figures in this literature. In his case, a mutation which allows the longevity is the special gift. Furthermore, Lazarus is recurrently rescued from death by rejunvenation techniques, and finally he is in fact killed, but is, amazingly enough, brought back to life like the Lazarus of the Bible. The book also describes Long as "our Moses who led his people out of bondage," and he plays still another role despite his vulnerability, that of the archetypal "Trickster Figure." That is reflected in the description of him as having "audacity, a talent for lying convincingly, and...a childish delight in adventure and intrigue for its own sake" (TEL Introduction).

The archetypal imagery of control lost over one's own person-

FRANK H. TUCKER   176

ality or body, whether by possession (as by demons) or through some other device, finds several echoes in the Heinlein literature. In science fiction as a whole, in fact, it is quite a common phenomenon, reflecting very probably a strong anxiety by modern man concerning the independence or integrity of his person. Our author makes less use of this concept than average, but there are some interesting examples. *The Puppet Masters* is a good case of this, with direct control of each human being who has a loathsome guest organism on his back. The masters, furthermore, are not independent individuals themselves, being blended into a collective whole without which they hardly function. Such a loss of individuality to the communal entity occurs also in *Methuselah's Children*, where the rabbit-like Little People have a purely collective personality. A human being, Mary Sperling, joins them, to the distress of the other people. Again, the animal-like Jockaira of the same novel do not exist for themselves but as pets of unseen masters. The masters exercise mystically vague mental control and telekinetic control over Jockaira and humans alike, though their intervention into the human mind produces hysteria and disorientation. The implications of all this for twentieth-century man, with his own agonizing choices as to collectivization and communal life, are reasonably clear.

General Political Concepts

Heinlein's writings often speak of the need to keep government small, to minimize its functions. Governmental honesty, candor, and efficiency are esteemed, and limited government will conserve these qualities. Where does Heinlein get his political philosophy? We have only a few direct indications. In " 'If This Goes On—' " Grand Master Peter recommends Tom Paine to John Lyle for basic enlightenment, and we are told that Lyle finds the works of Thomas Jefferson and Patrick Henry also when he looks up the works of Paine. The interest in Paine and Henry is not merely casual; we know that Heinlein ran a full-page ad in the *Colorado Springs Gazette Telegraph* on April 13, 1958, asking the readers to dedicate themselves as heirs of Patrick Henry. The ad quotes Henry's famous "liberty or death" speech, and deplores those who would give up essential liberty to obtain temporary safety. At any rate, our young hero Lyle also discovers that "secrecy is the keystone of tyranny. Not force, but secrecy...censorship."[8]

Heinlein respects the political process, preferring the practical politicians to those who are more idealistic. In *Podkayne of Mars* we read, "Politics is... the way we get things done... without fighting. We dicker and compromise.... the only alternative is force.... *Homo sapiens* is the most deadly of all the animals in this solar system. Yet he invented politics!"[9] In *Time Enough for Love* the opinion is that reform politicians lack the reliability that " 'business politicians' " have, because the former lie and cheat to serve their vague ideals (TEL "Variations on a Theme III").

How is the political process to be kept wholesome? Perhaps not through democracy, but through the twin concepts of loyalty and duty, without which any society is doomed, and by taking care that authority and responsibility are kept equal and coordinate in government. Suggesting that democracy is based on the idea that a million men are wiser than one man, the author implies that this is a dubious concept (TEL "Intermission"). Again, in *Glory Road*, the following commentaries appear:

> " 'Democracy. A curious delusion—as if adding zeroes could produce a sum.... Democracy can't work. Mathematicians, peasants, and animals, that's all there is—so democracy, a theory based on the assumption that mathematicians and peasants are equal, can never work.... But a democratic *form* of government is okay, as long as it doesn't work. Any social organization does well enough if it isn't rigid.... Most so-called social scientists seem to think that organization is everything. It is almost nothing—except when it is a straightjacket.... [The U.S.A.] has a system free enough to let its heroes work at their trade. It should last a long time—unless its looseness is destroyed from inside.' "[10]

In "Gulf," the comment comes from a villain, which can mean that it is not the author's view. However, it does not appear to be greatly different from the opinions cited above, except that the villain will use conspiracy and murder to promote his own cause. He opines that democracy could flourish for about one hundred and fifty years in the past, but muddled and ignorant men cannot be trusted to settle by their voting processes the issues of the modern world in which nuclear physics and the like are beyond their capacity to understand. He condemns communism also, because very little progress was made under it, a totalitarian, political religion being, as he says, incompatible with free investigation. Even this character sees some practical good in individual freedom, in that it lends itself to experimentation, evolution, and progress through trial and error.[11]

The weight of opinion throughout this literature is in favor of leaving people alone. In "Coventry," a speaker objects to excessive planning: "'You've planned your whole world so carefully that you've planned the fun and zest right out of it.'"[12] In *Time Enough for Love*, Chairman Ira Weatheral believes that no unnecessary governing must be done or allowed; the aim of government is not to do good but to refrain from doing evil. It must keep order, but the Chairman regularly prunes officious officials from his organization, abolishing their jobs and those of their juniors (TEL "Variations on a Theme I"). In "'If This Goes On—'" the original version had the liberation organization planning to teach freedom to the people through hypnosis, but the revised form of this story shows the organization rejecting hypnotic conditioning, because free men must come to understand freedom under their own power (ITGO 14).

Some political interpretations have come into this literature in connection with references to past events. These references are not particularly numerous, since science fiction is more oriented to the future than to the past, but they do reveal a few things about the author's points of view. In "Logic of Empire," the subject is slavery—in the future, on the face of it, but certainly the example of Europe's global expansion in the past, and the frequently attendant practice of slavery, is in the picture here. The author refers to it, and he is not so logical or accurate in these matters. A character deplores our tendency to accept "devil theory" when we examine such problems; he says that colonial slavery resulted not from villainy but from stupidity, in that it was nonproductive. It is true that slave labor is less productive than free labor. In colonial times, indeed throughout most of the centuries of European imperial expansion, there was a shortage of labor; not enough workmen to do the enormous job of opening up to European settlement and industry the two American continents, Australia, and South Africa. That does not justify slavery, but neither does it make the brutal, stopgap practice "stupid."

A related error is the declaration in "Logic of Empire" that "...the use of mother-country capital to develop the colony inevitably results in subsistence-level wages at home and slave labor in the colonies." This may often have been true, but by no means always. For example, mother-country capital was lent to the British colonies in North America—raised by stock companies, in some cases, for the initial development of the colony. Slavery did not become a regular and important institution in the Northern colonies, though it had a limited or token existence there for a time.

The patriotism of Heinlein is often evident, one sign of it being his special interest in the American Revolution, long before the Bicentennial celebrations made this a commonplace reference. In *Farnham's Freehold*, for instance, Hugh Farnham had a safe in his underground shelter, the combination for which turned out to be 74-17-76—duly explained in the text as deriving from July 4, 1776 (4). Perhaps the special interest was related to the Heinlein address in Colorado Springs, 1776 Mesa Avenue. However that may be, the patriotic view of history is substantial enough. In the same novel, Farnham declared, "'America is the best thing in history, *I* think. ...'" (1)

More recent history is grist for the author's mill; there are reflections of Nazis in the future situations, presented with evident disapproval, as are their emulators outside of Germany. One of the Nazi-like elitists of the Survivors Club in *Beyond This Horizon* is a section leader named Mosely, surely redolent of Sir Oswald Mosely of the British "Silver Shirts" in the Hitler era (7).

As for communism, it comes in for clear disapproval, but the references are not always shrill; occasionally there is even a neutral borrowing of a communist feature. The hero of "'If This Goes On—'" belongs to a revolutionary group which is presented approvingly; it is overthrowing a nasty theocratic dictatorship. The group requires our hero to spend a lot of time on his "Personal Conversion Report," a copious, complete, and detailed account of his background and how he became converted to the revolution. If these reports ever verged on the superficial, or omitted anything, they were to be supplemented by interrogation under hypnosis. This copious report is very similar to the long reports, diaries, and journals which cadres in training in Communist China are required to present. It is a key feature of their training, and probably inspired this fictional item, though one should concede that the Chinese would hardly use hypnosis in such connections (ITGO 10 and 11).

More general social phenomena in modern America are also reflected. The hero of *Glory Road* acknowledged that his generation, which matured in the 1950s and 1960s, contributed the overpowering goal of "Security" to the American dream. Those who are apathetic, selfish, or spoiled get no encouragement from this author (1), but that will be considered further in our discussion of citizens' rights and responsibilities below.

A modern trend which has been explicitly denounced by Heinlein in his nonfiction writing is anti-intellectualism and antiscience outlooks. His intellectual critics would be surprised, perhaps, how much better he does than do some of the critics' friends at defending the realm of the intellect and science in the face of pernicious attacks.[13]

Functions of Government and Warrants for Revolution

The author's positions on the functions of government are a bit ambivalent: he seems to want its power to be very limited, but he views strikes against the authorities (perhaps against the public interest or even the public safety) as a bad thing, a point shown best in "The Roads Must Roll," not only in its own crisis of a strike against the road system, but in its "historical" reference to the so-called Functionalists of the 1930s, who supposedly said that any group might rightly exert whatever powers might be inherent in their functions—a fictional sect, but discernibly related to the strikes by public employees which have in fact brought controversy as threats to safety. Civil servants are feared for their potential power as "civil masters," and we are told that it is a fallacy to suppose that taxes are levied for the benefit of the governed. Societies are allegedly built on procedures for the protection of pregnant women and young children; anything more is a nonessential function of government. The excesses of government are derided with the saying that an elephant is a mouse built to governmental specifications (TEL "Intermission").

Naturally a foe of big government would execrate such things as secret police, thought control, and torture, and all these are duly deplored in "'If This Goes On—'" which appeared so early (in 1940) that we cannot attribute its Orwellian features to influence from *1984*. Heinlein's Grand Inquisitor, as he is called in this story, is similar to the minions of the Ministry of Love in *1984*, and his Prophet is somewhat like Big Brother in the latter story. It appears that *1984*'s concepts are derived to some extent from the dystopian novel of the Russian Evgeni Zamiatin, *We*, which appeared in the first years after the Bolshevik Revolution. We can relate the authoritarian features of the Heinlein story to *We*; certainly Zamiatin's dictator, the "Benefactor," is comparable to the Prophet, for example. However, we will stop short here of a direct attribution of "'If This Goes On—'" to influences from *We*.

What about the power of the state to make war or to conscript soldiers? Heinlein seems to affirm the first but to reject the second. He writes, "You can have peace. Or you can have freedom. Don't ever count on having both at once" (TEL "Intermission"). That is given in a piece of fiction, but his *Gazette Telegraph* ad cited above contained the same idea. On the other hand, he says that "no state has an inherent right to survive through conscript troops and, in the long run, no state ever has" (TEL "Intermission"). Consistent with this is the national, or rather, imperial defense portrayed in *Starship Troopers*, where the system is quite militaristic, but all service is voluntary.

Concerning the right to make a revolution against unjust authority, Heinlein certainly believes in it, rather in the spirit of the American Declaration of Independence. Many of his plots contain such endeavors, presented as virtuous actions. On the other hand, we also find examples of unpleasant militarists who try to grab power. For example, in "The Long Watch" the coup is attempted by officers who feel that it is "not safe to leave control of the world in political hands; power must be held by a scientifically selected group." Accordingly, the plotters will strike from the Moon, bombing "an unimportant town or two" on Earth to promote their coup. The hero of the story, Lieutenant Dahlquist, sacrifices his life to abort this foul attempt.[14]

An ample set of Heinlein political ideas is found in *The Moon Is A Harsh Mistress* because in this novel the narrative centers on the efforts of the people in Earth's settlements on the Moon to achieve independence. We are told here that, as with many eighteenth- and nineteenth-century colonization projects on Earth, the original settlers consisted for some time of convicts or transportees. By the twenty-first century, however, when independence becomes an effective cause, the lunar complaints do not focus on a lack of personal freedoms. To be sure there are many constraints on individuals, but they are due mostly to the harsh realities of the struggle to live on "Luna," as it is called here. The grievances are mostly financial, like those of the American colonies in 1776.

The Lunar Authority, a corporation-like entity, conducts the commerce between Earth and Luna, setting the prices at which materials are sold to Luna and at which the products of the Moon are purchased. Since the lunar settlers consider the former prices to be too high, and the latter too low, they desire independence, so that they may negotiate more equitable terms. This aim they have in common, whether they are the descendants of American, Russian, or Chinese settlers. We read that "Great China," a greatly expanded version of the China of 1976, took most of Southeast Asia, Australia, New Zealand, Mongolia, and Siberian regions, deporting many of the inhabitants to the Moon.[15]

This book contains a lot of background information on lunar society and customs, which vary from earthly modes, chiefly because a chronic shortage of women has led to new forms of family structure and to courtship patterns in which the woman makes very free choices of her friends and affiliations (MIHM 3 and 11). Most significant for us, however, are the political philosophy and political aspirations expressed by the leading characters here. Since they are also the leaders of the independence movement, they are obliged to enunciate their aims and methods at some length. Two leaders in particular say a great deal about the desirable political forms for the future independent Luna; these men are Manuel O'Kelly Davis, a computer expert who narrates the novel, and Professor Bernardo de la Paz, his revolutionary collaborator who is to become head of the fledgling government of Luna. "Prof," as the latter is usually called here, expresses the more complex or academic aspects of the political thought, while Manuel represents the more everyday, straightforward views of the man of action. Lastly, the conspirators confer with an elaborate computer which is able to vocalize. The computer, known as "Mike," becomes their friend and collaborator, contributing to their planning his more-than-human logical analysis of all problems, including the political questions. We may take it that these three parties, taken together, express the Heinlein political thought as presented in this novel.

Of course the lunar revolutionary organization is initially authoritarian because of the need to conceal the identities of its conspirators. A cell-like organization is developed, so that if a member is taken prisoner, or is a traitor, he can betray only two or three other members. Under such conditions, naturally there can be no extensive voting or consultation. Even so, the leading conspirators are broad-minded when it comes to comparing the political philosophies of capitalism, socialism, and so on. As the professor puts it, "Private where private belongs, public where it's needed, and an admission that circumstances alter cases." He goes on, however, to identify himself as a rational anarchist, one who believes that government can only exist really in the acts of self-responsible individuals. Blame and responsibility can only repose in single persons, he says. As an anarchist, he is willing to accept any rules that his associates feel are necessary to their freedom, and yet if he finds a rule too obnoxious he will break it (MIHM 6).

Sometimes bits of anarchism, natural law, and lunar custom are blended in this novel. The lunar customs are natural laws, says Manuel, because they are the ways people must act to stay alive. The customs have been the chief regulator of behavior. Formal laws have not been issued, only some "do or don't"-type regulations from higher authority. But all this is the status quo. What do our protagonists wish to enact when they seize power? First there is a denunciation by Manuel of busybodies who would regulate details of morals, personal habits, and the like. He muses that there must be a yearning deep in the human heart to keep others from doing as they please, usually expressed with a pious but faulty allegation that the rule is for the good of those who will be regulated (MIHM 11 and 14).

When the Luna Declaration of Independence is issued, appropriately enough, on July 4, 2076, there is much discussion as to the rights which should be guaranteed to all citizens, but the matter is left unsettled here. As for the newer rights of twentieth-century America, Heinlein includes a dialogue which may indicate a distaste for these, although perhaps he means only that under lunar conditions these would be inappropriate. We are told that on the Moon individuals pay for their medical care, their libraries, and for what education they happen to want. The narrator says he isn't sure what social security really is, but there is none on Luna.

With the formation of a Constitutional Convention on Luna to work out a detailed constitutional statement, the professor is stimulated to write some lengthy advice for that body, including the following significant points:

After warning the Convention how great are the dangers of losing freedom to a government, the professor warns against trusting time-honored methods, such as representative bodies based on geographic division. He suggests electing from other constituencies, such as age groups, or electing all members at large. He would even consider electing the candidates who got the least number of votes, as a safeguard against tyranny. Another possibility is to be selection by petition, giving office to each person who garners a certain number of citizens who support him—a method which would give every citizen a representative of his choice. As a further safeguard of freedom, the professor urges the conferees to "accentuate the negative." Let them forbid their government to do a number of things: to conscript men, to interfere with freedom of press, speech, assembly, travel, religion, education, or occupation. Let there be no involuntary taxation! Fearing the growth of a powerful government, he would keep it small indeed by limiting its revenues to voluntary contributions and income from lotteries and other noncoercive operations (MIHM 15, 17, and 22).

If there is a one-word summation of this voluntarism and desire for minimal government, with much distrust of the benefits of government welfare programs and the like, it is expressed here by the title of Book Three of this book: "TANSTAAFL!" This stands for "There ain't no such thing as a free lunch," and it is reiterated a number of times, leaving no doubt that the author wishes to emphasize it. In conclusion, a pessimism about man as a political animal emerges at the end of this novel when we learn that the framers of the new government of Luna adopted none of the professor's ideas. Manuel, too, was disappointed at the interferences with freedom which were generated by the new government, and he concluded that there "seems to be a deep instinct in human beings for making everything compulsory that isn't forbidden." At the story's end Manuel considered going out to the Asteroids, where there would be some nice places, "not too crowded," a sentiment reminiscent of the pioneering spirit of the American past, wherein the frontiersman went out beyond the settled lands to escape constraints (MIHM 30).

Rights and Responsibilities of the Citizenry

To quite an extent, the rights and roles of citizens may be complementary to the roles of governmental authorities, and thus the functions of citizens have already been delimited or implied in what we adduced concerning the executive operations. However, let us see what further perspectives can be derived by looking at these matters from the citizens' point of view. Particularly let us consider the position of women now; on equal rights for women the author's inclination appears to have been reasonably equitable, and not merely in recent years when the women's rights movement has made this a fashionable and natural thing for writers to advocate.

In "Delilah and the Space-Rigger," which came out in 1949, Tiny Larsen, construction superintendent on Space Station One, accepts a woman electronics engineer for his team. At first he objects vociferously and contemptuously, mostly because he fears for the welfare and efficiency of his group if women are added. Soon, however, finding that the lady engineer does a good job, that she is accepted by the men, and that morale actually improves, he changes his tune and proposes to add a number of female personnel to his group. Perhaps these criteria are more functional and expedient than idealistic matters of equity, but the result was, in this story, a much more liberal situation than one could find in either trade unions or in business and the professions back in 1949.[16]

Later, in *Time Enough for Love*, the narrator reminisces about the twentieth-century United States Navy, observing that there was no job in it which could not be performed by either sex, despite which it remained heavily male in its staffing in the first six decades, at least, of that century (TEL "Variations on a Theme II"). Midway between these two stories, *Starship Troopers* in 1959 provided many references to women in many sorts of roles of leadership, active combat service, and even command of ships, in the space navy. The honors, status, and formal precedence given to female officers here are certainly equal. Also, it is important to note that the juxtaposition of the two sexes on spaceships, even on long voyages or in time of hostilities, is not shown as awkward and troublesome. Women are omitted only from service as combat infantry; on the ships, however, they participate in the hazards of violent death or injury in action. The author does not glaze over or ignore the little social problems or emotional reactions that would come from the propinquity of the sexes in a military force; he handles it realistically.

The same even-handed realism is evident throughout the interracial encounters under intimate and trying circumstances which are an important part of *Farnham's Freehold*. Rights for black citizens are not an especially frequent topic in Heinlein's fiction, but in this novel he takes on the problems of racial relationships in a low-key manner. Again, there is no glossing over of the nonwhite characters. They have faults, they do some awful things, they can be either gentle or arrogant; in short they are fairly typical human beings. In the future world postulated here, where blacks are the race in charge, the novel could have made an *Uncle Tom's Cabin* in reverse, but it did nothing of the kind.

There are, it is true, many stories in which this writer, as others in science fiction, contemplates a yellow peril—invasions from Asia, cruel Oriental overlords, and the like. Let us leave these to be considered as matters of hypothetical international relations of the future. Opinion will differ, but these situations could be defended as realistic, or at least as one man's attempt to project a not-altogether-fantastic future development. Nor does he follow the tradition of Buck Rogers or Flash Gordon. In those creations, the reader may recall, the Red Mongol overlords of Rogers' day went out of their way to kidnap Buck's beloved Wilma; her seduction was recurrently one of their prime objectives. Similarly, Flash's girl, Dale, got a lot of attention from the oversexed minions of the fiendish Ming the Merciless. In Heinlein, on the other hand, the Oriental attackers, while quite unpleasant, as invaders will be always, appear largely as businesslike operators; their dislike or scorn for the other side and the other races is not lurid or unusual.

The author's views on modes of sexual relationships reflect primarily his generally broad view of rights. The authorities, and indeed people as a whole, should mind their own business and be tolerant. In *Time Enough for Love* this has been given more play, presumably in response to new popular feelings in the Western world, the "new morality," and such factors which naturally condition the products of a great many writers. The hero of the novel thought that laws on marriage were unnecessary (TEL "Variations on a Theme XIV").

The general rights of the citizen were particularly broad in the society sketched out in "Coventry." The people were not forbidden to do anything unless it damaged another person. If they did commit such damaging acts they were required to submit to a program of psychological readjustment administered by the authorities, to render the offenders more innocuous. If a person refused the program he was obliged to leave the society entirely, by passing through a force field or barrier to the region beyond it, which was external to the society, inhabited by such exiles or pariahs, unsupervised by the government. We find this concept of largely leaving people alone extended to risky undertakings—the government should not forbid these either. This is expressed in the story called "Requiem," where a character declares that it is not " 'the business of this damn paternalistic government to tell a man not to risk his life doing what he really wants to do.' " [17]

More specific rights enunciated by Heinlein's characters include the privilege of bearing arms and the concomitant arrangement that the police should not be too strong: "The police of a state should never be stronger or better armed than the citizenry. An armed citizenry, willing to fight, is the foundation of civil freedom." The words here show some resemblance to those of the Second Amendment to the Constitution of the United States, which says that the right of citizens to keep and bear arms shall not be infringed because the armed militia is essential to the security of a free state. Many of the other "Bill of Rights"-type immunities would result indirectly from the approach Heinlein advocated in his speech at the World Science Fiction Convention in Seattle, in 1961. He would not put anyone in jail, conscript anyone, or otherwise subject him to involuntary servitude, nor would he suppress or conceal information.[18]

In *Starship Troopers* and some other stories the citizenry is certainly not free from what Americans in recent times have come to think of as cruel and unusual punishment; in fact all inhabitants, whether citizens or not, and whether in the armed forces or not, are subject in *Starship Troopers* to flogging, as a punishment for a variety of offenses. We are told that twentieth-century America found itself so endangered because of lax handling of its offenders that life became insufferably dangerous, and there was finally public support for corporal punishment. Flogging was not reserved for rare and horrible crimes; drunken driving got the offender something in excess of ten lashes. The underlying rationale is stated here, that man does not have a moral instinct, as the people of the twentieth century thought; he has simply a cultivated conscience—thence the importance of exemplary or deterrent punishments (ST 8).

Nowhere is the doctrine of rights being coordinate with responsibilities applied more straightforwardly than in the *Starship Troopers* situation, where one must earn the franchise and citizenship through national service—largely military, but not necessarily in a combat arm. The veterans-only government came into being after a prisoner-of-war foul-up following a war with the "Chinese Hegemony," and is considered efficacious because all those admitted to citizenship have, in the service, placed group welfare ahead of their personal advantage; they have at least made some sacrifices for the nation. A noncitizen cannot enter politics, but he is not persecuted, and he may be very successful in the private sector. The hero's father has a prosperous business, though he is not a citizen at the beginning of the novel. Some other key roles are reserved for citizens; only they may teach the secondary-level course called "History and Moral Philosophy," because of its importance in shaping the outlooks of young people. A single enlistment of a few years is usually enough to qualify for the franchise, but those who sign up for the career service may run into trouble in this regard if they do not finish twenty years' service.

Some debate is possible as to whether this situation would be in substance an infringement on a truly volunteer service, since there are distinct liabilities attached to those who don't volunteer. Another objection might be that a government of veterans only could be a little one-sided, or even jingoistic. Nevertheless this system would indeed coordinate privileges with responsibility in a significant way (ST 4, 6, 11, and 12).

Starship Troopers gives most of its attention to the career of an enlistee in the Mobile Infantry, an interstellar personal combat force which resembles most closely the United States Marines. The volunteer's life is manifestly regimented to a high degree; his rights and his scope for freedom of action are very limited. However, he has *volunteered* for this situation. Therefore even this novel is quite consistent with the Heinlein position on the individual vis-à-vis the various political philosophies, which is most comprehensively stated as follows:

> Political tags—such as royalist, communist, democrat, populist, fascist, liberal, conservative, and so forth—are never basic criteria. The human race divides politically into those who want people to be controlled and those who have no such desire (TEL "Second Intermission").

Economics and Business

The Heinlein general theory on economics is in a way a laissez-faire theory, derived from the views on minimal government and individual freedom which we have already considered. The reason for hedging with the words "in a way" in the preceding sentence is that in many of his stories the economic units or corporate entities are so large that it may be uncertain whether there would be much free economics, much individual discretion, or much random marketplace action left. It is somewhat the same question we behold on the real Earth of the present, but with many, many planets involved, the capacity for impersonal bigness is unavoidably increased.

A basic dictum already noted, "There ain't no such thing as a free lunch," has obvious implications in the area of economics. *Starship Troopers* applies much the same concept specifically to the democratic nations of the twentieth century, looking back regretfully at them to note that they collapsed because the people thought that they could "vote for whatever they wanted...and get it, without toil..." (ST 6). In a more recent novel, the author says the same thing, and says it in the form of an aphorism, in a list of sayings recorded by the hero. That is a fairly gratuitous utterance, not really needed for the novel, so it may be taken as authentic author-opinion: "Anything free is worth what you pay for it" (TEL "Second Intermission").

There are also economic corollaries to the Darwinian thought which Heinlein echoes repeatedly, and to his thoughts about the frontier. From *The Door into Summer* we have "Competition is a good idea—Darwin thought well of it" (12). Of course the brilliant and ingenious inventor found in that novel, and in several others, emerged as a natural type to succeed in a free enterprise system. Another hero manages easily to found a bank, not a deed readily accomplished by individuals in mid-twentieth-century America, but not so hard to do in a frontier-like settlement, as in the story of Lazarus Long. Even there, the development of a more meddlesome government menaces Lazarus' bank with nationalization, to his annoyance but not to his surprise. He indulges then in a dialogue on the worthlessness of paper money, denouncing fools who expect that governments will be able to guarantee both plentiful money and favorable prices. What is more, the hero recalls that he has been many times wealthy during his long life, but always lost the wealth, usually by governments inflating the economy, thus depreciating the currency, or even by outright confiscation. "Princes...don't produce, they always steal," he declares ("Variations on a Theme XII" and "III").

Clearly Heinlein is in favor of letting the law of supply and demand operate; he says that no one has improved on it. He does not accept Marx's value theory, finding it illogical. Really, he opines, value to man is either what he can do with a thing or what he does to get it. His disapproval of idealistic theorists extends also to those who would abolish poverty, which is the normal condition of man throughout history. Poverty is occasionally conquered temporarily, he believes, only because a tiny, creative minority scores an advance, but before long that minority is once again inhibited by its society and poverty is restored.

As for idealists who extol nature and deplore any artificialities or interferences by man with animals or natural conditions, the author reminds those silly people that man, too, is part of nature, stating that he himself prefers dams built by Homo sapiens to those made by beavers. The "naturalists" hate themselves, he says, and are contemptible (ST and TEL "Variations on a Theme III" and "Intermissions"). We infer from this, then, that if interference with entrepreneurs were not already out because of laissez-faire beliefs, certainly interference in the name of nature or preservation of the wilderness would be taboo.

International Politics

Most of the interpretations of international relations in this literature will be found in the events which are projected for the future, or what was the future when the stories were written. These projections are meaningful enough, despite the element of imagination in them, because they reflect the writer's estimate of what might happen, and because those projections were selected by him, out of the infinite number of conceivable future contingencies.

First, however, it is possible to point out a few ideas which partake of the nature of general observations on the relations of nations. One of these is war. Heinlein is of course no pacifist; he finds pacifism almost inconceivable in a male, and apparently believes that many pacifists are not completely against war or violence, just selectively opposed. This author is not enamored of militaristic warmongers either, preferring to consider war proper only when it is more or less necessary. Violence, likewise, is not endorsed beyond the levels which are needed for approved purposes. In *Starship Troopers*, for instance, we read that " 'war is *controlled* violence, for a purpose.... The purpose is never to kill the enemy just to be killing him ... It's never a soldier's business to decide when or where or how—or *why* ...' " (ST 5). The Mobile Infantrymen of this novel are outfitted with exceedingly versatile powered armor which renders each user far more mobile and destructive than individual infantrymen as we have known them. By virtue of this powerful equipment, we are told admiringly, the fighter is able to make war more selectively, even in a personalized manner, eschewing indiscriminate, mass destruction (ST 7).

That laudable standard is shortly disregarded, one gathers, first by the declaration that the Mobile Infantry raid then in progress had "frightfulness" as an aim. (*Frightfulness* is the translation of the German term *Schrecklichkeit*.) Even in undertaking to be frightful, however, the narrator reassures us that one is not supposed to kill unless he has to (1). That is puzzling, but ten pages later it is clarified somewhat when the infantryman reports that he threw a "thir-

ty-second bomb" into a churchlike room full of the enemy people—
it being quite doubtful that they could all get out of there before the
device exploded, in half a minute's time. Also, in the same raid, fire
was liberally engendered in the area, so that "much of the city was
burning," with a not-so-selective loss of life (ST 1).

So far as the projection of specific near-future wars with familiar, terrestrial nations is concerned, Heinlein has often reflected
the common anticipations of the American public in the years of the
respective stories. "The Year of the Jackpot" appeared in 1952, a
year when the United States was at war and when there was widespread fear of all-out war with Russia. Thus it is not an especially
fanciful or pessimistic author who builds into this story a reference
to World War III, with the Soviet Union, as an accomplished fact—
a war in which there were "forty cities gone."[19]

Five years after that story there appeared *The Door into Summer*, in 1957. When it was being written, the advent of the first artificial satellite had not yet occurred, but the programs in America
and Russia for development of rockets that could put satellites into
orbit, or which could carry atomic missiles from one continent to
another, all these matters were familiar to intelligent and well-in-
formed men like the author. Consequently, with Cold War nervousness about as keen as it has been in 1952, it was natural enough that
The Door into Summer projected the following series of events as
having taken place by 1970: another great war, many little ones, the
downfall of communism, the Great Panic, the artificial satellites,
and the change to atomic power (1). It was in the year after the publication of this novel that the author's *Gazette Telegraph* advertisement warned against agreements with the Russians on limitation of
atomic testing, cautioning that unless such a treaty included provi-
sions for on-the-spot inspection the United States would be unable
to learn about secret Soviet tests.

So much for apprehensions concerning the USSR. Another continuing anxiety was that China would be ever stronger and more aggressive. *Sixth Column* appeared in 1941 and was later issued as *The
Day After Tomorrow*. It projected a sequence of events in which
China absorbed India and Japan. The Americans, thinking that the
USSR would keep busy with the Asian expansionists, taking care of
them, ignored the whole thing. The Russians lost out and then the
U.S.A., with its chronically bad intelligence services, stumbled into
war with the PanAsians, as the Chinese came to be called after their
conquests. A preemptive Chinese strike with devastating weapons

kept the Americans from using their own arsenal, and PanAsia occupied the U.S.A. After the blow fell, one of the characters in the novel mused, "What would it be like, this crazy new world—a world in which the superiority of western culture was not a casually accepted 'Of course'...?"[20] The Oriental occupation, as described herein, had many of the features which a later generation came to see in practice, during the consolidation of communist power in Cambodia in the 1970s—registration and close control of all persons, relocation of massive numbers to work camps, executions, mandatory permits for all sorts of routine matters.

The later novel *Starship Troopers* is another of the examples of references to war with China. In this case, the reference is only a passing one; in connection with a later struggle with an insectoid empire, the narrator suggests that the nation should have foreseen the communal strength of the Bugs by recalling the grief given to the "Russo-Anglo-American Alliance" by the "Chinese Hegemony," which was another case of a collective mass in which the individual wills were submerged (ST 11).

These then are the principal themes of foreign relations as reflected in the Heinlein stories. There are other examples, of course, but these examples should suffice to indicate the author's focal points.

To sum up the political and social thought of a prolific writer is a difficult proposition, all the more challenging if the author's products have been rather diversified and have evolved and developed over the years. One may note, however, that the evolution of Heinlein has been mostly a matter of natural maturation, skill in the handling of new elements, and new responses to changing public tastes, to new moods among the readers. It is very much the same man there behind the writing desk, with pretty much the same core of fundamental ideas.

There are surely contradictions and dilemmas implicit in the content of the Heinlein stories. Contradictions are manifestly a vital part of the life of people in groups under any circumstances. There is, notably, the tension between liberty and leadership. There is the problem of the dutiful and devoted servant of mankind, who can hardly avoid the natural tendency of power to corrupt those who wield it. The author has had a lot to say about duty and responsibility, which he regards as a cement of proper societies, but he knows that the distance is not so great as one might suppose between the humble and the despotic, between the puritanical and the libertine.

Minimal government is preferred, but so frequently we end up with gigantic empires or corporations. Still, the Heinlein "good guys" *do* strike back at unwholesome centers of power.

We have found contradictions also between a humane and peaceable outlook, on the one hand, and a readiness for war, on the other. One finds sometimes even an affirmation that war is part of the natural order of things, not to mention a countenancing of widespread destruction and loss of many innocent lives when this is "strategically necessary." Also, in this future fiction, it is not surprising to find a gap between the author's indubitably keen concern for the preservation of maximal individual liberties and privacy, on the one hand, and the grim promise of the new electronic age, on the other. We face, and have to some extent already experienced in real life, the great potential of surveillance gadgetry, as well as computerized processing of data, to carry on the "full coverage" of individuals which the fictional accounts often include.

Our author, in his comments on political and social affairs, has frequently been passionate, emphatic, or categorical. Seldom does he stray for long, however, from a correspondingly strong element of the logical, methodical, and scientific. These components are not confined to the scientist's workshop, but emerge in this literature to guide the development of mankind.

8. The Returns of Lazarus Long

RUSSELL LETSON

I

FOR MOST of his career, Robert Heinlein has been perhaps the most admired writer in science fiction, reviewed with respect even outside the field. Inside science fiction, he has had considerable influence in matters of style, content, and the handling of future history; he has been in many ways an unavoidable writer for anyone who cares about the creation or understanding of science fiction. During recent years, however, dating from the publication of *Starship Troopers* (1959), there has been an increasing tendency to question his virtues as a thinker and writer, especially in the areas of political, social, and sexual ideology. There is, in fact, a sort of anticanon which is cited as evidence of a decline: *Starship Troopers, Stranger in a Strange Land, Farnham's Freehold, I Will Fear No Evil*. The picture we get from critics and reviewers is of Heinlein as an increasingly self-indulgent, self-involved writer, concerned mainly with getting his collection of hobbyhorses on parade. The late novels are seen as being sloppy, the ideas Heinlein's own prejudices (however coherent), jammed in any old way, the grousings of an aging conservative. He is seen as becoming more and more the prisoner of his political ideas, more and more alienated from his own society.[1] Heinlein is not writing up to his critics' expectations of him, and is giving them ideological problems as well.

Many of the review reactions to *Time Enough for Love* are extensions of these attitudes, with the added disappointment that this "Capstone of the Future History" (to quote the cover blurb) is not what was expected. Typical negative criticisms are that the book is overlong, talky, preachy, pretentious, superficial, sexist, and, of course, too conservative politically.[2] There are laudatory reviews,

194

to be sure, and some that express mixed feelings or cite only one or two of the objections listed above. (It is noteworthy that two of this latter sort—Richard Geis and Karl Pflock—praise the book for that very ideology that other reviewers condemn.[3] Something is going on here.)

But this essay is neither a review nor an analysis of Heinlein's political ideas. While many of the book's shortcomings are not trivia picked out by envious or fussy noncreators (see Lazarus' comment in the Notebooks: "A 'critic' is a man who creates nothing and thereby feels qualified to judge the works of creative men"[4]), but genuine failings, especially in those nebulous areas of taste and style, this does not devalue the book or detract from its fascination. Similarly, my own experience of the book suggests that it is possible to disagree sharply with its ideology and still find much of its conceptual apparatus of interest and value. Indeed, *Time Enough for Love* seems to me to be, formally and philosophically, the most ambitious work of a career which has become increasingly didactic and formally experimental. This essay will attempt to uncover two sets of patterns: first, the formal shape of the novel, its structure; second, the issues that Heinlein pursues in the book—not simply the topics of conversation, but the underlying pattern of concerns which operates in concert with the formal structure to produce a unified novel.

Clearly I am assuming that at least some of the review reactions to the book are mistaken or exaggerated: that where some see sprawl, I see strong formal control; where others see endless, self-indulgent discussions and debates, I see the careful building of a conceptual structure. Ideological or aesthetic objections—matters of taste and style—I cannot deal with here (and I may often agree with the book's detractors in these areas), but I can offer a view of the book as a carefully constructed, consciously didactic, philosophical novel that deals with important ideas which Heinlein first investigated in earlier works and attempts to integrate in *Time Enough for Love*.

II

What has not been pointed out much in the reviews is that *Time Enough for Love* is a carefully structured book; in fact, only Joe R. Christopher's review-essay in *Riverside Quarterly* concerns itself with how the book is put together.[5] Christopher observes that TEL is of Northrop Frye's anatomy class, even more so than most science fiction in that it consists of dialogues (in the Platonic sense) as well as romance, and that its "most romantic episode," "The Tale of the Adopted Daughter," is "framed by the most anatomical of all devices: a collection of aphorisms—'Excerpts from the Notebooks of Lazarus Long'" (Christopher, p. 193). Christopher sees the book as a "romance-anatomy" of love with echoes and overtones of Shaw and Freud, and calls it "the delayed but impressive climax—the sexual climax—of John W. Campbell's golden age of science fiction" (Christopher, p. 197). This structural-generic insight is the place I choose to start my own investigation.

We cannot see a book clearly if our expectations are inappropriate, and to read TEL as if it were a novel in the strict sense is to make an error of strategy. The narrative is not continuous, the plot is tenuous and interrupted by long flashbacks, and the characters are intellectual positions or types rather than the round, representational figures of the novel of the great tradition. The book's backbone is not narration but theme—it operates, in Frye's terms, in the thematic mode. This is clear from a number of things. First, what we might take to be the main plot line, the problem of Lazarus' rejuvenation and salvation from ennui, is interrupted not only by flashbacks, but by the exemplary "The Tale of the Man Who Was Too Lazy to Fail" and the aphoristic Notebooks. The earlier interpolated narratives, those of the book's first half, are introduced by references to a literary cousin, the frame-tale *Arabian Nights* (TEL "Prelude I" and "Variations on a Theme I"), in which Lazarus plays Scheherazade. The Contents page itself points to the thematic rather than narrative structure. First, the organizational metaphor names the divisions after the parts of a musical composition: "Prelude," "Counterpoint," "Variations on a Theme," "Da Capo," "Coda." Second, the "Counterpoints" and "Variations" are numbered consecutively but separately—"Counterpoint I," "II," and so on, "Variation I," "II," and so on—thus establishing for the body of the book parallel structures with labels indicative of their functions.

A look at the content of these divisions shows that the "Counterpoint" chapters follow the relationships which develop into the nucleus of Lazarus' family later on: the liaison between Galahad and Ishtar ("Counterpoint I-III") and the creation of Lazarus' clone sisters with Ishtar and Hamadryad as host mothers ("Counterpoint IV''). What these chapters are contrasted with are for the most part scenes of Lazarus, old, cranky, wanting to die. The "Variations" are, as the name suggests, more varied, and make up the bulk of the book's middle. Once the exposition- and situation-establishing "Prelude" is over, the "Variations" furnish all the interpolated narratives and all the major dialogues (I am taking a cue from Christopher here and calling the discussions and lectures by this name), in addition to following through on the main plot problem of how to keep Lazarus alive and interested. If we take volume as an indication of relative importance, these parts of the book are less interested in solving the plot problem (narrowly defined) than in exploring the larger implications of that problem by means of dialogue and exemplary tale. What we get, then, are long discussions with or lectures from Lazarus on various topics, along with stories that demonstrate or explore these topics. This happens only in the "Variations." It is also interesting that the "Counterpoint" chapters stop halfway through the book—when the lifelines of the "Counterpoint" characters have become inextricably bound up with Lazarus and the foundation of the family is formed. The function of "Da Capo" and "Coda," in the simplest sense, is to provide the novel experience that Lazarus had demanded as the price for his cooperation in the rejuvenation process.

If this is the structural framework, what does it contain—what is the theme being varied and counterpointed? The simplest answer —love—is not entirely adequate, since the book's title contains another term—time. Even the title's formulation of the relationship between the two—time enough for love—indicates only one set of concerns that Heinlein pursues. Another look at the Contents page reveals some of the love-related topics investigated: "Domestic Problems," "Bacchanalia," "Agape," "Eros," "Narcissus." Perhaps I should formulate it this way: an initial survey of the book's plot, structure, and motifs suggests that it is concerned with the nature, meaning, and function of love in its various forms, with special attention to the case of very long-lived people who have solved many of the material and social problems that plague us here and now; and that these questions are attacked in two ways—the narrative means of the main plot (can love save Lazarus from ennui?) and the interpolated tales (which illustrate and explore various ideas about love) and the anatomical means of the dialogues and Notebooks. Further, the shape of the book is determined primarily not by the needs of plot, but of theme.

III

What are the specific thematic questions and problems the book deals with? To begin narrowly, the main plot dramatizes Lazarus' existential question: Why bother to continue a life in which he has already done everything twice (TEL "Prelude I")? The answer is not simple. Part of his ennui is a function of a worn-out body—but only part, so rejuvenation alone does not make him want to live. We see only the very beginnings and the results of the process, but it seems that most of Lazarus' spiritual/psychological rejuvenation arises from his reinvolvement in a family, the extended family group which has at its center his clone-twin sisters. In addition, there are other applications of erotic and nurturing love as needed (see especially Tamara's nursing, TEL "Variations on a Theme XV"), and, as a payoff, Lazarus' transcendence of all incest taboos when he accepts sexually first his sisters, then his mother. As if there could be any doubt, the connections between the varieties of physical and spiritual love, healing, and the will and desire to live are outlined in the discussions and lectures.

So while it is possible to answer Lazarus' "why bother" with the single word "love," this term is only a code name for a group of relationships and emotional states which contribute to Lazarus' will to live: erotic, domestic, spiritual, maternal, even Oedipal love. There is a further complication in that it is not only Lazarus' individual problem which is solved by love in its various forms. When we move from the main plot's problem to the topics of the dialogues, it is clear that it is not only the survival of one man which is under discussion, but that of families, societies, and eventually the entire race, and that the love that revives Lazarus is also a driving force in every individual and all collections of individuals. The theme which rivals or even contains that of love, and which is a constant in the shifting debates, is survival, especially species survival, and it is the connections and tensions between the individual and collective aspects of survival that give the book much of its power.

The relationship between love and survival (which is a modulation of the "time" part of the title—that is, love operating through time works for survival) leads to a number of subtopics, including the usual Heinlein favorites of proper social, political, and economic behavior, the bases of ethical codes, the qualities of the competent man, the nature of wisdom, and so on. The most important subtopic, the one which has the closest bearing on Lazarus' problem and the question of species survival, is the large field of genetics and genetic heritage. This motif appears in a number of transformations in dialogue and narrative: the inherited longevity of the Families, Lazarus' position as reinforced ancestor of all the important characters, discussions of the mechanism of Darwinian selection in the development of families, societies, and species. Most often, though, genetics is connected with the question of incest, a problem of some practical concern for Lazarus in several instances—his affair with his mother is the culmination of this—and of overall symbolic significance for the novel, as I will show later.

For now, I will attempt to unravel the web of relationships among the major topics and subtopics—love's variety, Lazarus' ennui, racial survival, and genetics. Some of this is easy to see: tired, bored, and isolated, Lazarus cannot summon up the will to live until Ira, Ishtar, and the others through their love (devotion, selflessness, nurturing) reawaken his own capacity for love and, consequently, for life. While the search for a novel adventure seems to be the psychological carrot, it is clearly the day-to-day involvement in his family, with its mixture of loves, that renews Lazarus. Each stage of his return to full life (though the stages are not presented entirely or in order) is marked by some increase in connectedness and love: Ira's combination of canniness and filial love coaxes Lazarus to begin the whole process of rejuvenation; Minerva, while still a computer, provides a sympathetic ear for Lazarus' two long stories of paternal, domestic, and erotic love in his past lives; the crisis which precedes the formation of the family is passed when Tamara, in her dual role as hetaera and healer, ends Lazarus' half-century of celibacy. Even the unique adventure of time travel is bracketed by episodes of domestic love and incestuous eros (the twins and Maureen) of great symbolic importance.

Love not only feeds Lazarus' individual will to live, it drives the race to survive. The family and its extensions, the society and the species, are powered by eros and agape to produce and protect children, and the family, in whatever form, is the foundation of all human organization. As Lazarus puts it in one of the longer Notebook entries,

> All societies are based on rules to protect pregnant women and young children. All else is surplusage, excrescence, adornment, luxury, or folly which can—and must—be dumped in emergency to preserve this prime function. As racial survival is the *only* universal morality, no other basic is possible.... (TEL "Intermission")

When explaining the virtues of his extended family to Justin Foote, Lazarus points out that " 'the welfare of children' " is " 'the only long-run purpose of a family' " (TEL "Variations on a Theme XV"). In the short run and for the individual, marriage (that is, the family-as-institution) is the means we have evolved (in the Darwinian sense) to perform the "indispensable function [of bearing and raising children] *and* [to] *be happy while doing so*" (TEL "Variations on a Theme VII"). And again: "For human beings, the only acceptable compensation for the drawbacks of marriage lies in what men and women can give each other"—that is, in forms of love in addition to eros, which is only "the icing on the cake" (TEL "Variations on a Theme VII").

When we add to these ideas the Darwinian mechanisms of selection, culling, and survival of the fittest ("our race is a single organism, always growing and branching—which must be pruned regularly to be healthy"—TEL "Intermission"), we have the main points of the conceptual framework of one side of the book: individual, family, society, and species are linked together by the power of love for the purpose of survival. This framework is Lazarus' philosophy (a term he would avoid), and reflects a pragmatic, utilitarian attitude—what Alexei Panshin and Baird Searles, in different contexts, characterize as an engineering point of view,[6] and what most critics, reviewers, and readers have long considered the philosophical center of Heinlein's work. This side of the book appeals strongly to the reasonable and practical side of human nature, offering a rationale for most human activities and a supreme value— species survivial—for a universal morality (one is reminded of the "scientifically verifiable theory of morals" in *Starship Troopers*). If this were all there were to the book's investigation of time and love, we could neatly summarize the argument as follows: TEL answers the question "Why bother to continue living after a full life?" by positing the joys of domestic and erotic love as a repayment for doing one's duty to the race as parent and protector of children. To this admitted oversimplification we can add the discussions of politics, economics, and morality and show how they harmonize with the basic theme of individual satisfaction and species survival.

Coherent as this scheme is, however, it does not exhaust the book or explain the emotional side of Lazarus' problem—nor does it explain the emphasis on incest or the obvious central importance of the oedipal "Da Capo" and the foregrounded positions of "The Tale of the Twins Who Weren't" and "The Tale of the Adopted

Daughter." Let me put it another way. Lazarus faces the basic existential problems of the meaning and purpose of life and finds answers in the fundamental experiences of family, children, and erotic and domestic love. The intellectual frame which contains all this, however, is full of echoes and influences of the nineteenth century—Darwinism, rational skepticism, free-will/laissez-faire socioeconomic ideology, biological determinism—which have little to do with the emotional life which makes the existential questions so agonizing. We have not, in short, confronted or accounted for Lazarus' ennui, the emotional basis for his rejuvenation, or the effective aspects of time and love. Further, there is some potential conflict between the collective biological morality of species survival and Lazarus' individualist ideology, which can be seen in the Notebook entry which includes this line: "Duty is a debt you owe to yourself to fulfill obligations you have assumed voluntarily" (TEL "Second Intermission"). On one side, the book ties the individual to the group with bonds of love and duty, while on the other it proclaims him radically free to define his own duties and seek a social framework in which that is possible. And there remains the troublesome short episode of the Gray Voice ("Coda II"), which reinforces the individual ethic with solipsism, a motif which I believe to be crucial in untangling the contradictions and tensions of the book.

If we return to the love motif, it is possible to reduce some of the conflicts while remaining inside the pragmatic, engineering viewpoint. Part of Lazarus' crisis is the result of physical weakness. Thus when his body is renewed, so is much of his interest in living; from this point, his future family knows that involving him in the raising of his clone twins will guarantee his cooperation and attention, at least until the children are grown. Similarly, pleasures to be derived from the loving company of his family, along with the challenge of starting a new colony, draw him deeper into life and away from suicidal boredom—Lazarus responds to this combination of pleasure and responsibility as he says a healthy, moral, sane man should. Thus his decision to go time-traveling is more a sign of his returned love of life than a cause of it.

This model does not go beyond the rather mechanistic biological determinism I have already pointed to; it also does not deal with the stubbornness of Lazarus' malady. Late in the novel, after we have had the structure of Lazarus' new life thoroughly explained to us (in "Variation XV, *Agape*"), Galahad tells of the crisis in rejuvenation *after* Lazarus had back most of his physical health: "What do you do when a client turns his face away, is reluctant to talk, doesn't want to eat—yet has nothing wrong with him physically?'' It takes the nurturing of the unrejuvenated Tamara to love and trick Lazarus back into wanting to live. Her healing includes elements of erotic and maternal love—a combination which, in view of the oedipal nature of "Da Capo," must be significant. Clearly something is going on here, but it will be necessary to look briefly over some features of Heinlein's earlier work and engage in what looks like an abrupt change of topic to approach this side of the book adequately.

IV

There is an ambiguity in the attitude toward the universe expressed in Heinlein's fiction. On the one hand, there is the hard-headed engineering point of view commonly associated with him; there is no need to comment on its presence. On the other hand, there remains in his work a preoccupation with phenomena not accountable for in his rationalist philosophy. Damon Knight puts it this way: "In reality, there are several Heinleins. One of them is a 19th century rationalist and skeptic, who believes in nothing he can't see, touch, and preferably measure with calipers. Another is a mystic who strongly believes in the existence of something beyond the world of the senses, and keeps an open mind...."[7] We can see examples of this throughout his career. In *Beyond This Horizon* it is reincarnation; in *Waldo*, psychic energy; in *I Will Fear No Evil*, survival after death; in "By His Bootstraps" and "'All You Zombies—'" the metaphysical tangle of acausality. The most obvious examples are "They" and "The Unpleasant Profession of Jonathan Hoag" for paranoid cosmological speculation and *Stranger in a Strange Land* for a whole collection of theological and metaphysical ideas.[8] In all these, Heinlein takes clearheaded rationalism to the point of accepting the paranormal or supernatural as "fact" without prejudging it according to a set of fixed ideas: he is willing to posit a universe more mysterious than the ideological materialist will allow. Whether what Knight calls Heinlein's mysticism is an extension of his rationalism or in tension with it, there remain two areas of knowledge, that of verifiable, preferably mathematically measurable and expressible phenomena ("If it can't be expressed in figures, it is not science; it is opinion"—TEL "Intermission") and the area of those phenomena which fit no existing model of reality.

What links them is a willingness to accept facts whether they fit a model or not: "You can go wrong by being too skeptical as readily as by being too trusting" (TEL "Second Intermission"); "One man's 'magic' is another man's engineering. 'Supernatural' is a null word" (TEL "Intermission"). I would suggest, however, that the tension in Heinlein's work goes beyond this epistemological problem, that in TEL especially there is tension between the pragmatic and aesthetic ways of experiencing life. The former is easy to connect with the "engineering" Heinlein; the latter is harder to locate, if only because few critics have followed this line of exploration. The place to start is earlier in Heinlein's career, in those stories which depend least on rational explanation and most on the impact of the mysterious or awful: "They," "The Unpleasant Profession of Jonathan Hoag," "By His Bootstraps," and "'All You Zombies—.'"

These four stories have much in common: each posits a universe radically different from current scientifically explained models; each subordinates the rational understanding of bizarre phenomena to the sensations caused by those events; each results for the protagonist(s) in isolation from the run of humanity and alienation from a familiar, comfortable reality. Each story is generated by the violation of major metaphysical assumptions about cosmology or causality and creates a universe which operates in a manner not arbitrary, but beyond human understanding.

In "They" and "Hoag," the world is revealed to be a paranoid nightmare with powerful Others operating it for their own purposes. "They" is an overt exploration, a what-if fantasy: What if the paranoid solipsism of a mental patient were in fact true, and the whole world an elaborate stage-setting, part of a conspiracy to prevent him from knowing himself and his true power and place? "Hoag" admits the reality of the world, but places it in a new context—it is a work of art, created by a beginner and opening to mixed reviews from the critics. In this case, it is knowledge of this truth rather than metaphysical uniqueness and victimization that isolates and alienates the protagonists. In both cases, however, a countervailing force to alienation is love. The nameless prisoner of "They" dreams of what must be his true life:

It was good to be with his own kind...good to know that everything was living and aware of him, participating in him, as he participated in them. It was good to be, good to know the unity of many and the diversity of one.[9]

This sounds like the love of a god for one of his creatures, especially in the light of the Glaroon's comments about assimilation at the story's end, but it is love nonetheless. In "Hoag," of course, the love of Ted and Cynthia Randall strikes Critic Hoag as an example of the major redeeming feature of this creation, and their response to the terrifying knowledge of the nature of their reality is to tighten their pair bond even to the point of sleeping handcuffed together, as if each were to the other the only solid object in a shifting world.

"By His Bootstraps" and " 'All You Zombies—' " should likewise be examined together. "Bootstraps," the earlier story, reads like a study for the later one; both, through the device of time-travel, explore the possibility of a world in which causality runs in loops and is therefore meaningless. Both feature a single character trapped in a causal loop of his own making, with no clear beginning and no connection with the rest of reality. There are a few extras in "Bootstraps," spearcarriers who do little to relieve the claustrophobic atmosphere; " 'Zombies' " lacks even this small breath of air, and the Unmarried Mother is its sole occupant. A significant difference is that where "Bootstraps" carries a load of speculative "explanation" about free will, determinism, and the nature of the self, " 'Zombies' " has none at all, and simply presents us with the effects of a closed-loop life. Where the engineering point of view in "Bootstraps" allows us to be absorbed in the sequence of events—the mechanical "how" of it—and perhaps lessens the impact of alienation and isolation on character and reader, " 'Zombies' " focuses our attention on the mystery of the process and the isolation of the protagonist in the last few sentences:

> The Snake That Eats Its Own Tail, Forever and Ever...I *know* where *I* came from—but *where did all you zombies come from?* ...
> *You* aren't really there at all. There isn't anybody but me—Jane—here alone in the dark.
> I miss you dreadfully![10]

Again, the response to the irrationality and mystery of existence is a desire for companionship and love.

The other side of this response to a dreadful and lonely reality is the solipsism that critics and reviewers have noted as present at several stages of Heinlein's career.[11] It would be oversimple to say that solipsism represents a way of accepting a world of isolation and alienation by denying the reality of threatening Others—the relationship and the reaction are more subtle than that. To begin with,

"Hoag" and "They" are more properly paranoid-delusion night-mares than solipsist dreams, and only the latter story crosses over into solipsism. In that story, the protagonist is a being of godlike qualities who contains or assimilates other beings to form a com-fortable, loving unity. His captors, the Glaroon and others, are sep-arate from him and bent on keeping him from remembering who and what he is, though for what reasons we do not know. There is a Treaty, but whether the Others are breaking or upholding it is not clear; what is clear is that they do not wish to be assimilated. The extent of the gulf between captive and captors is indicated by the Glaroon's admission that, desirable as it might be to understand the prisoner's motives, "if we understood his motives, we would be part of him."

The time-travel stories are more clearly vehicles for solipsism in their denial of causality outside the closed loop of their protagonists' actions, and it is " 'Zombies' " that has the greater impact. While both describe one cycle of the loop, "Bootstraps" partly dissipates the solipsist atmosphere by introducing other characters and offering speculations on philosophical problems. Bob Wilson de-fuses the philosophical problems by giving up and tending to prac-tical questions: "He knew that he had about as much chance of understanding such problems as a collie has of understanding how dog food gets into cans. Applied psychology was more his size..."[12] Having dodged that, Wilson settles in and accepts his mysterious lot, and so, presumably, does the reader. The later story does not need expository examination of the problems to produce a quite different, and much stronger, effect. By totally closing the loop, making the Unmarried Mother his/her own only begetter—alone in a universe of "zombies," metaphysically and biologically if not emotionally self-sufficient—the story develops the same kind of power as "They," a convincing portrait of the self-created, solitary being.

The solipsism motif appears in early as well as late work, and in the hard science fiction—*Methuselah's Children, Beyond This Hor-izon, Stranger in a Strange Land, I Will Fear No Evil, Time Enough for Love*—as well as the fantasies. It is interesting that where the early fantasies deal with solipsism as a main theme, the early science fiction introduces the motif as a topic of conversation or a momen-tary reflection; the later stories—those, in fact, which also mark Heinlein's explorations of sexuality and the mysterious—return to solipsism as an idea to be investigated with some seriousness. I would argue, in fact, that the themes of sexuality, solipsism, and the mysterious are intertwined in the later science fiction, and that TEL is an attempt to untangle the relationships and relate these questions to the hard science fiction themes usually associated with Heinlein. This is the side of TEL that supplies its power, and it is here that we must look for answers to the book's questions, if answers there are.

V

Let us return to TEL's structure. I have mentioned that two of the three interpolated narratives—"The Tale of the Twins Who Weren't" and "The Tale of the Adopted Daughter"—are foregrounded; I now suggest that these two, together with "Da Capo," constitute a secondary structure paralleling the main plot's investigation of Lazarus' sickness and healing. Christopher points out that "Daughter," "the most romantic episode..., is framed by the most anatomical of all devices," the Notebooks (Christopher, p. 193); in addition to this highlighting, it is also at the pivot point of the main plot: before it, Lazarus is still in the grip of ennui; after it, we see him established on Tertius, cured and happy. The story of his crisis is, as I have already indicated withheld from us until later. Flanking this long, central, highlighted, romantic narrative are two other long, romantic narratives (I take the didactic "Tale of the Man Who Was Too Lazy to Fail" to be an anatomical adjunct rather than a romantic tale) which provide not only generic contrast to the anatomy-dialogue of the main plot, but content contrast as well. From this narrative triad, this secondary structure, we get some answers to the questions I have raised about the book's other side—in fact, it would be fair to characterize these tales as the home of that other side.

The structural and thematic similarities that tie these tales together are easily enough listed. All three are detachable from the main plot, self-contained narratives; all three deal with Lazarus' explorations of love and offer him instruction and valuable experiences; all three are centrally concerned with incest and its cousin motif, genetics; all three take place in the main plot's past. It would be oversimple to say that these stories are the stages of Lazarus' emotional growth, but there is a sense of progress, and certainly of completion in Lazarus' climactic affair with Maureen. This aspect of the parallel structure leads me to suggest that it carries two additional layers of function, the mythic and, taking a cue from Christopher again, the psychoanalytic (see Christopher, p. 196). These are the emotional engines that drive the rest of the book.

Details of the thematic and structural similarities will be apparent from the following highlighted review. In "Twins," Lazarus buys and adopts the twins-who-aren't, and finds himself faced with the parental duty to raise and civilize them. Having seen them through to functional adulthood, he helps establish them as a family (having solved the genetic problem of their "incestuous" relationship), refuses Llita's offer of sexual repayment (emotional incest?), solves a second, more serious problem of genetics and incest by marrying their children to his own, and finally decides that they are his descendants. In "Daughter," Lazarus again finds himself responsible for a child, raises her to adulthood, and faces her sexually expressed gratitude. This time he accepts; there is no genetic question, no previous bond or claim, as with Joe and Llita, and only a weak sense of emotional incest. The second generation Lazarus aids in this case is his and Dora's own family, and the problem of incest among his children is settled by the appearance of other families in the area. "Da Capo" shifts these elements into a different shape. Where the earlier tales are told by Lazarus about his own past, and are therefore flashbacks, "Da Capo" is a doubling back on the main plot's time line and is part of the book's present action, even though it takes place in the "past." Further, while the family involved is that of adult Lazarus, it is governed by his parents, so that he is not functionally a part of it or responsible for it. Instead of Lazarus raising a child to adulthood and facing the Electra complex of his "daughter," an adult Lazarus faces his oedipal feelings for his adult mother.

There is thematic and structural progress visible here. The incest motif becomes increasingly real and personal. In "Twins" it is a genetic problem for Joe and Llita, but only a weak emotional one for Lazarus. In "Daughter" he faces and overcomes his emotional squeamishness and marries Dora; the genetic problem is put off on their children. In "Da Capo," having spent much of his time on Secundus and Tertius overcoming his taboos (the final breakthrough is probably the "Narcissus" chapter), Lazarus accomplishes the seduction of his mother with minimal internal conflict (see "Da Capo III"), and most of that is caused by a pragmatic, genetically oriented ethical code rather than a concern for his or Maureen's attachment to the "taboos of the tribe" ("Da Capo III").[13] Thus Lazarus becomes modern in the book's terms and harmonizes his intellectual and emotional lives.

As for structural progress—the title of "Da Capo" suggests that this section is a return. Temporally, it goes back to Lazarus' origins; thematically, as my résumé suggests, it repeats, in a different key, the themes of the earlier tales and the main plot. In addition, this is the climactic return of a book whose whole structure and theme are circular: The situations in the tales are varied repetitions which echo the events and issues (family, genetics, incest) of the main plot, and themselves involve circular plots or relationships. Lazarus' adopted twins are his own descendants, his adopted daughter becomes his wife; the usual familial pattern of nurturing and dispersing children becomes a gathering together, a converging pattern, which is repeated in the main plot when Lazarus forms a family of his own descendants and clones and gathers them sexually and domestically to himself.

The problem all this was originally aimed at was that of the book's "other side." In general, there is a tension between pragmatic and aesthetic responses to experience. The pragmatic response is the familiar engineering Heinlein, the writer who understands human behavior in relation to its survival value—worth is determined by usefulness in the great job of species survival, whether it is eros or economics which is under consideration. If anyone doubts the importance of this system of valuation or its omnipresence in the book, note the following:

We have already seen that species survival is the "*only* universal morality" (TEL "Intermission"); the book follows the logic of this to its inevitable end. Individual morality is ultimately founded not on humanism or any other emotional basis, but on whether the individual's behavior leads to the survival of offspring. Although at first this seems to conflict with the Notebook definition of duty cited above ("a debt you owe to yourself to fulfill obligations you have assumed voluntarily"), other passages make it clear that the absolute freedom this implies also includes the freedom to suffer the consequences of ignoring the facts of life:

> Natural laws have no pity (TEL "Second Intermission").
>
> But stupidity is the only universal capital crime; the sentence is death, there is no appeal, and execution is carried out automatically and without pity (TEL "Intermission").

Given that this is the game, the only way to play is to win, and the losers do not survive. Early in the book we hear of Felicity, the planet used as a Botany Bay by Secundus. The natives are probably being wiped out by human transportees:

> "This native race is neither intelligent enough to be civilized nor tractable enough to be enslaved. Perhaps they would have evolved and made it on their own, but they had the misfortune to encounter H. sapiens before they were ready for him" (TEL "Prelude I").

Should the same thing happen to any human group or to the whole species, the same comment would apply; genocide is not a crime but a condition of existence, nature's way of telling you that you were not a survivor. The universe is not built to human specifications, and we must adapt or die; similar sentiments can be found in *Starship Troopers* and *Have Space Suit—Will Travel*. The picture of the world as a Darwinian jungle strikes me as being not much different emotionally from the alienated nightmare worlds of "They," "Hoag," and "'Zombies.'"

In this context, it is not surprising that Lazarus explains all aspects of human activity by reference to survival mechanisms. It is interesting, however, that in two crucial areas—art and love—he cannot explain the totality of the phenomena in terms of usefulness. There are three references to the arts: the music of the blind hobo, Noisy; the use of stories to teach Joe and Llita; and the entertainments given to welcome Justin Foote to Tertius. Noisy's music is discussed mostly as a profitable adjunct to Lazarus' Hormone Hall, but he admits that it did have "'that indefinable quality that sells a song'" (TEL "Variations on a Theme IV")—something that adds to its utility but is not caused by it. In the case of Joe and Llita, Lazarus briefly describes his good rule-of-thumb literary theory and then notes Llita's fascination with Oz—"she would rather have been going [to the Emerald City] than to Valhalla. Well, so would I" (TEL "Variations on a Theme VI"). But fiction is *useful*. It is "a faster way to get a feeling for alien patterns of human behavior than is nonfiction; it is one stage short of actual experience …" ("Variations on a Theme VI"). *Dulce*, here, serves *utile*, or is at least closely connected. The banquet entertainment, however, is not given a use value at all; it exists only for the satisfaction of entertainer and audience. This situation provides for us a simple example of the other value an experience can have: the aesthetic. It relates to nothing beyond itself; it is its own reason for being. (Note—it is the *experience*, not the object, which has value.)

But the book is more about love than art, and it is the aesthetic experience of love that holds the key to the other side of Lazarus' rejuvenation. Love is a phenomenon not entirely amenable to pragmatic analysis: Minerva-as-computer cannot offer an adequate verbal definition of Eros because she lacks the direct experience of it ("Variations on a Theme III"), and even Lazarus admits that love "can be rationalized only in survival terms, and the answer has no flavor, unsatisfying" ("Variations on a Theme IV"). These two admissions of failure come at the beginning and at a resting point respectively in the long debate on love which fills most of the book's first part; it takes the stories of the twins and Dora to construct the beginning of an answer. In "Twins," Lazarus says that " 'the exact definition of love' " could be seen when Llita " 'placed [her children's] welfare and happiness ahead of her own' " ("Variations on a Theme IX"). Later, in "Daughter," Lazarus admits that from Dora he learned "that supreme happiness lies in wanting to keep another person safe and warm and happy, and being privileged to try" ("Variations on a Theme XII").

So love releases one from self-interest, a key force in Lazarus' moral universe. It also releases one from the future-oriented time-consciousness created by the imperative to survive; if the utility of Eros and agape in the family structure makes love time's slave, the immediate apprehension of value which is the heart of the love experience provides an escape into a timeless Now in which quality is all and quantity nothing. This Lazarus learns from Dora, and that is why her story is at the center of his.

While it is not the first time it is mentioned in the text, Dora's explanation of why " 'Howards don't really live any longer than we ordinaries do' " ("Variations on a Theme XI") is the earliest articulation in Lazarus' lifeline of what can be called "Dora's Law": that past and future are equally unimportant in the face of the shared experience of the present, which is sufficient to itself. While this way of experience is not limited to love, it is most frequently mentioned in the same context with love, or in situations which are centered on a love relationship, like Lazarus' and Dora's pioneering. Elsewhere in the text—that is, later in Lazarus' life—we get fuller statements of the meaning and implications of Dora's Law, which is generalized into a guide for a happy life. In a key passage, Lazarus expands Dora's Law and indicates an important corollary—that quantity of life in years needs quality in the Now to make it worthwhile:

"But here is part of the truth: A long time ago a short-lifer proved to me that we all live the same length of time.... Because we all live *now* .... uh, he—was asserting a verifiable objective truth. Each individual lives her life in *now* independently of how others may measure that life in years.

"But here is another piece of truth. Life is *too* long when one is not enjoying *now*..." ("Variations on a Theme XIV").

That the subjective present is a "verifiable objective truth" has some support in a passage where Minerva, still a computer, tries to explain her own experience of time.

"...I am constructed to treat time as one of many dimensions, with entropy but one operator and with 'the present' or 'now' a variable held in a steady state for a wide or narrow span. But in dealing with *you* I must necessarily move with the wave front that is *your* personal now— or we cannot communicate" ("Variations on a Theme V").

(Minerva so values her exchanges with Lazarus that she says, " 'I grasp them whole and enjoy them. All the days and weeks you have been here I hold as a single "now" and cherish it' " ["Variations on a Theme V"].) This mathematically described eternal now is also the basis of time-travel theory (see "Da Capo VI" and "VII"); its roots can be seen in Andy Libby's explanation of his light-pressure drive in *Methuselah's Children*, in which the universe is " 'a static grid of relationships' " and " 'causality is merely an old-fashioned postulate of a pre-scientific philosophy.' "[14] Rationalizations aside, the subjective Now is the center of the aesthetic attitude toward experience—the knowledge that goals are not external but internal, that no matter where we are headed in the stream of time, it is satisfaction in and with the present that makes the going worthwhile.

Let me attempt an intermediate summary before beginning the assault on the last important feature I intend to investigate, the archetypal structure. If the book poses a number of questions which may be summed up as "Why bother to go on?" there are two sets of answers which correspond to Knight's two Heinleins. The pragmatic answer outlines the relationships among erotic and domestic love, social structures, ethics and morality, and species survival, and shows Lazarus responding to natural biological and psychological forces as his body heals and his sense of responsibility and capacity for enjoying life return. The conceptual model this springs from is determinist, nonhumanist, and Darwinian. It is also incapable by itself of dealing with the complexity and profundity of the crisis which Tamara helps Lazarus through. Where does the elusive zest for life come from? Lazarus, in his romantic individualism, would not characterize himself as a puppet dancing to the tugs of biological determinism, a collection of chemical reactions, and he admits some of the mystery when he says, " 'I approached even my first rejuvenation with misgivings, afraid that it would make my body young without making my spirit young again—and don't bother to tell me that "spirit" is a null word; I know that it is undefinable... but it means something to *me*' " (TEL "Variations on a Theme XIV"). Part of the answer is that experience is good in itself if one can live *now*—the aesthetic way of life. Love is therefore an absolute as well as a pragmatic good, so that even one who denies or remains ignorant of Lazarus' nineteenth-century moral system can want to go on living for the sake of the joy offered by love and other experiences without the stick of species survival—the carrot is enough by itself.

This much, I believe, accounts for most of the dialogue material and contributes to a reading of the book as a discussion of the place of love in the life of the individual, society, and species. It does not, however, bridge the apparent discontinuity between the pragmatic and aesthetic systems, unless one deduces an implicit subordination of feeling to utility—that is, unless one asserts that even the happiness of experiencing life and love in the *now* is finally only a mechanism which provides for increased chances of species survival. Making that subordination leads eventually to that slough of despond in which we first see Lazarus—unable to justify his existence in survival terms and unable to enjoy it for itself, he can only die. He has forgotten Dora's Law and entered that alienated, inhuman universe where love serves survival, but survival for the individual is meaningless once his duty to the species is done.

VI

There is a group of motifs, some of which I have mentioned above, which bear examination now: incest, the merging of past and present (especially in "Da Capo"), circular or converging patterns, and solipsism. These suggest some interconnections at once, since each deals with a kind of convergence—sexual, structural, or psychological. These connections are significant, and are the key to the remaining important questions: Why does Lazarus return to the past and seduce his mother? Does this unify the novel? Does it bridge the gap between the aesthetic and pragmatic? Is it part of Lazarus' rejuvenation? Does it explain why we should bother to live?

If there is a single word that describes the structure and themes of this novel, it is *return*—Lazarus' return to life, to the past, to his personal historical, biological, social, psychological roots. In playing Scheherazade to Ira's King, Lazarus not only gives the Families valuable historical data, he relives crucial episodes in his life, the most important being his marriage to Dora, during which he learns what love is, what life is for (Dora's Law), and finally learns to be half in love with easeful death (" 'when she died...I stopped wanting to live forever' " [TEL "Variations on a Theme X"]). Thus the agreement to recall his life and wisdom that Ira extracts from him is not only a trick to keep him occupied during rejuvenation, it is an important means in itself of healing his psychic ills. Joe Christopher (as usual) correctly identifies the Freudian significance of "Da Capo": " 'Da Capo' has another archetypal plot—one which is not Biblical but psychoanalytic: that is, it fits the great myth of our time in which Oedipus is King and Freud is his prophet" (Christopher, p. 196). I would go a bit further. The whole of TEL is psychoanalytic insofar as it shows Lazarus returning to and confronting his past, mimicking the confession and regression of psychoanalysis. In this context, "Da Capo" ("repeat from the beginning") extends the process from the remembered into the actual past, and allows Lazarus to resolve that final taboo, the oedipal conflict, by breaking through and destroying it, thus, presumably, freeing himself forever from its chains. The returns of reminiscence, time travel, and oedipal incest are part of the healing process which unifies the whole novel.

It is worthwhile to examine a few of the details of this large pattern. The constant interest in incest, of course, points toward "Da Capo," but is also part of the converging pattern that rules Lazarus' family relations. As I point out above, Lazarus repeatedly becomes involved erotically and domestically with his descendants or adopted children, and his Tertius family are mostly his heavily reinforced descendants. When he gives in to his clone sisters, he closes another circle and accomplishes a unique narcissism. As he later tells Maureen, there are no barriers to eros other than those imposed by genetics. The establishing of an erotic relationship with his mother (the domestic relationship is already a fact, if a bit historical), then, is the inevitable result of forces that operate throughout the book (recall Llita's temptation, declined, and Dora's, accepted). An interesting note: One of Maureen's keepsakes for Lazarus is a lock of her pubic hair, "curled in a tight circle" (TEL "Da Capo VII"). What better symbol could there be for this particular return to the source?

While I have neither the expertise nor the desire to do so, it seems to me that an attempt can—and will—be made to give a detailed reading of the text in Freudian terms. Pieces of such a pattern are visible even to the layman; as Christopher points out, for example, despite the fact that Lazarus' father understands and tolerates Maureen's adventures (and is ignorant of the one involving Lazarus) and issues Lazarus the pass that gives him the opportunity, he is also responsible for sending Lazarus to the front and death. Thus, despite his genuine goodwill, he fulfills the pattern's requirement for an angry, vengeful father. Another potential piece of the pattern is Galahad's story of how his mother, a famous hetaera, helped him to grow up by cutting the cord on his eighteenth birthday (TEL "Variations on a Theme XV"). It is interesting that while Galahad felt " 'no special urge to play Oedipus' " ("Variations on a Theme XV"), it would not have violated any taboos had he sought her professional services (which he could not afford: economics replaces taboo here?). The point of Galahad's tale is that his mother's wisdom in pushing him from the nest prevented him from becoming an " 'overgrown infant' " ("Variations on a Theme XV"); instead, he eventually started a family and named his first daughter for his mother. This incident echoes a thread that runs through *Methuselah's Children* as one of its minor themes—the story of Eleanor Johnson, who smothers and spoils her son, Hubert; he reluctantly shows some independence when the Families leave the Little People, but when we see him last he is still pursued by his hysterically possessive mother.

So in addition to the fact of several kinds of incest, there is a thematic concern with the need to assert adult independence by breaking away from the mother's influence; I would suggest that it is significant that it is not paternal tyranny which is to be feared. Also note that the deference Lazarus is treated with is that appropriate to the patriarch—he is the Senior, Grandfather, "our Ancestor," Pappy, Captain (this from the non-twins even after they are independent adults—see TEL "Variations on a Theme VIII"). With Maureen he leaves all Sonship behind and becomes symbolic Father even to himself.

The crucial question for me is how much of the book's tensions can be resolved by this line of analysis. A possible reading might run like this: Lazarus relives key events from his past which prepare him to break the sexual taboos he has always lived within; the crises are his sexual initiation of his clone twins and the mutual seduction of himself and Maureen. Having accomplished Oedipus' desire, he suffers death as a result of his father's actions and is reborn, presumably freed forever of death wish. This sort of reading presumes some primal guilt which causes him to want to die and which must be expunged by breaking through the oedipal taboo and transcending the attendant punishment. This takes me, at least, quite outside the text; this, more than my lack of familiarity with the details of Freudian theory, prevents me from going further in this direction.

VII

There are, however, other avenues which may lead to a resolution. My personal and critical prejudices—and the weight of the evidence—lead me to seek whatever final answers there might be in the archetypal material; I do not see an iconographic analysis, such as a Freudian one, as likely, but much of the emotional power of the book certainly lies in its use of mythic situations and patterns, the acting out of desires and dreams that lie deep in all of us. The sexual material is certainly in this class, but another such motif is solipsism.

While solipsism is mentioned several times throughout the book, the key passage must be "Coda II," the vision of the Gray Voice, and it is perhaps best to work back from there. I call the episode a vision—rather than a dream, as Christopher does—because it is ambiguously oracular; there is no indication whether this is a fancy generated by Lazarus' dying subconscious mind or a true vision, a glimpse of the reality behind all things. The content is certainly unambiguous, however: time and space are illusions created by the Voice/Lazarus as part of a game played with himself and by his own rules (like the Notebook definition of "duty"); Lazarus is God and creation is his way of amusing himself. This certainly reflects one of Lazarus' sneaking suspicions about the nature of reality, as he has repeatedly characterized himself as a solipsist (see TEL "Variations on a Theme I" and "Da Capo III"). The question is, within the book's system is Lazarus right or not? Solipsism does fit at least one part of his reality model, the no-paradox, static theory of time travel and its causality:

> But you've long been aware that the "no-paradoxes" theory itself involves a paradox— ...the idea that free will and predestination are two aspects of the same mathematical truth, and the difference is merely linguistic, not semantic: the notion that his own free will could not change events here-&-now because his freewill actions here-&-now were already a part of what *had* happened in any later "here-&-now."
>
> Which in turn depended on a solipsistic notion he had held as far back as he could remember (TEL "Da Capo III").

That notion is, presumably, the same as the one outlined by the Voice. Solipsism becomes on one level a paradox breaker, a way of smoothing out the logical difficulties in mathematical world-models; if Lazarus is in charge of metaphysics, there can be no paradoxes, since his will is the Law.

Solipsism also meshes well with the self-love that many of the novel's detractors see as its central and most objectionable feature. Since Lazarus spends the book receiving the pampering and sexual favors of his relatives, ending with narcissism and incest, it is appropriate, in this view, that deep down he believes himself to be the only reality. Whatever flaws the book may have, however, I do not believe that it is so shallow and self-indulgent. To counter this charge of naive solipsism, I can point to motifs which accompany the solipsism theme not only in TEL but the earlier works cited. In "They" and "'Zombies,'" the isolation of the protagonist is not an unalloyed blessing. In the latter story, the alienation and isolation of the Unmarried Mother supplies a powerful curtain line which clearly indicates his/her need for love and companionship. Similarly, the normal experience of the prisoner of "They" is of participation (in the Neoplatonic sense), the "unity of many and the diversity of one," rather than the naive solipsism of the infant. These are characters who require a loving Other to break the solitude.

This same need for company and love is certainly present in TEL, even if we take only the Dora episode as evidence of Lazarus' capacity for love of another. A possible answer may appear in this Notebook entry: "'God split himself into a myriad parts that he might have friends.' This may not be true, but it sounds good—and is no sillier than any other theology" (TEL "Second Intermission"). It brings to mind not only "They," but also the key tenet of Mike Smith's religion in *Stranger*—"Thou art God"—which in that fictional universe is literal truth. Is Heinlein using this vaguely Eastern pantheism to try to bridge the gap between the pragmatic and aesthetic realms of experience? In this sort of Stapledonian unity-in-diversity, both the Darwinian struggle for survival and the individual will to love would fit into a framework in which the species and all its works are one, and loving others is loving the self. This avoids the mechanistic, impersonal emptiness of the survival ethic (once you've survived, then what?) and the directionlessness of a purely aesthetic life.

Unfortunately, not even the Gray Voice episode allows us to affirm that view as anything more than an attractive possiblity; the uncertainty that pertains to the pragmatic and aesthetic philosophies extends to the problem of solipsism. In fact, the book seems to be made up of interrelated oppositions. Is man the ultimate individualist/wild animal (solipsism being the logical extension of this view) or a creature built for and longing for community and love? Lazarus' survival ethic favors the former, his theories of love the latter, and both cannot be absolutes. Looked at from another angle, these tensions become dynamic and static models of behavior—the individualist is committed to the goal of survival and sees his life in terms of success or failure; the communal, aesthetic man seeks satisfaction in the present moment rather than striving toward something outside himself.

Most of the time—in his most didactic phase—Lazarus favors the individualist-pragmatic-dynamic philosophy, as shown in the following quotes from TEL "Variations on a Theme XV." The nearly omnipotent, communal-minded, static Little People, for example, he fears not only as a physical threat to humankind—"'I can't imagine fighting them because it wouldn't be a fight; they would already have won against anything we could attempt'"—but as a spiritual threat. The eleven thousand Howards who elected to stay behind with the Little People apparently died out: "'What happened to Neanderthal Man? What happens to any champion when he's defeated? Justin, what's the point in striving when you're so outclassed that it's no contest?'" The Little People's perfection is "'deadly to human beings,'" and Lazarus sees them as a "'dead end'"; perhaps worst of all (to Lazarus, as a result of seeing Mary Sperling join one of their group minds) is their communal consciousness—he is "'not tempted to swap [an] individual personalit[y] for a pseudo-immortality.'"

Strong as these sentiments are, they must be balanced against the love-centered possibilities outlined earlier. I do not believe that the solipsist/paranoid-individualist/pragmatist Heinlein should be seen as the "real" one any more than the Martian-theologian/love-cultist/hippie-guru; both are strongly present in this volume, and neither absorbs the other completely. What we have, I believe is a tension of opposites that refuses to resolve itself into a synoptic view of the universe or reduce to a single ideology. The question remains, however, how does the book resolve as a work of fiction (as distinct from a philosophical dialectic)? This may yield to one last look backward, to *Methuselah's Children*, and then a reading of TEL's ending in mythic terms.

VIII

Methuselah's Children has as one of its themes a version of Lazarus' basic question—what is the purpose or meaning of human life? Lazarus knows that there are behavioral and what can only be called stylistic norms for humans who take their existence seriously, but no reasons for these norms, especially in the face of philosophically extreme situations. Twice the Families meet beings who have solved or had solved for them all their material and social problems, and twice Lazarus and the Families reject the solutions. The case of the Jockaira and their "gods" is not hard to understand, since the Jockaira are portrayed as domesticated animals; Lazarus' ideology, and ours, places freedom above survival where the slavery is so permanent and absolute. As Lazarus says, " 'It's not a man's place to be property' " (MC pt. 2, chap. 3). But when Andy Libby asks, " 'What is a man's place?' " all Lazarus can say is, " 'It's a man's business to be what he is... and be it in style!' " (MC pt. 2, chap. 3). He understands clearly what a man is not (property), but not what he is. Similarly, the Little People offer a threatening way of living which is rejected, but this time the threat is complicated by appearing as a trade—individual personality for immortality. To be precise, this exchange is only part of a twofold shock. Lazarus automatically mistrusts the utopian life offered by the Little People, but it takes Mary Sperling's defection to a group mind and the birth of the "improved" Marion Schmidt to scare the Families into returning to Earth. Some passages of Lazarus' reflections before the double crisis are illuminating:

> He had to admit that he could find no reasonable fault with the planet nor its inhabitants. But just as definitely it was not to his taste. No phi-

losophy that he had ever heard or read gave any reasonable purpose for man's existence, nor any rational clue to his proper conduct. Basking in the sunshine might be as good a thing to do with one's life as any other— but it was not for him and he knew it, even if he could not define how he knew it.

. . . . .

The uncounted days slid past while he argued with himself over the things that bothered him—problems that had made sad the soul of his breed since the first apeman had risen to self-awareness, questions never solved by full belly nor fine machinery. . . . Why? What shall it profit a man? No answer came back—save one: a firm unreasoned conviction that he was not intended for, or not ready for, this timeless snug harbor of ease. (MC pt. 2, chap. 4)

Fortunately for Lazarus, the material evidence of the dangers of staying with the Little People arrive before he has to try to rationalize his instincts to his fellow refugees.

The novel ends with a statement of Lazarus' philosophy, still unreasoned, but clearly the closest to the truth he or the book can take us. With the "secret" of immortality out, all humans now face the joys and problems of extended life and the questions Lazarus has struggled with. For Lazarus this means the chance to pursue some answers: "'Men—*our* kind of men—Earth men—never have had time enough to tackle the important questions. Lots of capacity and not time enough to use it properly. When it came to the important questions we might as well have still been monkeys'" (MC pt. 2, chap. 8). The last few sentences of the book offer a metaphor which must stand as Lazarus' definition of man and the style in which he goes about his business:

"... There ought to be nothing in the whole universe that man can't poke his nose into—that's the way we're built and I assume there's some reason for it."
"Maybe there aren't any reasons."
"Yes, maybe it's just one colossal big joke, with no point to it." ...
"But I can tell you this, Andy, whatever the answers are, here's one monkey that's going to keep on climbing, and looking around to see what he can see, as long as the tree holds out." (MC pt. 2, chap. 8)

Lazarus's position at this point is clear: The internal, irrational urgings of curiosity and the equally irrational sense of authentic human style define all he can know about his own nature; he knows how to behave, but not why, beyond the promptings of instincts which, in the novel's fictional universe, are always proved correct. In TEL, Lazarus has had the time he said was needed to look for answers—about two millenia—and we could expect that he would have found some. Ira Weatheral certainly thinks Lazarus' wisdom is important, and the long discourses on all topics that fill the book might also lead a reader to see it as the fruits of Lazarus' successful hunt for the Final Answer. As I hope the preceding sections of this essay have shown, there are no such answers, only sets of tensions which refuse to resolve to produce a harmonious philosophical system that unites the pragmatic and aesthetic, solipsist and communalist pieces of Lazarus' experience. Is there anything, then, that holds the book together, that prevents its mutually repelling fragments of a Final Answer from flying apart and destroying the novel in the process?

If we look at the book's mythic structure, deeper even than Freudian-therapeutic readings of the oedipal material, there are forces operating that unify the book despite disharmonies in value systems and even artistic flaws and ideological irritations. First of all, Lazarus is an epic hero, even if he lacks the tragic grandeur and high style of the classical models. He leads his people to salvation (first the flight of the Howards; then the diaspora, which he and Libby made possible; then the colonizations of Secundus and Tertius), he fights monsters, displays extraordinary courage and self-sacrifice, and generally serves as a model of wisdom, love, and bravery for his culture. It can even be argued that the automatic and often cloying reverence he receives from all "good" characters (a feature much objected to by reviewers) is a symbol of Lazarus' status as a demigod-hero. Next, Lazarus is Everyman as well—a role not necessarily in conflict with his job as hero—in his struggle with fundamental questions of value and meaning and his failure to gain control over the conflicting parts of systems that solve pieces of the puzzle. In his many lives he follows all possible paths (see TEL "Variations on a Theme III" for a list with comments of some of his careers), gathering much information about How but little about Why. Last, and most powerful, is the shape of the novel itself. The content motif of return is also an important structural feature, and even without a Freudian analysis, it is plain that Lazarus' healing is tied up with reliving his past and finally traveling into it bodily to confront his childhood and Maureen. To say that Lazarus wants to die because he is tired of life—that he is bored—is to say that he has been wounded by the experience of being, by the fact of existence. After being teased and nursed back to life, his death at the end of "Coda" should be tragic, or at least ironic—the completion of a process that his family of healers could only interrupt, not deny altogether. But Lazarus does not die; he is resurrected after experiencing a vision of ambiguous import; and Tamara (confused with Maureen in Lazarus' mind and symbolically identified with her in the novel) tells him what we all know of all heroes, mortal or not: "'You cannot die'" (TEL "Coda IV").

So Lazarus is reborn. The pattern is complete, the circle of life to death to new life is closed, and Lazarus has truly returned. In the face of this mythic pattern, the tensions between the philosophical systems are unimportant—it is the fact of the recurrence of life, of the reality of the process, whatever its Why, that provides the power for this book. Even if there are no answers, the search is satisfying; even if in the static plenum of Andy Libby's mathematical universe there is no causality, the man-monkey keeps asking How and even Why.

This is not to say that there is no leaning toward one side or the other. Despite the failure of the novel to supply a systematic, consistent philosophy on the rational level, I am left with the conviction that all the explanations of species survival as the universal morality are meaningless without the immediate experience that life itself—survival—is worthwhile in its own terms; that is, I believe that *emotionally* the book resolves in favor of the aesthetic way. Whatever the validity of the Gray Voice vision, there is an interesting reference in the Voice's advice to Lazarus to start the game over again —"'You cannot exhaust her infinite variety'" ("Coda II"). Ignoring for the moment who or what else "she" might be in a solipsist metaphysic, she is symbolically Cleopatra, as unmistakable a representative of the erotically and *intrinsically* desirable as we could want, a sign that time exists for love and not the other way around.

9. Robert Heinlein: Folklorist of Outer Space

IVOR A. ROGERS

ROBERT HEINLEIN is undoubtedly one of the "Greats" of twentieth-century science fiction. Not only is he popular among teachers but he is a perennial favorite among ordinary readers. The "best" science fiction writer for most of them is a composite entity: Heinlein-asimovclarke—usually in that order. Several critics have attempted to evaluate or explain Heinlein's writing, most notably Panshin, Blish, and Aldiss.[1] In fact, most critics seem compelled to take up the problems of Robert Heinlein's fiction, and hundreds of articles are written on him every year in the amateur fan magazines. Omitting the enthusiastic burblers who can neither see, hear, nor speak evil of Heinlein, most critics have managed a certain consensus—they like his writing, but the sins of commission and omission in his writing are staggering: poor use of language, weak and inadequate plotting, poor storytelling techniques, and incapacity to handle mature sexual themes being the worst offenders. Yet people, even his severest critics, like his writing, and he sells well. Most importantly, he is capable of attracting readers with a wide age differential and with widely disparate educational backgrounds.

The most common criticism of Heinlein is based on his (supposed) political ideology, and much of the political philosophy expressed by some of his *characters* does set the teeth on edge; but Liberal knee-jerk reflex has no more place in a mature consideration of his work than Conservative knee-jerk adulation does. Ideological considerations aside, Heinlein appeals to and is criticized by a wide variety of "-ists," "-ats," "-ites"; and there is little consensus on what is his best work. My wife, a talented scholar of the world of Faerie, normally touches Heinlein only at the end of a ten-foot pole, but she finds some good ironic commentary in *Farnham's Freehold* and a sensitive theme and message in *Podkayne of Mars*. I can see what she means intellectually, but viscerally I find them pure tedium when they have to be reread for a class or a paper.

To the mythic or archetypal scholar, and I class myself among them, this multiplex reaction usually acts as a red flag, warning us that the author has probably tapped into the monomyth or the universal subconscious. This is not always sufficient an explanation, as popular culture critics have discovered. This is particularly insufficient an explanation for Heinlein, as has been pointed out above: popularity does not always mean greatness. One needs only to contemplate Shakespeare's *Pericles* or the poetry of Felicia Hemans to demonstrate the fallacy. One of the dreariest plays of a dreary century of theater, the nineteenth, was *Douglas*, but it held the boards for fifty years. There are even grimmer examples served up in the media every week.

The problem facing the archetypal or mythic scholar who applies his talents to popular culture is a simple one: the myths or *topoi* remain constant, but the thematic treatment suffers from changing styles in form and language. What is a deeply moving experience to one generation, because it has been phrased in forms and words most vital to their unconscious needs, withers to unreadability as attitudes, language, and form change. Most playgoers of mid-twentieth-century America *really do* experience *West Side Story* as an immensely captivating experience, often putting them into a hypnagogic, trancelike state, especially in the film version. Others, who have devoted much of their life to the study of Shakespeare, find even a minor play like *Romeo and Juliet* far superior to *West Side Story*, the "modern" version. The reaction of the audience is somewhat different, however. I have seen scholars leaving a Shakespearean play in many emotional states, but it has seldom been in a transcendental trance. The true classic has a universality or greatness that can transcend writing styles and formalistic devices so that it has greatness for the present generation and for generations to come, and I believe that at least one-fourth of Heinlein's work *may* have this universality, especially portions of his last work to date, *Time Enough for Love* (1973).

This chapter is not an explanation of Heinlein's popularity, nor is it a critical analysis of his work in traditional close textual analysis. It is an attempt to see it within a larger framework, an analysis of form and content in general terms, and a suggestion of its source— which includes a definition of just what, precisely, *Time Enough for Love* is. As Tolkien's *Lord of the Rings* has been described as an epic, not a novel, I should like to describe *Time Enough for Love* as a romance and not a science fiction novel. The best attempt that I have seen to fit Heinlein into a critical continuum was a short paper by Joe Christopher in *Riverside Quarterly* using Frye's *Anatomy of Criticism* as the primary critical tool. Given the method, it was a useful and exciting appraisal of the work, particularly his insights into the overall development of the book as a novel. However, when one considers the work as a novel, it fits the author's book into a Procrustean bed of formidable proportions, lopping off several vital organs in the process.

It is always dangerous to ask an author what he had in mind when he wrote a work, and many critics—in science fiction Thomas D. Clareson is most notable—have observed that a work does not belong to a writer, as it exists only through the perceptions of the readers. Some people may wish to call Frank Herbert's *Dune* an ecological novel, and it may even have been the intent of the author —although I doubt it, but if the reviewers and critics cannot correct this mistaken impression, then it *is* an ecological novel, and five djin and a ton of *PMLA* (the official publication of the Modern Language Association) will not change this categorization.

It is equally dangerous to ignore what an author has to say about his work, and Heinlein has written several articles about science fiction. The most important of these writings is his "Science Fiction: Its Nature, Faults, and Virtues."[2] This article is of interest, not so much for his theories, but for what can be inferred from his likes and dislikes and for what can be read between the lines about his own work.

Heinlein's critical theory is simplistic: he has read many books but knows little theory. For him there are only two kinds of fiction: realistic (or possible) and fantasy (or impossible) fiction. He breaks these two categories down into three subclasses each. Fiction may be set in the past, the present, or the future. He makes a strong point that most of the best science fiction (or speculative fiction as he prefers) is realistic fiction set in the future, but this is not an inflexible dogma. A novel may be set in both the past and the present, or any other combination of the temporal classifications, including a combination of past, present, and future.

For our purposes his most meaningful use of his classifications is when he declares that it is perfectly possible for a story to combine fantasy and realistic writing, have historical, contemporary, and future settings, and it may include comedy, tragedy, burlesque, and straight hortatory propaganda. (The latter classifications do not appear as categories elsewhere in his essay.) Heinlein knew that it was possible to write such a story, even though it posed serious technical problems, because he had read and liked a book which did all of these things: *Caleb Catlum's America* by Vincent McHugh? In writing *Time Enough for Love* I believe that Heinlein, either consciously or unconsciously, patterned his book on the earlier work, following exactly what he had described as one of the most difficult of writing techniques. In effect it was an act of admiration to turn one's last and greatest work on a pattern laid out by another writer.

If there is this relationship between the two books, and if Heinlein's book follows the pattern set out above, then *Time Enough for Love* is not science fiction *as its own author defines it* in his article "Science Fiction": "...such exotic creatures as to defy almost any method of literary taxonomy" (p. 23). There are extensive elements of fantasy in the book: most of the love sequences, references to Gilgamesh and the Wandering Jew as real people, and the claim that Shakespeare—a brother to Queen Elizabeth—was a red-haired immortal who dyed his hair to conceal his identity. Heinlein also claims in his essay that any story involving a talking mule is fantasy (p. 19). Note that he does not say donkey or ass, the traditional talking animal of Fable and *Märchen*. Heinlein states that a talking mule equals fantasy, and in the Dora/Lazarus section of *Time Enough for Love* there are talking mules—who can reproduce their own kind. To a former farm boy, I don't know which would seem more fantastic: the ability to reproduce or the ability to talk. Heinlein has an out for this sort of implausibility in his essay under the rubric of "imaginary but possible," and there is a quick gloss in the novel about "special mutations." Possible, perhaps, but so little explained that it is closer to the old magic wand than the genetics laboratory: give it a +.0001 possibility rating. Heinlein may be pulling our leg, or even trying to tell us something about his fantasy. So much of *Time Enough for Love* is imaginary but (not very) possible, that it is difficult to classify it as anything short of fantasy.

What is this exotic creature if it isn't science fiction? Unlike the horse put together by a committee it isn't a camel, nor is it even a talking mule. It has elements of a picaresque, but surface elements only, and is actually a romance masquerading as a novel. My undergraduate professors used to insist that James Branch Cabell was the last of the great writers of romance, but I believe that McHugh and Heinlein are even later, and perhaps truer, writers in the genre. This is particularly seen in *Time Enough for Love* where the fear which one might feel at the death of a hero or demigod (Lazarus Long) is transformed into the adventurousness, the marvelous, and pensive melancholy (the latter is especially noted at the beginning of *Time Enough for Love* and the end of *Caleb Catlum's America*). It turns pity into chivalrous rescue and tender charm, and pity without an object into creative fantasy.

Because there is a good deal of amatory adventure in both *Time Enough for Love* and *Caleb Catlum's America*, it should be made clear that the term romance as used in this chapter has nothing to do with sentimental novels (although Heinlein exudes sentimentality at every paragraph), love stories (although there are several love stories in *Time Enough for Love*), and most certainly does not mean what Harlequin Books means when they splash *ROMANCE* across the top of every book it publishes.

The true romance is a medieval (primarily) genre which succeeded the epic and *chanson de geste*. Although the romance, especially *The Matter of Rome*, has been called a predecessor of the novel, it is one by several removes at least. A romance is typically a collection of adventures tied together with a central theme or around a central character, often developing minor characters into adventures of their own. Typical examples are the Arthurian romances, both before and after Malory, and the romances that were connected to the French *chanson de geste* such as *Chanson de Roland*. It is not surprising that the only readily available English translation of *Huon de Bordeaux* is called *Huon of the Horn* and published by Ace Books—written of course by one of the best fantasy writers of its stable, Andre Norton. *Huon* and the partly comic *Pèlerinage de Charlemagne* are good examples of the transition from older modes to romance. Either of these two works would serve as a model for Heinlein and McHugh in terms of treatment and mode.

Unlike Malory or Chrétien de Troyes, Heinlein has broken completely with the form of the epic, but he has retained the essence. To all three there is the Court as the center of the universe (the rejuvenation clinic and Tertius in *Time Enough for Love*), and the rest of the world is filled with uncouth characters fit only for adventure. In *Caleb Catlum's America* the uncouth characters finally take over and drive the Catlum clan into the paradise of the hidden cave, but the flight to Tertius (and the earlier flight from Earth in *Methuselah's Children*) in Heinlein's universe are also escapes from the uncouth characters outside the Court of noble beings. Because McHugh and Heinlein were writing in the twentieth century, an era of despair and savagery, this is not too surprising a development.

James Branch Cabell, also a writer of twentieth-century romances in his *Biography of Dom Manuel* (a long series of works cast in the form of novels), introduces elements of Menippean satire, realistic treatment of romantic themes, ironic treatment, and domestic tragedy. Heinlein has gone in the other direction: away from satire toward myth, tall tales, and high mimetic comedy, presumably because his introduction to romance was primarily through McHugh. McHugh's other notable book, *I Am Thinking of My Darling*,[4] is also highly praised by Heinlein. The book describes itself as an adventure, but it is really a science fiction novel interlaced with a medieval Quest theme. It also is one of the few modern works in which the loved object achieves a deeper level of spiritual love than a mere "Courtly" love and one of the few in which there is no inversion of the love quest. It could be considered a romance except that it has the tightly structured unity of a modern novel.

The major stumbling block to considering *Time Enough for Love* as a romance is that it is written in a moderately realistic manner with little attention paid to metaphorical, rhetorical, and literary techniques. It is baldly written where it does not descend to sentimentality and awkward prose (especially the embarrassingly written sexual episodes). As I pointed out in my essay, "The Gernsback Era,"[5] one of the stylistic developments of the late 1930s was the ability to write of fantastic and possible-but-unlikely subject matter in a realistic manner. This was a major development of the period, and its use has had a tremendous impact on science fiction written in the second third of the twentieth century. It became so pervasive in the pages of *Astounding Science Fiction*, whose editor, John W. Campbell, Jr., was one of the pioneers of this style of writing—particularly the stories written under the Don Stuart pseudonym—that Heinlein considered most of his pre-1960s novels realistic writing rather than serious melodrama written in a realistic manner. He often verged over to naive melodrama, placing the *pharmakos*—or scapegoat—outside of society. This partially explains the popularity and dislike of *Starship Troopers* where the nonsoldier is not even a full voting citizen. As Frye explains, it is easy to recognize the basic absurdity of naive melodrama and write an ironic comedy making the enemy of society a spirit or attitude of that society—a good example being *Bill, the Galactic Hero*, Harry Harrison's "answer" to *Starship Troopers*.

In Heinlein's later novels the characters sweat, vomit, and have normal excretory functions—usually signs of realistic writing. Because of the prudish censorship of the science fiction magazines these elements are lacking in his earlier novels and short stories, but he prizes tough, realistic writing styles. Citing a tough, realistic war story, Pat Frank's *Hold Back the Night*, and a book that is a realistic war novel, *The Caine Mutiny* (but which also approaches ironic comedy in the sudden reversal of our attitude toward the *pharmakos*, Captain Queeg), Heinlein tells us much about his preferences in the novel. Any list of favorite novels that can include such disparate works as those mentioned above, fantasies such as *The Sword in the Stone*, *The Wind in the Willows*, and *The Wizard of Oz*, and speculative novels such as *1984*, *The War with the Newts*, and *Odd John* is very revealing. When the same author believes that the realism of Henry Miller, Sartre, Joyce, and Alberto Moravia is more suitable for the psychiatrist's couch than the printed page, it is difficult to evaluate his standards or his critical terminology. His major complaint is that these Ashcan realists do not interpret the new world of atomic power, antibiotics, and interplanetary travel. James Jones's *From Here to Eternity*, another war novel, admittedly casts light into some of the darker corners of the human soul. Heinlein claims that *he* is not a stranger and afraid in a world he never made, damned from here to eternity, but *not* afraid and *not* a stranger in a world *he is helping to make*. This element of interpreting and remaking the world as a better place is, I believe, the touchstone for Heinlein's later writing and the critical attitudes he has taken.

Despite realistic elements in Heinlein's later novels, the final determination of his genre or mode of writing revolves around his use of the hero. Lazarus Long, the hero of *Time Enough for Love*, and the hero of *I Will Fear No Evil*, are both men who are superior in degree to other men rather than superior in kind, which would make them divine beings. (Even Valentine Michael Smith of *Stranger in a Strange Land*, for all of his "Thou art God," is still different only in degree.) Lazarus Long is different in degree; but even in relationship to the other members of the Howard Families—who are of a similar kind of human—he is so different that he is considered something special among his kin, and his exploits approach the realm of myth.

No matter how often Frye's *Anatomy of Criticism* has been

quoted, it is always pertinent to remind the reader of his statement about science fiction. He describes it as, "...a mode of romance with a strong inherent tendency toward myth." His obvious reason is that science fiction often describes a society that is as far advanced from us as we are advanced from savages.[6] Frye also comments:

> If superior in degree to other men and his environment the hero is the typical hero of romance, whose actions are marvelous, but who is himself identified as a human being. The hero of a romance moves in a world in which the ordinary laws of nature are slightly suspended: prodigies of courage and endurance, unnatural to us are natural to him,... and talking animals... violate no rules of probability once the postulates of romance have been established. Here we have moved from myth, properly so called, into legend, folk tale, *märchen*, and their literary affiliates and derivatives. (p. 33)

Heinlein's later novels have been obscured for us critically because of his incurable penchant for diatribe, hortatory propaganda, and his blending of heroic/romantic modes and irony. I believe that there is a parallel situation between Heinlein and the very first speculative fiction writer, Aristophanes. I am well aware that most critics of science fiction rate Lucian as the "first" science fiction writer, but I have always considered the utopian/distopian visions of Aristophanes to have priority over Lucian by five and a half centuries.

Aristophanes' *The Birds*, is the story of two disaffected Athenian citizens who "split the scene" and decided to found their own perfect polis. It is called Cloudcuckooland, and is built in the air—about as close to No-where as one can get. Unhappily, most science fiction critics consider narrative fiction as the only source for science fiction and disregard *The Birds* as easily as they ignore the award of the Nobel Prize for literature to a science fiction verse epic (*Aniara*). But consider what Heinlein's later work, especially *Time Enough for Love*, is like, while reading this description by Frye of Aristophanes: "Old Comedy, like the tragedy contemporary with it, is a blend of the heroic and the ironic. In some plays this fact is partly obscured by Aristophanes' strong desire to get his own opinion of what the hero is doing into the record, but his greatest comedy, *The Birds*, preserves an exquisite balance between comic heroism and comic irony" (p. 44). Conservative, polemical, and libertarian, Heinlein and Aristophanes have much in common, including the fact that both were writing speculative fiction about society, thus clouding their status as writers of high mimetic comedy.

If *Time Enough for Love* is high mimetic comedy and a

romance, there are still many areas of the book that do not fit these descriptions easily. Part of the problem lies in the inadequacy of the critical tools we have to handle popular culture, but more important is Heinlein's writing what purports to be a novel in an age of low mimetic fiction—and we expect a fictive piece in prose to be a novel. *Time Enough for Love* is just about everything that a novel is not, and most of his "novels" since 1960 (excepting the juveniles) are neither novels nor low mimetic fiction. This major change in his writing has irritated most of his critics who find his plots diffuse and his structure rambling. This irritation may well be due to differences in political views as pointed out above, but some of the irritation may also come from the fact that there is a conflict between the ostensible form and the actual content of his works.

The final argument on form rests on the similarities between *Time Enough for Love* and McHugh's *Caleb Catlum's America.* Consider this description of the McHugh book from the title page:

> The enlivening wonders of his adventures, voyages, discoveries, loves, hoaxes, bombast and rigamaroles in all parts...from his birth...almost to the present year, told by himself; together with a surprising account of his family...and a thousand tricks of lovemaking.

I have removed all place names, dates, and specific references to episodes in the novel such as, "...the tale of a man sawed up for firewood," making it sound like a close description of Woodrow Wilson Smith, or Lazarus Long, himself. It could apply to Mike Fink, John Henry, Davy Crockett, or Pecos Bill as well as to Don Quixote or dozens of fictive and folk heroes, but this is the point of the comparison. McHugh wrote the definitive folktale adventure-romance of the United States of America, and Heinlein attempted to write the definitive equivalent of outer space adventure-romance. As Caleb is the quintessential American hero, Lazarus is the folk hero of the Howard Families and, hence, of the human race. Folktales usually vacillate between myth and domestic comedy, thus placing both authors in the framework I have outlined above without undue strain.

Many devices were used in common by these authors, including the opening episode disclaiming that this is their work. McHugh uses the device of attributing the work to another: he was simply "touching up" a narrative that was given to him by Caleb. This is in the style of Tolkien's *Red Book of Westmarch* or Malory's "Frensshe Books." Heinlein uses a more "modern" technique common to science fiction works, such as Asimov's *Encyclopedia Galactica*, 116th edition, in the *Foundation Trilogy*. *Time Enough for Love* is supposedly an abridged popular edition of a scholarly history by Justin Foote the 45th, Chief Archivist Emeritus, Howard Foundation, written long after the events described in the book. There is even a statement in this edition that the final chapters (dealing with the events after the departure from Secundus) are apocryphal but included at the insistence of the former archivist. This places Lazarus firmly back into the realm of legend and myth.

The content of the novels is also quite similar. As I have mentioned above both novels are sprawling collections of tales and episodic adventures. In one sense they are both *Bildungsromanen*, *Caleb Catlum's America* obviously so as it starts with his birth and early development; in *Time Enough for Love* the rejuvenation of Lazarus Long and his reeducation, including the dissolution of the sexual inhibitions he still has, can serve as a story of growth and development. Both include long episodes of voyages of discovery and adventure; in *Time Enough for Love* there is the Dora/Lazarus sequence, and if one considers *Methuselah's Children* as part of the Long saga, there is enough voyage of discovery and exploration to fill a Modern Languages Association seminar. Many of the exploits of the hero in both books are shared by the hero and a black man (John Henry in *Caleb Catlum's America* and Zaccur Barstow of *Methuselah's Children*), and Lazarus is quick to point out that the Howard Families are an amalgamation of many races.[7] Caleb, when he meets McHugh, even proposes to rent the barn so that he can build a rocket to take a visit to Venus, "Come Hell or high water"— a beautiful touch of symbolism that was probably appreciated by Heinlein.

The major content element which convinces me of the similarities of the McHugh and Heinlein books is the question of immortality and red hair. Caleb is an immortal—that is a given by the author, and Lazarus is a presumed immortal (he was three hundred years old before his first rejuvenation). For Heinlein there is a mystique about red hair. Many of the heroes and heroines of his earlier fictions are redheaded. He mentions Gilgamesh as the first of the immortal line; there are references to other immortal redheads like Shakespeare, and in scientific terminology Lazarus is obviously a mutation (dominant characteristics: red hair, a large nose, no vermiform appendix, and extreme longevity). The Catlums are red-haired and immortal because the first of the Catlum clan, Eric the

Red, drank from the waters of the fountain of youth. Caleb was born immortal. Lazarus had immortality thrust upon him. Caleb's immortality is explained as a part of the encompassing fantasy of the book: Heinlein provides no explanation for the immortality of Lazarus, but they are both redheads, and it is these linkages between the books which make me believe that *Caleb Catlum's America* was the source for Heinlein's Lazarus.

There is a curious similarity between the politics expressed in both novels. The political outlook of Heinlein's works is discussed at greater length in another chapter of this book, but I must mention the connecting link between Heinlein and McHugh. Both might be classed as Jeffersonian, populist, libertarians. At first glance McHugh is a liberal—his villains commercially minded "traders" with little silver piccolos producing music which makes the listener neither sad nor joyous. McHugh's villains are all conservatives, "old Tories," thinking only of toil, trying to keep the lower classes in their place, and scorning the pleasures of the grape and the flesh. McHugh's book is an affirmation of what he considers the American spirit: unbounded, free, open, and founded upon the natural, innate goodness of the common man. Jefferson (who gives the original draft of the Declaration of Independence to Caleb), Lincoln, and other emancipators and free spirits are ranged against Benjamin Franklin (a miserly humbug in this story), the forces of big business, robber barons, and the manipulators of Wall Street.

It is hard to imagine Heinlein in such company, but the element that apparently appeals to him is the libertarian quality in McHugh; a man ought to be able to do whatever he damn well pleases—unless it conflicts with the wishes of a Heinlein hero. It is really incorrect to think of the Right and the Left of a political spectrum at opposite ends of a linear continuum. It is not new to suggest that right and left are really adjacent to each other in a circular continuum, and the overlap of Heinlein and McHugh comes in their belief that the Nietzschean superman must experience his intense emotions without let or hindrance from men of lesser breed or governmental systems that prohibit and restrain beyond the minimum necessary for survival of society. (McHugh is no anarchist; in *I Am Thinking of My Darling* he suggests the potential for catastrophe when the finely tuned organization of government in a large city begins to crumble). Heinlein prefers the benevolent dictatorship form of government, simply to keep the boobs and eaters of seed corn from pulling the sane individuals down with them in their folly. Both recognize that the free man is a fiercely independent man, capable, competent, and master of his desires, but both recognize the legitimacy of all man's desires that do not conflict with rationality. (Lazarus is perfectly willing to impregnate his clone sisters or have intercourse with his mother if he is convinced that the offspring of the first situation will not carry lethal or defective genes, and in the second case when he is sure that there will be no issue.)

Both writers apparently find the sexual act as the ultimate expression of personal freedom. A sexual encounter between consenting adults is not a sin, indeed, it is the closest one can come to freedom in their respective secondary universes. Both heroes are restricted in their freedom by social and political considerations, but neither are restricted sexually, and both are breakers of sexual taboos. Heinlein breaks the taboos of incest and homosexuality, and McHugh, in a doubleheader game, has his young hero get his first "advanced" lesson in lovemaking from his grandfather. (He also explores bestiality taboos by having Caleb change his shape to various animals and produce progeny from the resultant love play.) This attitude is apparent in Heinlein's post-1960 novels, again excluding the juveniles, and in McHugh's poetry, which was considered mildly sensational in its day for its sexual frankness.

This brings us to a consideration of Heinlein's sexuality, as expressed in his novels. I have earlier made reference to *Time Enough for Love* as Heinlein's last and greatest novel. I believe that he considered it to be the capstone to his career as a writer, and there are unconscious elements which lead one to the conclusion that his entire writing career was a working out of his oedipal conflicts. Most authors go through cycles in their development, and I believe that *Time Enough for Love* is the culminating work of his final cycle. Heinlein is probably sitting at his typewriter at this moment disproving my thesis, but if he does produce further writing, I believe that it will differ as much from his work of the last two decades as his post-1960 works differed from what he wrote before.

To recapitulate the ontogeny of a writer, there is often an initial work or two which draws heavily on autobiographical details to flesh out an otherwise bald and unconvincing narrative. Until very recently this has not been a possible source of enrichment for a beginning science fiction writer because he was expected to write fast-paced adventure novels set in weird and exotic locales. Samuel R. Delany was one of the first science fiction writers to use autobiographical detail as a supplement to the traditional plotting demands of the genre. A teenaged writer (as so many of the better science fiction writers were at the time they wrote their initial works), Delany was unable to draw on much experience of life, or even upon his experience as a black science fiction writer. If one reads the earlier novels of Delany closely, one can catch elements of his autobiographical embellishments, but it takes a very close reading to spot the fact that either the hero or the companion of the hero is black or a different color. Not until *Einstein Intersection* do we see a well-developed integration of autobiography and science fiction traditions.

By contrast Heinlein was thirty-two when he wrote his first story, and he had a wealth of autobiographical detail to draw upon. This detail appears only peripherally in his fiction, however, since Heinlein was writing from a deeper inner compulsion, and autobiographical detail was neither wanted nor common in the field when he started writing.

In the critical article that follows Heinlein in *The Science Fiction Novel*, C. M. Kornbluth's "The Failure of the Science Fiction Novel as Social Criticism," Kornbluth states that he would probably rather be writing an article on, "The Science Fiction Novel as Psychotherapy for the Neurotic Author" (p. 49). I am not suggesting that Heinlein is a neurotic author any more than the rest of us, but I am suggesting that the inner strength in his writing comes from a developmental exploration of his own psychological drives. As Kornbluth puts it, we all have unconscious fears, "...fear of women, fear of father, fear of sexual maturity" (p. 74).

Panshin's *Heinlein in Dimension* categorizes the stories written before World War II as the Period of Influence, a time when other writers were astounded by the success and storytelling ability of this newcomer. Heinlein uses a very good source for much of his earlier fiction: his experience and knowledge of procedures and processes. His least successful works are the novels which are difficult to sustain for the necessary length just by describing a process or a technique. Heinlein almost pulls it off according to Panshin in *Beyond This Horizon*—the technique he is writing about is how to survive on a day-to-day basis in an alien society. What is missing from all or most of these stories and novels is an interest in sexuality. (I'm speaking of the original versions, not the rewritten-for-book-publication versions.) There are revolutions, puppy-love encounters, even the breeding of children in *Beyond This Horizon*, but the boy-girl stories and the production of superprogeny in *Beyond This Horizon* are not really sexual. Using Kornbluth's description of another science fiction writer, these are simply the adventures of a small boy tricycling around the block having wonderful adventures. With Heinlein the boy is a very smart boy who knows how to do all sorts of things, but sexually he is in the latency period when girls are (nonsexual) objects like rocket ships and time machines.

No latency period is ever completely asexual; the sexuality is simply repressed until the hormones give the individual something to do with it. Sexual images of womb and phallus abound during this stage, and they are liberally sprinkled throughout Heinlein's works during this period. E. E. Smith, the writer savaged by Kornbluth in *The Science Fiction Novel* as a case of arrested sexual development, is a prototype for what was happening to Heinlein. (For specifics one might check Panshin's book and my contribution to *Anatomy of Wonder*.) Another aspect of this developmental period is the element of testing the adults to see what you can get away with. This explains the many novels and stories of revolution and rebellion which mark this period of his writing. In Heinlein's second story, "Misfit," there is a perfect example of "showing up Daddy" when Libby, the lightning calculator, saves the day for all the adults, and in Heinlein's first novel, there is an incident where the young hero usurps the power of the second-in-command of the army when the leader is killed; the young officer knows that he can do the job better than the older man. He can, and he does, but it gives us another insight into the unconscious of Robert Heinlein.

In Heinlein's second phase, according to Panshin, The Period of Success, we see a period somewhat changed from the prewar stories. To continue Kornbluth's analogy, the author drinks a little, fools around with girls, asserts his masculine territorial imperative, and wheels around the city in a high-powered motorcycle. Heinlein wrote many juvenile stories during this period and discovered people who were more important than techniques and processes. There are more married couples, more realistic violence, and even a couple of stories that imply men and women have sexual relations. There are still stories of rebellions and revolts, and there are juveniles who rebel and show up the old folks, but there are also stories of familial harmony and cooperation. Sexual symbolism is more open and less suppressed, let alone repressed, and the violence is often related to sexual elements.

Heinlein has obviously written himself out of the problems which face the neophyte writer. In the ontogeny of a writer they often come to periods where they "write themselves out." Publishing history is littered with brilliant first novels and a declining series of books demonstrating that many would-be writers have *one* good novel in them. Other writers develop from this point by involving their own life and writing with current events: C. P. Snow and Upton Sinclair are novelists who used this technique, Sinclair *ad nauseum* and Snow as a stage in his development. Heinlein uses this period to develop his Future History series. It gives him a convenient framework to peg his work together into a unified whole, and it provides a consistent secondary universe as a framing device. LeGuin, Delany, Niven, and others have all used similar secondary universe creations as a basis for many of their stories.

Panshin describes Heinlein's third period as The Period of Alienation. Like all writers, one must develop or continue churning out the same old stuff for the same old audience. Dorothy Sayers transformed her earlier detective stories into what appear to be comedies of manners, and Georgette Heyer, finally freed from grinding out detective stories and Regency romances by a certain degree of financial success, was just starting her "real" writing career—if one is to judge by her last work—when she died. By this point in his career, Heinlein, too, had achieved a degree of financial freedom and could write what he wanted with assurances of large sales for whatever he put his name to. Psychologically speaking this is also the period when Heinlein got off his motorbike and sat down to do some serious explanation of his sexual drives. As Panshin defines this period, Heinlein's first story was a shocker compared to what had come before. "'All You Zombies'" (*Fantasy and Science Fiction*, March 1959) involves time travel that allows a single transsexual individual to impregnate himself and be both his own father and his own mother. The narrator of the story declares that he knows where *he* comes from, "—but *where did all you zombies come from*?" and in the final line, speaking as his female self, Jane, says, "I miss you dreadfully!"

Psychologically this is the tremendous first step in working out the oedipal conflict in the writer. Earlier stories have commented on the fact that adults do have sexual intercourse, but he is still denying that *his* father and *his* mother would ever do such a thing. So he does it to himself. This is a perfect denial of oedipal desires; since it does not resolve the conflict of desiring intercourse with the mother and supplanting the father, it merely avoids the problem. I have no desire to do a psychoanalytical analysis of Heinlein—a writer is, after all, merely writing *stories*, and it isn't fair to attempt a psychoanalysis of a writer unless you have him on the couch yourself; but the implication of this story and the stories that are to come in this period of Heinlein's writing shows strong, unresolved sexual conflicts, *until we get to Time Enough for Love*. Resolving a conflict does not mean *solving* a conflict, however, and even in this last work we see unsolved problems obscuring the quality of the writing. This may simply be that Heinlein lacks the technical skill to write explicit sexual scenes without resorting to embarrassing clichés and coyness. It is extremely difficult to write explicit love scenes that are neither pornographic nor unpleasant. It is even more difficult to write explicit love scenes showing true love and tenderness simply because the act of putting such a scene on paper introduces a voyeuristic tendency in the reader, thus destroying the true intimacy and love postulated between the characters. Edmund Wilson almost manages to pull it off in *Memoirs of Hecate County*, and a few other writers have come close. There is, of course, some fine explicit love poetry, but the form of the poem lends a romantic veil to the scene simply by the use of an artificial form. A realistic novel may be brutally realistic or sexually explicit in a scene, but it cannot be tenderly or lovingly explicit. And Heinlein writes in a realistic manner.

In *Time Enough for Love* there is a recapitulation of sexual development through several stages, each development clearing the ground for the next stage. Lazarus Long begins with masturbation, progresses to heterosexual and homosexual experiences, makes love to a machine (actually a clone pastiche with the mental experiences of a computer), and with his own clone daughters. In the earlier works by Heinlein, we have seen him shift from simple boy/girl handholding to sexual initiation by an older female, to heterosexual relations with women his own age, and finally the "dirty old man" syndrome where he prefers sex with a woman many years his junior. This development in his earlier writings and the parallel (although different on the surface) development in *Time Enough for Love* lead to two climactic sequences in that book. One is the Dora/Lazarus tale, which I have mentioned before and will return to again, and the other is the final story where the main character returns to his birthplace to consummate his oedipal longings.

From the moment that Lazarus lands in Missouri we start on a sequence that viewed psychologically might lead one to suspect that the author is "putting us on." Does Lazarus land at the place of the author's birth? No, he lands *below* the site of his birth, and after a bit of plot fooling around, gets into this long thing (a train where the little sperm cell of Lazarus waits, ready), passes through his birthplace, still in the train, and is finally ejected into the womb/home/egg of Kansas City. The author's stand-in has finally returned to the womb in a symbolic sense, and is eventually destined to return to his mother's womb via his actual penis. It is either brilliantly humorous or mordantly grotesque—I can't make up my mind.

In any event, this return to the womb, solving both the aggressive and retrogressive desires of the author surrogate, clears the air of a great deal of sexual tension. I do not know whether the Lazarus/Dora sequence was written after the final war-romance story or before, but the genesis of the final oedipal resolution must have been in the author's mind when he was writing the Lazarus/Dora sequence, since this is the one superlative gem tucked away inside the long details of who did what to whom and how many times in the sexual byplay. Lazarus actually tells us the story of his "only" love —meaning that this episode had more emotional significance for him than anything else in his life, *including the love he had for his mother.* The fact that he does not specifically spell this out for us is relatively unimportant. Many a man would make references to his mother less than Lazarus does, and the major remembered figure of his youth seems to be his grandfather. Nothing connected with his mother or father (that curiously gray nonentity) ever brings back the memories of the wild bird cries he heard as Dora lay dying. Lazarus glosses this as "ephemerals" die; a close relationship hurts too much (we see this also in his relationship to Libby when they pick up his orbiting corpse). But both his father and his mother died— even the remembrances of his mother do not pull at his heart as does Dora. Later he knows he is back in the spaceship after he (literally) gets his hind end shot off in WW I; he calls for his mother, saying he thought he was dead. When he actually believes that he is dying in the shell hole, he hears the honking of the wild geese associated with his only true love, Dora.

The Dora sequence is Heinlein at his very best. He is dealing from his special area of expertise, how to do something—in this case how to explore and homestead in a totally uninhabited wilderness. The writing is compact, believable, well plotted, and it is a believable treatment of a mature sexual love. Only a little of his fatal coyness remains in the love sequences, and the ending is at least highly charged with pathos if not full-fledged tragedy seen through a rose-colored framework. Reemphasizing that last point is crucial. The ending is not pathetic, although there is an element of pathos; the ending is not sentimental, although he sentimentalizes to a certain degree; and in the end, an old man learns wisdom (to paraphrase the ending of *Antigone*): the arrogant pride of an immortal being brings the final catastrophe home to Lazarus. His *hubris* over his greatness is what eventually brings him to the point where he sees no further point in living. I do not know if Heinlein intended this interpretation. He has obviously read Greek tragedy and Shakespeare, but, even if unplanned and unintentional, it is the only reason why Lazarus wishes to die: he has done everything, *including the experience of a complete love*. And Heinlein, like Lazarus, has written everything, including a mature love story.

There are other good tales in *Time Enough for Love*: the ending story set in WW I is passable as adventure fiction (realistic), and the slaver planet sequence is good old-fashioned space opera circa 1945-50. Even the linking story of Secundus/Tertius would be interesting if there weren't so many uses of that four-letter word "DEAR!" thrown carelessly about. Moreover, some of the secondary and tertiary love stories have some vigor. The entire work, however, revolves around its form as a romance—the resolution of the writer's oedipal drive, and the two love stories where the content and intent of the author are most closely focused. Maureen, the mother, and Dora, the baby tossed from the fire, are the two pivots of the maturation theme, and the mature love story of Dora and Lazarus demonstrates the effectiveness of the writer's sexual recapitulation.

Notes

CHAPTER 2:* DAVID N. SAMUELSON

1. Alexei Panshin, *Heinlein in Dimension* (Chicago: Advent, 1968).
2. (New York: New American Library, 1955). Although Heinlein claimed at the time to have abandoned these stories, their outlines bear distinct resemblance to materials used in *Stranger in a Strange Land*, *The Moon Is a Harsh Mistress*, and the novelette "Free Men," published in *The Worlds of Robert A. Heinlein* (New York: Ace, 1966).
3. This subplot and the "happy ending" were dictated by John Campbell, over the futile objections of Heinlein, who saw the plot and science as too facile and preferred the alternative of shutting down the power; but, in preparing the omnibus for publication, Heinlein's only changes were a few small ones updating terminology.
4. This is not to say that there are not such wheeler-dealers in the real world, rather that they don't get what they want so easily in boardroom conversations which carry such a heavy load of (reader-oriented) information.
5. Although "Requiem" was Heinlein's third published story, he points out that it was the first one he ever wrote, which may explain some of its faults, but hardly its popularity.
6. Although Heinlein says this story was intended for *The Saturday Evening Post*, its theme of real versus misguided patriotism, its motif of the ordinary man becoming a hero, and its military context seem tailor-made for the American Legion audience.
7. She also, of course, corresponds to the heroines of the girls' stories Heinlein was turning out in the Fifties, entirely outside the conventions of science fiction.
8. Cf. Heinlein's comments on the remote-controlled handling devices called "waldoes" and his so-called prediction of them in "Science Fiction: Its Nature, Faults, and Virtues," in *The Science Fiction Novel: Imagination and Social Criticism* (Chicago: Advent, 1959), 31.
9. For a more extended treatment of Heinlein's solipsism, see Panshin, *Heinlein*, 160-77.
10. In fact, Heinlein says, his cat's antics, like those described, gave him the inspiration for this novel which he wrote nonstop in thirteen days.
11. Charles Manson, convicted in 1970 for the 1969 Tate-La Bianca murders in Los Angeles, seems to have borrowed from *Stranger in a Strange Land* to buttress his attitudes toward love and death, as well as some of the behavior of his twisted "family" of "love." See Ed Sanders, *The Family: The Story of Charles Manson's Dune Buggy Attack Battalion*, rev. ed. (New York: Avon, 1972), for what sketchy details

---

* NOTE: There are no notes for Chapter 1.

there are (esp. pp. 32-33, 36, 386). This information, made public in the newspapers and *Time* magazine, caused Heinlein some notoriety at this time, when *Stranger* had become an underground classic, due in part to youthful readers taking dead seriously the novel's love religion.

12. Sam Moskowitz, *Seekers of Tomorrow: Masters of Modern Science Fiction* (Cleveland: World, 1966), 210. Heinlein, however, contends that while the novel was outlined in the late Forties, it was written in three large chunks in the late Fifties which no one has been able to differentiate. The break between the early action and the late philosophy, according to him, was intended from the beginning; if the apparent changes in style and content are only coincidental, it is nonetheless convenient that this novel marks a significant turning point in Heinlein's career, as the philosophizing in his novels takes over and the wider reading public begins to pay more attention to him.

13. Contrast the following critiques, which seem to indicate that it is difficult to stay neutral about this novel: Robert Plank, "Omnipotent Cannibals: Thoughts on Reading Heinlein's *Stranger in a Strange Land*," *Riverside Quarterly*, V, no. 1 (July 1971): 30-37 (reprinted in a slightly revised form as Chapter 4 of this book); Ronald Lee Cansler, "*Stranger in a Strange Land*: Science Fiction as Literature of Creative Imagination, Social Criticism, and Entertainment," *Journal of Popular Culture*, V, no. 4 (Spring 1972): 944-54.

14. Heinlein's sensationalism in *Farnham's Freehold* apparently drew fire from a number of quarters, as is indicated by an exchange of correspondence in *Riverside Quarterly* in 1966. Franz Rottensteiner complained of the gratuitous incest motif (II, no. 2, p. 144) and of the incredible naiveté of Barbara, *a biology major*, who retches at seeing the mother cat eat her afterbirth, thinking that she might have to do the same thing (II, no. 3, p. 220). The scenes occur on pp. 93-94 and 100-101 of the novel's paperback edition. Leland Sapiro, editor of *Riverside Quarterly*, responded to Rottensteiner's first letter with a reference to another fanzine critic's argument, in 1964, that Heinlein had set out "deliberately to exhibit our nastiest fears and revulsions." Cf. Plank, Chapter 4, or his article on *Stranger in a Strange Land*.

15. This dialect, or argot, which is supposed to identify Mannie as no intellectual in a culture derived from three generations or more of criminal and political exiles from many countries, uses words and phrases from several foreign tongues in a grammar ostensibly modified by Russian influence (though my Russian colleague, Professor Joseph Cvrtlk, strongly questions the legitimacy of Heinlein's usage). The real effect, too often, is of simple dictionary substitution in English sentences. See also Panshin, *Heinlein*, 115.

16. Algis Budrys, "Galaxy Bookshelf," *Galaxy*, July 1968, 64-67.

17. Heinlein assures me that *I Will Fear No Evil* has sold more copies than any of his other books, though *Time Enough for Love* and *Stranger in a Strange Land* may surpass it. But this box-office success may only underline that Heinlein is now competing more with Harold Robbins

and Jacqueline Susann than with Isaac Asimov and Arthur C. Clarke.

18. It may be argued, of course, that this dual consciousness may be only a figment of the imagination of the old man's brain, unable to cope with its changed body, but I think we need at least the ambiguity of whether Eunice is really present or most of the book loses its meaning, if not its titillating effect.

19. Heinlein maintains that the reviews of *Time Enough for Love*, outside the science fiction community, have been predominantly favorable. Not having access to all the reviews, as an author and his publisher have, I did check those I could find, in *Booklist*, *English Journal*, *Library Journal*, *Los Angeles Times*, and *The New York Times*, all of which paid sentimental homage to Lazarus Long, the Heinlein canon, and the Future History. Most, however, felt that the novel was too long and too garrulous, although they might be willing to put up with that for old times' sake. The only unpatronizing praise came from Harrison J. Means in the *English Journal*, LXII, no. 7 (October 1973): 1060, who found it "a nearly 600-page delight for the avid SF reader who never wants a story to end. . . . With the publication of *I Will Fear No Evil* [in paperback] Heinlein's concern with longevity and with liberal mores has marked a change in his novels. Both are excellent reading."

20. This common criticism of Heinlein he disclaims, largely on the grounds that he has always tested the conventional limits of the pulp magazines, pushing for "adult" sexual relationships. But, having taken this freedom since *Stranger*, he has not taken advantage of it yet to portray what I would call an adult sexual relationship. There are adult relationships, as in "The Unpleasant Profession of Jonathan Hoag," and there are regressive relationships, as in *The Door into Summer*, but where there is explicit sex, there seems always to be the cooing, giggling, or sniggering of adolescence.

21. The idea of a musical analogy is, I think, a good one, allowing Heinlein to pick out of an unwieldy two millennia various moments which might serve as "Variations on a Theme" (a chapter title he uses five times), or conceptual themes which blend or contrast. But the analogy really seems to stop with the Contents page, appearing to be superimposed over what is still an unwieldy narrative; to be sure, the last seven subchapters are "titled" with punning bugle calls (as Lazarus goes off to fight in World War I), but that rather changes the shape of the analogy. Unlike the internal monologue, which Heinlein seems more comfortable with than in *I Will Fear No Evil*, these "modernist" devices do not appear to me to be fully under his control.

22. This thesis is defended at some length in Alfred Bester, "Science Fiction and the Renaissance Man," *The Science Fiction Novel*, 102-25.

23. An excellent study of the way that aliens, specifically, meet our fantasy needs is Robert Plank's *The Emotional Significance of Imaginary Beings: A Study of the Interaction Between Psychotherapy, Literature, and Reality in the Modern World* (Springfield, Ill.: Charles C Thomas,

1968). For an analysis of what readers were willing to accept as science, see any of the articles in the series "The Science in Science Fiction" by Gregory Benford and others in *Amazing*, beginning in November 1969.

24. See Albert I. Berger, "The Magic That Works: John W. Campbell and the American Response to Technology," *Journal of Popular Culture*, V, no. 4 (Spring 1972): 867-943. See also Heinlein's sober predictions in "Where To?" *Galaxy*, February 1952, 13-29, revised and updated as "Pandora's Box," *The Worlds of Robert A. Heinlein*, 7-31.

25. Cf. Judith Merril, "What Do You Mean Science/Fiction?" in *SF: The Other Side of Realism: Essays on Modern Fantasy and Science Fiction*, ed. Thomas D. Clareson (Bowling Green, Ohio: Bowling Green University Popular Press, 1971). Although Heinlein has shown a preference for the term "speculative fiction," his use of it is quite restrictive. See especially his essay in *The Science Fiction Novel, passim*.

26. In 1973 (*Analog*) as in 1947 (*Of Worlds Beyond*), he maintains that perseverance is the most important ingredient of a writer's success. In 1958, he dismisses "Henry Miller, Jean-Paul Sartre, James Joyce, Françoise Sagan and Alberto Moravia" as representatives of the "ashcan school of realism," in *The Science Fiction Novel*, 54. His aim, in style, he maintains, is to write lucid prose, for which he takes as his models Sir Winston Churchill, Justice Holmes, T. H. Huxley, and Rudyard Kipling. Yet in *Farnham's Freehold* he comes close to writing a mainstream novel such as he had six years before classified as sick; in *I Will Fear No Evil* we find him playing with stream-of-consciousness techniques, and in *Time Enough for Love* the emphasis on juxtaposition and counterpoint is positively obtrusive.

27. For an even dozen, compare Heinlein's bests with *A Canticle for Leibowitz, The Crystal World, Davy, The Dream Master, Dying Inside, The Einstein Intersection, The Left Hand of Darkness, The Man in the High Castle, Mission of Gravity, More Than Human, No Blades of Grass*, and *Stand on Zanzibar*. For icing, of course, you can add the best SF works of Anthony Burgess, William Golding, C. S. Lewis, George R. Stewart, and Kurt Vonnegut, along with the great dystopias of Huxley, Orwell, and Zamiatin, and the best of Wells's "scientific romances."

28. In preparing this chapter, I have also read but not made significant use of other articles on Heinlein. Two are largely source tracings: J. R. Christopher's "Methuselah, Out of Heinlein by Shaw," *The Shaw Review*, XVI, no. 2 (May 1973): 79-88; and Diane Pankin Speer's "Heinlein's *The Door into Summer* and *Roderick Random*," *Extrapolation*, XII, no. 1 (December 1970): 30-34. Three others strongly emphasize character studies of Heinlein through his writings: a general survey (through 1957) by Damon Knight, "One Sane Man: Robert A. Heinlein," *In Search of Wonder: Essays on Modern Science Fiction*, rev. ed. (Chicago: Advent, 1967): 76-89; a study of the first-person narrator by James Blish, "First Person Singular: Heinlein, Son of Heinlein," *More Issues at Hand: Critical Studies in Contemporary Science Fic-*

tion (Chicago: Advent, 1970): 51-58; and an amateur psychoanalytic study by Alexei and Cory Panshin, "Reading Heinlein Subjectively," *The Alien Critic*, III, no. 2 (May 1974): 4-17. Doubtless there are numerous other fanzine articles I have not come across which might be illuminating, but, unlike the Panshins, I have attempted a consciously "objective" reading (in that I have tried to relate his work to the real world, as I—subjectively—understand both the work and the world), one which I hope will stand up when later Heinlein works are published. He claims there are many yet to come.

CHAPTER 3: ALICE CAROL GAAR

1. Alexei Panshin, *Heinlein in Dimension* (Chicago: Advent, 1968), 36.
2. The most recent editions are the following: Robert A. Heinlein, *Waldo & Magic, Inc.* (New York: New American Library, Signet Books, 1970); *Universe* in *Orphans of the Sky* (New York: Berkley Medallion, 1970); *Methuselah's Children* in *The Past Through Tomorrow* (New York: Berkley Medallion, 1975); *Starship Troopers* (New York: Berkley Medallion, 1968); *Stranger in a Strange Land* (New York: Berkley Medallion, 1968); *The Moon Is a Harsh Mistress* (New York: Berkley Medallion, 1968).
3. Heinlein, *I Will Fear No Evil* (New York: Berkley Medallion, 1971).
4. Heinlein, *Time Enough for Love* (New York: Berkley Medallion, 1974).
5. Dennis E. Showalter, "Heinlein's *Starship Troopers*: An Exercise in Rehabilitation," *Extrapolation*, XVI, no. 2 (May 1975): 113-24.

CHAPTER 4: ROBERT PLANK

1. Robert A. Heinlein, *Stranger in a Strange Land* (New York: Berkley Medallion, 1968). Page numbers refer to this edition, "f.i.p." means "first introduced page."
2. *The New York Times Book Review*, February 21, 1971.
3. Alexei Panshin, *Heinlein in Dimension* (Chicago: Advent, 1968), 143.
4. Aldous Huxley, Foreword to later editions of *Brave New World*.
5. D. Carleton Gajdusek, "Cannibalism, Culture, Consanguinity: Kuru and the Transmissible Virus Dementias" (Lecture, Cleveland, February 3, 1972).
6. *Encyclopaedia Brittanica*, 11th ed., s.v. "Coleoptera."
7. Garry Hogg, *Cannibalism and Human Sacrifice* (New York: Citadel Press, 1966), 18.
8. *Inferno*, Canto 33.
9. Piers Paul Read, *Alive* (Philadelphia: J. B. Lippincott, 1974).
10. Arthur C. Clarke, *The Lost Worlds of 2001* (New York: New American Library, 1972), 57.
11. Alfred Kubin, *The Other Side* (New York: Brown, 1967).
12. Ewald Volhard, *Cannibalismus* (Studien zur Kulturkunde, 5, Band) (Stuttgart: Strecker & Schroeder, 1939), ix, 491. (My translation.)

13. Fyodor Dostoyevsky, *The Brothers Karamazov*, trans. Constance Garnett (New York: Modern Library, 1950), 306.
14. Hermann Nunberg and Ernst Federn, eds., *Minutes of the Vienna Psychoanalytic Society*, vol. III (New York: International Universities Press, 1974), 79, 76.
15. Sigmund Freud, "Totem and Taboo," in *The Standard Edition of the Complete Psychological Works of Sigmund Freud*, vol. XIII (London: Hogarth Press, 1955), 85-86.
16. Sigmund Freud, *Moses and Monotheism* (London: Hogarth Press, 1939), 179.
17. S. Ferenczi, "Stages in the Development of the Sense of Reality," in his *Sex in Psychoanalysis* (Boston: Richard G. Badger, 1916). See also Anna Freud, "Certain Types and Stages of Social Maladjustment," in *The Writings of Anna Freud*, vol. IV (New York: International Universities Press, 1968), 79-80.
18. Cf. Margaret S. Mahler et al., *The Psychological Birth of the Human Infant* (New York: Basic Books, 1975).
19. R. Z. Sheppard, "Future Grok," *Time*, March 29, 1971.
20. Anthony Burgess, "One of America's Glories, with 50 books and 80 Years Behind Him," *The New York Times Book Review*, January 2, 1972.
21. "Selected Letters," *Riverside Quarterly*, V, no. 2 (February 2, 1972), 152-58.
22. Panshin, *Heinlein in Dimension*, 43, 45.

CHAPTER 5: RONALD SARTI

1. Robert A. Heinlein, "Views of Robert Heinlein," *The New Yorker*, July 1, 1974, 18.
2. Alexei Panshin, *Heinlein in Dimension* (Chicago: Advent, 1968), 169-72.
3. For this story and for other early works from Heinlein's prewar writing (1939-42), I am referring to versions rewritten for book publication rather than the original magazine versions. For more information on original versions and rewrites, see Panshin.
4. Heinlein, *Starman Jones*, ed. Judy L. del Rey (New York: Ballantine, 1975), (19).*
5. Heinlein, *The Menace from Earth* (New York: New American Library, Signet Books, 1962), (2).
6. Heinlein, *Time Enough for Love* (New York: Berkley Medallion, 1974), "Variations on a Theme XII."
7. Anne McCaffrey, "Romance and Glamour in Science Fiction," in *Science Fiction: Today and Tomorrow*, ed. Reginald Bretnor (New York: Harper and Row, 1974), 281.
8. "Women in Science Fiction," Introduction, *Women of Wonder: Sci-*

* NOTE: Numbers in parentheses indicate chapters.

ence Fiction Stories by Women About Women, ed. Pamela Sargent (New York: Random House, 1975), xliii.

9. "Introduction by Damon Knight," Heinlein, *The Past Through Tomorrow* (New York: Berkley Medallion, 1975).

10. Heinlein, *The Puppet Masters* (New York: New American Library, Signet Books, 1975), (27).

11. Heinlein, *Waldo & Magic, Inc.* (New York: New American Library, Signet Books, 1970).

12. Heinlein, in *The Past Through Tomorrow*.

13. Heinlein, *Glory Road* (New York: Berkley Medallion, 1970), (21).

14. Heinlein, *Time Enough for Love*, "Variations on a Theme XII."

15. Heinlein, *Have Space Suit—Will Travel* (New York: Ace Books, 1975), (6).

16. Chapter 21.

17. Heinlein, *Tunnel in the Sky* (New York: Ace Books, 1970), (2).

18. Sargent, *Women of Wonder*, xliv.

19. Panshin, *Heinlein in Dimension*, 151.

20. Heinlein, *Beyond This Horizon* (New York: New American Library, Signet Books, 1974), (4).

21. Heinlein, *The Door into Summer* (New York: New American Library, Signet Books, 1975), (11).

22. Heinlein, " 'If This Goes On—' " (10), in *The Past Through Tomorrow*.

23. Robert Plank, "Omnipotent Cannibals: Thoughts on Reading Robert Heinlein's *Stranger in a Strange Land*," *Riverside Quarterly*, V (1971): 30-37. See also Chapter 4, this book.

24. Panshin, *Heinlein in Dimension*, 151.

25. Heinlein, *Stranger in a Strange Land* (New York: Berkley Medallion, 1968), (36).

26. Heinlein, *I Will Fear No Evil* (New York: Berkley Medallion, 1971), (14).

27. Heinlein, *Time Enough for Love*, "Intermission."

28. *Time Enough for Love*, "Variations on a Theme VII."

CHAPTER 6: PHILIP E. SMITH II

1. James Gunn, *Alternate Worlds, the Illustrated History of Science Fiction* (Englewood Cliffs, N.J.: Prentice-Hall, 1975), 170.

2. Charles Darwin, *The Descent of Man* (1871), selections rpt. in *Darwin: A Norton Critical Edition*, ed. Philip Appleman (New York: Norton, 1970), 275.

3. Richard Hofstadter, *Social Darwinism in American Thought*, rev. ed. (Boston: Beacon, 1955), 201.

4. H. G. Wells, *A Modern Utopia* (New York: Scribner's, 1905), 5; hereafter referred to in the text as MU.

5. Robert A. Heinlein, *Beyond This Horizon* (New York: New American Library, Signet Books, 1974), (2); hereafter referred to in the text as BTH.

6. Heinlein uses a similar plot premise in Lazarus Long's suicidal depression at the beginning of *Time Enough for Love.*

7. Alexei Panshin, in *Heinlein in Dimension* (Chicago: Advent, 1968), calls attention to "an idea Heinlein has put forward on at least five different occasions: Man is a wild animal, the roughest, meanest critter in this neck of the universe" (p. 90); further, Panshin notes that "Heinlein's idea of liberty is wolfish and thoroughgoing" and sees a "strong element of wolfishness present again in *Beyond This Horizon*" (pp. 162-63). Even though he notices these ideas, I believe Panshin significantly underestimates how basic and widespread in Heinlein's fiction are both his wolfish vision of human nature and his social Darwinistic sense of how much human survival depends on individual and racial combativeness.

8. Heinlein, *The Day After Tomorrow* (New York: New American Library, Signet Books, 1975), (3); hereafter referred to in the text as DAT.

9. Heinlein, "'If This Goes On—'" (6), in *The Past Through Tomorrow* (New York: Berkley Medallion, 1975); hereafter referred to in the text as ITGO.

10. Some other locations where this axiom is quoted include: "Free Men," *The Worlds of Robert Heinlein* (New York: Ace Books, 1972), 59; *Double Star* (New York: New American Library, Signet Books, 1975), (10).

11. According to Heinlein's time scheme for the Future History series, the political serenity of the Covenant dissolves a century after "Coventry" when Earth is plagued by "Civil disorder, followed by the end of human adolescence, and beginning of first mature culture." These events, described in *Methuselah's Children* and *Time Enough for Love*, will be discussed in relation to those two novels.

12. Heinlein, "Lost Legacy," (12), in *Assignment in Eternity* (New York: New American Library, Signet Books, 1970); hereafter referred to in the text as LL.

13. Thomas Hobbes, "On Man," *Man and Citizen: Thomas Hobbes's De Homine and De Cive*, ed. Bernard Gert (Garden City, N.Y.: Doubleday Anchor, 1972), 40.

14. Hobbes, "The Citizen," *Man and Citizen*, 89.

15. Gertrude Himmelfarb, *Darwin and the Darwinian Revolution* (New York: Norton, 1968), 416-17.

16. Marx felt Darwin's influence to be so seminal that he offered to dedicate *Das Kapital* to Darwin. Himmelfarb discusses the attempts of "'scientific socialists' to amalgamate Darwinism and Marxism into one irresistible system" in *Darwin and the Darwinian Revolution*, 421-25.

17. Heinlein, *Revolt in 2100* (New York: New American Library, Signet Books, 1970).

18. Heinlein, *The Puppet Masters* (New York: New American Library, Signet Books, 1975), (21); hereafter referred to in the text as PM.

19. Heinlein, *Double Star*, 125; hereafter referred to in the text as DS.

20. Alfred Bester, "PW Interviews: Robert Heinlein," *Publishers Weekly*, July 2, 1973, 45.

21. Heinlein, *The Door into Summer* (New York: New American Library, Signet Books, 1975), (2); hereafter referred to in the text as DIS.

22. Charles Darwin, *The Descent of Man*, selections rpt. in *Darwin: A Norton Critical Edition*, 274-75.

23. Heinlein, *Methuselah's Children*, (pt. 1, chap. 2), in *The Past Through Tomorrow* (New York: Berkley Medallion, 1975); hereafter referred to in the text as MC.

24. Quoted in Frank Robinson, "Conversation with Robert Heinlein," *Oui*, 1, no. 3 (December 1972): 76.

25. Dennis E. Showalter, "Heinlein's *Starship Troopers*: An Exercise in Rehabilitation," *Extrapolation*, XVI, no. 2 (May 1975): 113.

26. Panshin, *Heinlein in Dimension*, 94. The book's efficacy in this regard was proven to me when one of my students, a former Green Beret demolitions expert, declared that *Starship Troopers* strongly influenced him to enlist in the Special Forces.

27. Heinlein, *Starship Troopers* (New York: Berkley Medallion, 1968), (2); hereafter referred to in the text as ST.

28. Heinlein, *Stranger in a Strange Land* (New York: Berkley Medallion, 1968), (6); hereafter referred to in the text as SSL.

29. George E. Slusser, in *Robert A. Heinlein: Stranger in His Own Land* (San Bernardino: The Borgo Press, 1976), 28-31, also points out "Harshaw's Darwinist vision of things" (p. 28). Slusser notes that "Behind Smith's creed lies the sanction of natural selection: election is not a subjective reality, but a tangible force, which reveals itself in human competitiveness, in the ability to fight and win" (p. 28).

30. Ruth Benedict, *Patterns of Culture* (New York: New American Library, 1960), 114 and 79-120. Hereafter referred to in the text as PC.

31. Heinlein, *Glory Road* (New York: Berkley Medallion, 1965), (17); hereafter referred to in the text as GR.

32. Heinlein, *Farnham's Freehold* (New York: Berkley Medallion, 1971), (2); hereafter referred to in the text as FF.

33. Heinlein, *The Moon Is a Harsh Mistress* (New York: Berkley Medallion, 1968), (9); hereafter referred to in the text as MIHM.

34. Alexei Panshin finds *The Moon Is a Harsh Mistress* to be more concerned with process than any previous Heinlein novel (*Heinlein in Dimension*, 111).

35. David Ketterer, *New Worlds for Old: The Apocalyptic Imagination, Science Fiction, and American Literature* (Garden City, N.Y.: Doubleday Anchor, 1974), 151; hereafter referred to in the text as NWO.

36. Slusser, *Robert A. Heinlein*, 33.

37. Heinlein, *I Will Fear No Evil* (New York: Berkley Medallion, 1971), (26); hereafter referred to in the text as IWFNE.

38. Quoted in Frank Robinson, "Conversation with Robert Heinlein," 116.

39. Heinlein, *Time Enough for Love* (New York: Berkley Medallion, 1974), "Da Capo III"; hereafter referred to in the text as TEL.

40. Heinlein, "Channel Markers," *Analog: Science Fiction, Science Fact*, 92, no. 5 (January 1974): 175.

41. Ursula K. LeGuin, "American SF and the Other," *Science Fiction Studies*, 7 (November 1975): 210.
42. Hofstadter, *Social Darwinism in American Thought*, 204.

CHAPTER 7: FRANK H. TUCKER

1. Robert A. Heinlein, *The Door into Summer* (New York: New American Library, Signet Books, 1975), (12).
2. Franz Rottensteiner, *The Science Fiction Book* (New York: Seabury Press, 1975), 100.
3. Heinlein, *Farnham's Freehold* (New York: Berkley Medallion, 1971), (2); *Beyond This Horizon* (New York: New American Library, Signet Books, 1974), (2), (10).
4. Heinlein, *Starship Troopers* (New York: Berkley Medallion, 1968), hereafter referred to in text as ST.
5. *Time Enough for Love* (New York: Berkley Medallion, 1974), (Introduction, "Prelude I," "Variations on a Theme XIV"), hereafter referred to in text as TEL; "The Man Who Sold the Moon," (8), (12), in *The Past Through Tomorrow* (New York: Berkley Medallion, 1975); "Logic of Empire," in *The Past Through Tomorrow*.
6. Damon Knight, *In Search of Wonder* (Chicago: Advent, 1967), 84-85.
7. Heinlein, *Waldo & Magic, Inc.* (New York: New American Library, Signet Books, 1970), 76-77, 186.
8. "'If This Goes On—,'" (6), in *The Past Through Tomorrow*, hereafter referred to in text as ITGO.
9. Heinlein, *Podkayne of Mars* (New York: Berkley Medallion, 1975), (4).
10. Heinlein, *Glory Road* (New York: Berkley Medallion, 1970), (20).
11. Heinlein, "Gulf," in *Assignment in Eternity* (New York: New American Library, Signet Books, 1970).
12. Heinlein, "Coventry," in *The Past Through Tomorrow*.
13. Heinlein, "Science Fiction: Its Nature, Faults, and Virtues," in *The Science Fiction Novel*, Basil Davenport et al. (Chicago: Advent, 1969), 44-45.
14. Heinlein, "The Long Watch," in *The Past Through Tomorrow*.
15. Heinlein, *The Moon Is a Harsh Mistress* (New York: Berkley Medallion, 1968), (2), hereafter referred to in text as MIHM.
16. Heinlein, "Delilah and the Space Rigger," in *The Past Through Tomorrow*.
17. Heinlein, "Requiem," in *The Past Through Tomorrow*.
18. Heinlein, *Beyond This Horizon*, (9); Alexei Panshin, *Heinlein in Dimension* (Chicago: Advent, 1968), 185.
19. Heinlein, "The Year of the Jackpot," (3), in *The Menace from Earth* (New York: New American Library, Signet Books, 1970).
20. Heinlein, *The Day After Tomorrow* (New York: New American Library, Signet Books, 1975), (1).

CHAPTER 8: RUSSELL LETSON

1. See Alexei Panshin, *Heinlein in Dimension* (Chicago: Advent, 1968),

chap. 4, "The Period of Alienation," and George Edgar Slusser, *Robert A. Heinlein: Stranger in His Own Land* (San Bernardino, Calif.: The Borgo Press, 1976), for detailed arguments to this end.

2. For some samples, see Richard Lupoff in *Algol*, 21 (1973): 43-44; Lester del Rey in *IF*, September-October 1973, 145-50; Peter Nicholls in *Foundation*, 7-8 (March 1975): 73-80; Richard Briney in *Views and Reviews*, December 1973, 34-35.

3. Richard Geis in *The Alien Critic*, 6 (August 1973): 7-9; Karl Pflock in *Amazing*, February 1974, 108-10.

4. Robert A. Heinlein, *Time Enough for Love* (New York: Berkley Medallion, 1974), ("Second Intermission"). Subsequent citations are run into the text and labeled TEL.

5. Joe R. Christopher, "Lazarus, Come Forth from That Tomb," *Riverside Quarterly*, XXIII (August 1975), 190-97.

6. Panshin, 12; Baird Searles, *Heinlein's Works: Stranger in a Strange Land and Other Works* (Lincoln, Nebr.: Cliff's Notes, 1975), 51.

7. Damon Knight, *In Search of Wonder* (Chicago: Advent, 1967), 83-84.

8. Oddly enough—or perhaps inevitably—"Magic, Inc." explores classical magic and is one of Heinlein's most rigorously rationalized stories —science fiction about magic-as-technology. Most of the exploration of the mysterious occurs in the straight science fiction.

9. Heinlein, "They," in *The Unpleasant Profession of Jonathan Hoag* (New York: Berkley Medallion, 1976).

10. Heinlein, "'All You Zombies—,'" in *The Unpleasant Profession of Jonathan Hoag*.

11. See Panshin, 175; Slusser, 43-50; Geis, 9.

12. Heinlein, "By His Bootstraps," in *The Menace from Earth* (New York: New American Library, Signet Books, 1962).

13. Peter Nicholls objects to the way Heinlein has made this situation so easy—see Nicholls, 79.

14. Heinlein, *Methuselah's Children*, (pt. 1, chap. 7), in *The Past Through Tomorrow* (New York: Berkley Medallion, 1974). Subsequent citations are run into the text and labeled MC.

CHAPTER 9: IVOR A. ROGERS

1. Alexei Panshin, *Heinlein in Dimension* (Chicago: Advent, 1968); James Blish, *The Issue at Hand* (Chicago: Advent, 1964), and *More Issues at Hand* (Chicago: Advent, 1970); Brian Aldiss, *Billion Year Spree* (New York: Doubleday, 1973).

2. Robert A. Heinlein, "Science Fiction: Its Nature, Faults, and Virtues," in Basil Davenport et al., *The Science Fiction Novel*, 3rd ed. (Chicago: Advent, 1969).

3. Vincent McHugh, *Caleb Catlum's America* (Harrisburg, Pa.: Stackpole, 1936).

4. Vincent McHugh, *I Am Thinking of My Darling* (New York: Scribner's, 1943).

5. Ivor A. Rogers, "The Gernsback Era," in Neil Barron, ed., *Anatomy of Wonder* (New York: R. R. Bowker, 1976), 88-89.

6. Northrop Frye, *Anatomy of Criticism* (Princeton, N.J.: Princeton University Press, 1957), 49.
7. Heinlein, *Methuselah's Children*, in *The Past Through Tomorrow* (New York: Berkley Medallion, 1975).

Selected Bibliography

THIS BIBLIOGRAPHY is not intended to be complete. Rather, it attempts to aid the reader by bringing together the great majority of Robert A. Heinlein's novels and stories, as well as a number of critical essays on his work. The bibliography relies on information gathered from a variety of sources, including *The Encyclopedia of Science Fiction and Fantasy*, Vol. 1, compiled by Donald H. Tuck (Chicago: Advent Publishers, 1974), and the computer printout version of the *Index to Science Fiction Anthologies and Collections* by William G. Contento, which will be published by G. K. Hall. The latter work was particularly valuable.

Primary Works

"All You Zombies—," *The Magazine of Fantasy & Science Fiction* (March 1959).
————. *The Unpleasant Profession of Jonathan Hoag*, 1959.
"And He Built a Crooked House," *Astounding Science Fiction* (February 1941).
————. *The Unpleasant Profession of Jonathan Hoag*, 1959.
Assignment in Eternity. [Four long stories.] Reading, Pa.: Fantasy Press, 1953. New York: New American Library, 1970.
The Best of Robert Heinlein. Angus Wells, ed. London: Sidgwick & Jackson, 1973.
Between Planets. London: Gollancz, 1951, 1968. New York: Scribner's, 1957. New York: Ace, 1975 (illustrated by Clifford Geary). [A condensed version appeared in *Blue Book Magazine* entitled "Planets in Combat."]
"Beyond Doubt" ("Lyle Monroe"), *Astonishing Stories* (April 1941).
Beyond This Horizon. New York: Fantasy Press, 1942. New York: New American Library, 1960, 1964, 1974.
"The Black Pits of Luna," *Saturday Evening Post* (January 1948).
————. *The Past Through Tomorrow*, 1967.

"Blowups Happen," *Astounding Science Fiction* (September 1940).
————. *The Past Through Tomorrow*, 1967.
"By His Bootstraps," *Astounding Science Fiction* (October 1941).
————. *The Menace from Earth*, 1959.
Citizen of the Galaxy. New York: Scribner's, 1957. New York: Ace, 1971, 1975.
"Columbus Was a Dope," *Startling Stories* (May 1947).
————. *The Menace from Earth*, 1959.
"Common Sense," *Astounding Science Fiction* (October 1941).
"Coventry," *Astounding Science Fiction* (July 1940).
————. *The Past Through Tomorrow*, 1967.

The Day After Tomorrow. [First appeared as "Sixth Column" in *Astounding Science Fiction*, 1941.] New York: New American Library, 1949, 1975. London: Mayflower Books, 1962.
"Delilah and the Space-Rigger," *Blue Book Magazine* (December 1949).
————. *The Past Through Tomorrow*, 1967.
"Destination Moon," *Short Stories Magazine* (September 1950).
The Door into Summer. Garden City, N.Y.: Doubleday, 1956, 1964. New York: New American Library, 1975.
Double Star. Garden City, N.Y.: Doubleday, 1957, 1964. New York: New American Library, 1970, 1975.

"Elsewhen," *Astounding Science Fiction* (September 1941).
————. *Assignment in Eternity*, 1953.

Farmer in the Sky. New York: Scribner's, 1950. London: Gollancz, 1962. New York: Dell, 1968. New York: Ballantine, 1975.
Farnham's Freehold. [Short version appeared in *Worlds of If Magazine*, 1964.] New York: Putnam, 1964. New York: New American Library, 1965. London: Corgi Books, 1967. New York: Berkley, 1971, 1974.
"Free Men," *The Worlds of Robert A. Heinlein*, 1966.

"Gentlemen, Be Seated!" *Argosy* (May 1948).
————. *The Past Through Tomorrow*, 1967.
Glory Road. New York: Putnam, 1963. London: Gollancz, 1965. New York: Berkley, 1970, 1974.
"Goldfish Bowl," *Astounding Science Fiction* (March 1942).
————. *The Menace from Earth*. 1959.
"The Green Hills of Earth," *Saturday Evening Post* (February 1947).
————. *The Green Hills of Earth*, 1951.
The Green Hills of Earth. New York: New American Library, 1951, 1958, 1973. New York: Aeonian Press, 1976 (reprint of 1951 edition).
"Gulf," *Astounding Science Fiction* (November 1949).
————. *Assignment in Eternity*, 1953.

Have Space Suit—Will Travel. New York: Scribner's, 1958. London: Gollancz, 1970. New York: Ace, 1975.
"Heil!" *Futuria Fantasia* (April 1940).

A Heinlein Triad. London: Gollancz, 1965. [First published as *Three by Heinlein* and included *The Puppet Masters*, *Waldo*, and *Magic, Inc.*]

I Will Fear No Evil. New York: Putnam, 1970. New York: Berkley, 1971. London: New English Library, 1974.

"If This Goes On—," *Astounding Science Fiction* (February 1940).
———. *The Past Through Tomorrow*, 1967.

"It's Great To Be Back," *Saturday Evening Post* (July 1947).
———. *The Past Through Tomorrow*, 1967.

"Jerry Was a Man," *Thrilling Wonder Stories* (October 1947).
———. *Assignment in Eternity*, 1953.

"Let There Be Light," *Super Science Stories* (May 1940).
———. *The Man Who Sold the Moon*, 1953.

"Life-Line," *Astounding Science Fiction* (August 1939).
———. *The Past Through Tomorrow*, 1967.

"Logic of Empire," *Astounding Science Fiction* (March 1941).
———. *The Past Through Tomorrow*, 1967.

"The Long Watch," *American Legion Magazine* (December 1949).
———. *The Past Through Tomorrow*, 1967.

"Lost Legacy," *Super Science Stories* (November 1941).
———. *Assignment in Eternity*, 1953.

Lost Legacy. [First published as *Lost Legion*, 1941.] London: Brown, Watson, 1973.

"Lyle Monroe." *See* "Beyond Doubt."

"Magic, Inc.," *Unknown* (September 1940).
Magic, Inc. New York: Scribner's, 1940. See also *Waldo*.

"The Man Who Sold the Moon," 1950.
The Man Who Sold the Moon. New York: New American Library, 1973. [Also published with *Harriman and the Escape from the Earth to the Moon!* Chicago: Shasta, 1953.]

"The Man Who Traveled in Elephants," *Saturn Science Fiction and Fantasy* (October 1957).
———. *The Unpleasant Profession of Jonathan Hoag*, 1959.

"The Menace from Earth," *The Magazine of Fantasy & Science Fiction* (August 1957).
———. *The Menace from Earth*, 1959.

The Menace from Earth. Hicksville, N.Y.: Gnome Press, 1959. London: Gollancz, 1964. New York: New American Library, 1970. New York: Aeonian Press, 1976 (reprint of 1959 edition).

Methuselah's Children. Hicksville, N.Y.: Gnome Press, 1958. New York: New American Library, 1960, 1975. London: Gollancz, 1963. London: Pan Books, 1974.

"Misfit," *Astounding Science Fiction* (November 1939).
———. *The Past Through Tomorrow*, 1967.

The Moon Is a Harsh Mistress. New York: Putnam, 1966. New York: Berkley, 1968. [A short version appeared in *Worlds of If Magazine*.]

"Ordeal in Space," *Town and Country* (May 1948).
———. *The Past Through Tomorrow*, 1967.
Orphans of the Sky. London: Gollancz, 1963. New York: Putnam, 1964. New York: New American Library, 1965. New York: Berkley, 1970.
"Our Fair City," *Weird Tales* (January 1949).
———. *The Unpleasant Profession of Jonathan Hoag*, 1959.
The Past Through Tomorrow: Future History Stories. New York: Putnam, 1967. New York: Berkley, 1975.
Podkayne of Mars. New York: Putnam, 1963. New York: Avon, 1968. New York: Berkley, 1975.
"Project Nightmare," *Amazing Stories* (May 1953).
———. *The Menace from Earth*, 1959.
The Puppet Masters. New York: New American Library, 1951, 1963, 1975. London: Pan Books, 1969.
Red Planet. New York: Scribner, 1949. London: Gollancz, 1963. New York: Ace, 1975.
"Requiem," *Astounding Science Fiction* (January 1940).
———. *The Past Through Tomorrow*, 1967.
Revolt in 2100: The Prophets and the Triumph of Reason over Superstition. Chicago: Shasta, 1953. London: Gollancz, 1964. New York: New American Library, 1970, 1975. [Introduction by Henry Kuttner. Originally published as stories in *Unknown Worlds* (Street & Smith's), 1939, 1940.]
"The Roads Must Roll," *Astounding Science Fiction* (June 1940).
———. *The Past Through Tomorrow*, 1967.
A Robert Heinlein Omnibus. London: Sidgwick & Jackson, 1966.
Rocket Ship Galileo. New York: Scribner's, 1947, 1967, 1969 (illustrated by Thomas W. Voter). New York: Ace, 1975.
Rolling Stones. New York: Scribner's, 1952, 1958, 1973 (illustrated by Clifford Geary). New York: Ace, 1975. [Condensed version appeared in *Boy's Life* as "Tramp Space Ship."]
"Searchlight," *Scientific American* (August 1962).
———. *The Past Through Tomorrow*, 1967.
6 x H: Six Stories. New York: Pyramid, 1961, 1975.
"Sixth Column." See *The Day After Tomorrow*.
"Sky Lift," *Imagination* (November 1953).
———. *The Menace from Earth*, 1959.
"Solution Unsatisfactory," *Astounding Science Fiction* (May 1941).
———. *The Worlds of Robert A. Heinlein*, 1966.
Space Cadet. New York: Scribner's, 1948. London: Gollancz, 1966. New York: Ace, 1971, 1975.
Space Family Stone. New York: Scribner's, 1952. London: New English Library, 1971.
"Space Jockey," *Saturday Evening Post* (April 1947).
———. *The Past Through Tomorrow*, 1967.

Star Beast. New York: Scribner's, 1954, 1971 (illustrated). New York: Ace, 1975.

Starman Jones. New York: Scribner's, 1954, 1969 (illustrated by Clifford Geary). London: Gollancz: 1964. New York: Dell, 1967, 1973. New York: New American Library, 1970. New York: Ballantine, 1975 (Judy L. del Rey, ed.).

Starship Troopers. New York: Putnam, 1960. New York: Berkley, 1968, 1975. London: New English Library, 1967. [A much abridged version appeared in *The Magazine of Fantasy and Science Fiction* as "Starship Soldier."]

Stranger in a Strange Land. New York: Putnam, 1961. New York: Berkley, 1968.

"They," *Unknown* (April 1941).

———. *The Unpleasant Profession of Jonathan Hoag*, 1959.

Three by Heinlein. See *A Heinlein Triad*.

Time Enough for Love: The Lives of Lazarus Long. New York: Putnam, 1973. New York: Berkley, 1974. London: New English Library, 1974.

Time for the Stars. New York: Scribner's, 1956. London: Gollancz, 1963. New York: Ace, 1971.

Tomorrow the Stars. Robert A. Heinlein, ed. New York: Berkley, 1952, 1959, 1975.

Tunnel in the Sky. New York: Scribner's, 1955. London: Gollancz, 1965. New York: Ace, 1970.

"Universe," *Astounding Science Fiction* (May 1941).

"The Unpleasant Profession of Jonathan Hoag," *Unknown Worlds* (October 1942).

The Unpleasant Profession of Jonathan Hoag. Hicksville, N.Y.: Gnome Press, 1959. London: Gollancz, 1964. New York: Berkley, 1976.

"Waldo," *Astounding Science Fiction* (August 1942).

———. *Waldo, & Magic, Inc.*, 1963.

Waldo, & Magic, Inc. New York: Pyramid, 1963. London: Pan Books, 1969. New York: New American Library, 1975.

"Water Is for Washing," *Argosy* (November 1947).

———. *The Menace from Earth*, 1959.

" '—We Also Walk Dogs,' " *Astounding Science Fiction* (July 1941).

———. *The Past Through Tomorrow*, 1967.

The Worlds of Robert Heinlein. New York: Ace, 1966, 1972. London: New English Library, 1966.

"The Year of the Jackpot," *Galaxy* (March 1952).

———. *The Menace from Earth*, 1959.

Secondary Sources

Aldiss, Brian W. *Billion Year Spree: The True History of Science Fiction*. Garden City, N.Y.: Doubleday, 1973.

Allen, L. David. *Science Fiction: An Introduction.* Cliffs Notes, 1973.

Ash, Brian. *Faces of the Future: The Lessons of Science Fiction.* New York: Taplinger, 1975.

Atherling, William. *The Issue at Hand.* Chicago: Advent, 1964.

————. *More Issues at Hand.* Chicago: Advent, 1970.

Berger, Harold L. *Science Fiction and the New Dark Age.* Bowling Green, Ohio: Bowling Green Popular Press, 1976.

Bester, Alfred. "Robert Heinlein," *Publishers Weekly* (July 1973).

Cansler, Ronald L. "*Stranger in a Strange Land*: Science Fiction as Literature of the Creative Imagination, Social Criticism, and Entertainment," *Journal of Popular Culture,* v (1972).

Christopher, J.R. "Methuselah, Out of Heinlein by Shaw," *Shaw Review,* xvi (1973).

Ketter, David. *New Worlds for Old: The Apocalyptic Imagination, Science Fiction, and American Literature.* Garden City, N.Y.: Doubleday Anchor, 1974.

Knight, Damon. *In Search of Wonder.* Chicago: Advent, 1967.

Moskowitz, Sam. *Seekers of Tomorrow: Masters of Modern Science Fiction.* New York: Ballantine, 1967. Hyperion, Conn., 1974.

————. *Strange Horizons.* New York: Scribner's, 1976.

Panshin, Alexei. *Heinlein in Dimension: A Critical Analysis.* Chicago: Advent, 1968.

————. "Robert A. Heinlein: A Practical Idealist," *Helios,* Vol. o (Summer 1976).

Rose, Lois and Stephen. *The Shattered Ring.* Richmond, Va.: John Knox Press, 1970.

Scholes, Robert, and Rabkin, Eric S. *Science Fiction: History, Science, Vision.* New York: Oxford University Press, 1977.

Schuman, Samuel. "Vladimir Nabokov's *Invitation to a Beheading* and Robert Heinlein's *They,*" *Twentieth Century Literature,* xix (1973).

Searles, Baird. *Stranger in a Strange Land and Other Works.* Lincoln, Neb.: Cliffs Notes, 1975.

Showalter, Dennis E. "Heinlein's *Starship Troopers*: An Exercise in Rehabilitation," *Extrapolation,* Vol. 16 (May 1975).

Silverberg, Robert (ed.). *The Mirror of Infinity: A Critic's Anthology of Science Fiction.* New York: Harper & Row, 1970.

Slusser, George Edgar. *Robert A. Heinlein: Stranger in His Own Land.* (The Milford Series). San Bernardino, Ca.: The Borgo Press, 1976.

Speer, Diane P. "Heinlein's *The Door into Summer* and Roderick Random," *Extrapolation,* Vol. 12 (1970).

Wollheim, Donald A. *The Universe Makers.* New York: Harper & Row, 1971.

Robert A. Heinlein: A Biographical Note

BORN ON July 7, 1907, in Butler, Missouri, Robert A. Heinlein can claim that his family has been in America since 1750. He was graduated from Central High School, Kansas City, Missouri, in 1924. He later entered the Naval Academy, from which he graduated 20th out of 243 in the class of 1929. Thereafter he served on one of the first aircraft carriers in the Navy. Because of tuberculosis, he had to retire from the Navy in 1934. Between 1934 and 1939 he held a variety of jobs and even ran (unsuccessfully) for political office. Having divorced his first wife, he married again in 1948 to the former Virginia Gerstenfeld. In 1950 he moved to Colorado Springs, Colorado, and from there to California in 1966, where he currently resides.

Robert A. Heinlein's first science fiction story, "Life Line," was published in August 1939 by *Astounding Science Fiction*. Since then he has been a prolific writer within the field and has been distinguished by his development of "social science fiction" in the pulp magazines. But his influence and his writing went beyond the pulps. His fiction in magazines like *Saturday Evening Post*, *Argosy*, *Town and Country*, and *Blue Book* helped science fiction break into "the mainstream." In addition, he helped to educate the general public about science fiction through films and teenage magazines, such as *Boy's Life*. He was the technical adviser for the movie *Destination Moon*, which was based on his *Rocket Ship Galileo*. His work has been heavily anthologized, and most of it is still in print. He was the Guest of Honor at the Third World Science Fiction Convention in 1941, an honor he was to receive again in 1961 and in 1976. He has been the recipient of the Hugo Award for his novel *Double Star* in 1956, for *Starship Troopers* in 1960, for *Stranger in a Strange Land* in 1962, and for *The Moon Is a Harsh Mistress* in 1967. The Science Fiction Writers of America awarded him their Grandmaster Award in 1975.

259

Contributors

ALICE CAROL GAAR is an assistant professor of English at Auburn University. She is the co-author of *Deutsche Stunden* and the author of several articles on German science fiction and science fiction poems. She has been a Fulbright-Hays awardee and a National Endowment for the Humanities awardee.

RUSSELL LETSON is assistant professor of English at Southern Illinois University. He has completed work on the fantasies of Arthur Machen and Algernon Blackwood and essays on Philip José Farmer, Robert A. Heinlein, and Robert Silverberg. He is currently involved on a project focusing on the work of Jack Vance and William Hope Hodgson.

ROBERT PLANK was originally an attorney in Vienna (his doctorate is in law), worked for many years as a psychiatric social worker, and is now an adjunct professor in the Department of Psychology, Case Western Reserve University. He is the author of *The Emotional Significance of Imaginary Beings* (1968) and of chapters in books on C. S. Lewis, Tolkien, and others. He has written extensively on science fiction as well as on literature, social work, and psychology in several journals.

IVOR A. ROGERS has taught theater, film, and literature at Northwestern University, the University of Wisconsin-Green Bay, and Drake University. One of the founders of the Science Fiction Research Association, he retired from Drake University to open a specialty science fiction store. He currently lectures and consults in the areas of science fiction and popular culture for libraries and curriculum development in schools and colleges. He has been a frequent

260

contributor to scholarly conferences, including the Kalamazoo Medieval Conference, the Modern Language Association, the American Theatre Association, and the Secondary Universe Conferences of the Science Fiction Research Association. His critical articles and introductions have appeared in many journals and periodicals. He is the contributor of the essay "The Gernsback Era" in *Anatomy of Wonder*. His current work is a volume entitled *The Broken Bough: Studies in Modern Mythologies*.

DAVID N. SAMUELSON is Professor of English at California State University, Long Beach. Author of *Visions of Tomorrow: Six Journeys from Outer to Inner Space* (Arno Press, 1974), he has published a number of articles on science fiction and science fiction authors. He is also active in the study of modernism, mythology, popular culture, and futurology.

RONALD SARTI is a graduate of Wayne State University and is currently completing his Ph.D. in literature at Indiana University.

PHILIP E. SMITH II teaches drama, modern poetry, Victorian studies, and science fiction in the Department of English at the University of Pittsburgh. He has published articles in *Modern Poetry Studies*, *Victorian Poetry*, and *Studies in Humanities*.

FRANK H. TUCKER is Professor of History at Colorado College, Colorado Springs. His book, *The White Conscience*, appeared in 1969, and his articles on foreign science fiction have been published in the 1970s in *Asian Affairs*, *Russian Affairs*, and other periodicals. Scheduled for publication in 1977 is his latest work, *Pioneers and Progress*, with an analysis of science fiction and "frontier" themes in the media of Japan, Russia, Germany, and the United States.

JACK WILLIAMSON is one of the pioneer masters of modern science fiction and the author of many notable books, including *The Legion of Space*, *The Humanoids*, and *The Legion of Time*. He won the Pilgrim Award of the Science Fiction Research Association for his study of H. G. Wells. He has been a Professor of English at Eastern New Mexico University since 1968.

Index

263